RTI

in **Middle** *and* **High** SCHOOLS

WILLIAM N. BENDER

Solution Tree | Press

a division of
Solution Tree

555 North Morton Street

Bloomington, IN 47404

800.733.6786 (toll free) / 812.336.7700

FAX: 812.336.7790

email: info@solution-tree.com

solution-tree.com

Visit **go.solution-tree.com/rti** to download the reproducibles for this book.

Printed in the United States of America

15   14   13   12   11   1   2   3   4   5

Library of Congress Cataloging-in-Publication Data

Bender, William N.

  RTI in middle and high schools / William N. Bender.

    p. cm.

  Includes bibliographical references and index.

  ISBN 978-1-934009-51-2 (perfect bound) -- ISBN 978-1-935249-28-3 (library edition) 1. Reading--Remedial teaching. 2. Reading (Middle school) 3. Reading (Secondary) 4. Response to intervention (Learning disabled children) I. Title.

  LB1050.5.B457 2012

  372.43--dc23

                          2011034069

Solution Tree

Jeffrey C. Jones, CEO & President

Solution Tree Press

President: Douglas M. Rife

Publisher: Robert D. Clouse

Vice President of Production: Gretchen Knapp

Managing Production Editor: Caroline Wise

Copy Editor: Rachel Rosolina

Proofreader: Elisabeth Abrams

Text and Cover Designer: Rian Anderson

Table of Contents

PART I

Chapter 1

Response to Intervention: A Catalyst for Change 7

Chapter 2

Existing RTI Structures in Middle and High Schools 43

Chapter 3

Differentiating Instruction in Middle and High School Classes 65

Chapter 4

Developing Tier 1 Differentiated Instructional Lessons for Middle and High School Classes

Chapter 5

Supporting RTI and Differentiated Instruction With Modern Instructional Technologies

PART II

Chapter 6

RTI and Differentiation in Reading

Chapter 7

Chapter 8

Epilogue

About the Author

William N. Bender, PhD, is a leader in instructional tactics with an emphasis on differentiated instruction, response to intervention, brain-compatible instruction, and classroom discipline. He is an accomplished author and presenter who consistently receives accolades for his workshops from educators at every level. Dr. Bender began his education career teaching in a junior high school resource classroom, working with adolescents with behavioral disorders and learning disabilities. After earning his doctorate from the University of North Carolina, he taught at Rutgers University in New Jersey, Bluefield State College in West Virginia, and the University of Georgia. He consults full time, writes professional development books, and presents over forty workshops each year for educators throughout North America.

Dr. Bender has written more than sixty research articles and twenty-six books in education. His numerous best-selling titles include *Response to Intervention*, *Differentiating Instruction for Students With Learning Disabilities*, *Introduction to Learning Disabilities*, *Relational Discipline*, *Reading Strategies for Elementary Students With Learning Difficulties*, and *Beyond the RTI Pyramid*.

To book Dr. Bender for professional development, contact pd@solution-tree.com.

Introduction

Response to intervention (RTI), differentiated instruction, and technology are fundamentally changing middle and high school instruction. Combined, they have an impact much greater than each factor in isolation (Bender & Waller, 2011). While RTI is used widely in elementary schools, it is not as common in the upper grades, and yet these students still experience large deficits in reading, writing, and math. Using all three catalysts, *RTI in Middle and High Schools* walks readers through the process of adjusting the RTI structure to best serve middle and high schools.

Throughout, I include real-world examples of RTI implementation in middle and high schools, sample RTI documentation forms in various content areas, guidelines and lists of instructional procedures, and suggestions for lesson plans and further resources. In addition, each chapter discusses many different instructional strategies, curricula, and progress-monitoring programs that address all major tasks within the core subjects. Virtually every teacher in the middle and high school grades can benefit from the strategies in this text. Part I introduces each of the three catalysts for change: RTI, differentiated instruction, and technology.

In chapter 1, I present an overview of RTI basics, including what RTI is and what the pyramid of intervention looks like for middle and high schools. I also cover common RTI elements and the role of a professional learning community, and I include a sample RTI documentation form for a ninth-grade reading intervention in the context of a U.S. history class.

Chapter 2 covers how RTI can be structured in the upper grades. I present several real-world examples from across the United States for comparison along with analysis of each.

I begin chapter 3 with a discussion of differentiated instruction in middle and high school classes. I present an overview of the initiative and discuss the importance of brain-compatible instruction, specifically for students who have grown up surrounded by technology. I also introduce several tools teachers can use to begin the differentiation process.

In chapter 4, I discuss practical hands-on advice for using differentiated instruction in the upper grades, such as tips on modifying traditional lesson plans to include differentiated elements. I also discuss the advantage of creating various centers in content-area classrooms.

Chapter 5 introduces technology in conjunction with RTI and differentiated instruction. I explore the basic technology requirements necessary to bring technology into middle and high school classrooms and provide many examples of hardware, software, and lesson plan ideas.

Part II moves away from the individual catalysts and shows their combined impact in various content-area classes, specifically focusing on reading, writing, and math interventions.

Chapter 6 discusses RTI and differentiation in middle and high school reading instruction. I present the challenges specific to upper grades, as well as strategies, suggested curricula, and monitoring tools for addressing these challenges. The chapter ends with a real-world example of how a Nevada school district approached RTI in reading instruction and a sample case study of an RTI in reading within a ninth-grade biology class.

Chapter 7 moves on to writing instruction in the upper grade levels. I explore the different types of writing assignments, various strategies to teach writing skills, and supplemental curricula. This chapter ends with a sample case study of an RTI in writing in a ninth-grade biology class.

Chapter 8 presents RTI in middle and high school mathematics instruction. I discuss strategies such as peer tutoring, problem-based learning, and problem solving. I also suggest supplemental curricula and monitoring procedures. The chapter ends with a sample case study in a tenth-grade general mathematics course.

These research-proven strategies and curricula are only a limited sample of those available, but they represent best practices. Therefore teachers should be applying these RTI procedures and differentiated instructional ideas across the board in their middle and high school classes, and professional learning communities should do everything possible to facilitate this transition.

The case studies and real-world examples I present involve an array of academic deficits in various subjects. These examples are not exhaustive, of course, but they should suffice as examples of what effective, best-practice instruction now requires. Furthermore, teachers should be able to utilize the forms, examples, and instructional ideas, coupled with their own curricula, to develop high-quality, effective Tier 2 and 3 interventions for their students.

I also describe many hardware, software, and web-based options every modern instructional program should use (Partnership for 21st Century Skills, 2007). Of necessity, the number of programs described is limited. However, these examples illustrate how much technology has affected instruction and how it is now impacting both RTI and differentiated instruction.

RTI, coupled with differentiated instruction and increased use of technology, will very soon create classrooms that look quite different from traditional middle or high school instruction. This book is intended to prepare all teachers for that change as well as to prepare leadership teams in the schools to guide and facilitate those changes. The excitement and energy of this three-catalyst interface in middle and high school instruction indicates how technology, RTI, and differentiation can and should work together to benefit all students.

Part I

Chapter 1

Response to Intervention: A Catalyst for Change

Perhaps more than any other single initiative, response to intervention (RTI) is likely to restructure how middle and high school teachers teach in a profound and fundamental way (Geisick & Graving-Reyes, 2008; Gibbs, 2008; James, 2010; National Association of State Directors of Special Education [NASDSE], 2006; National High School Center [NHSC], National Center on Response to Intervention, & Center on Instruction, 2010; Protheroe, 2010; Rozalski, 2009). Virtually every state and province is currently implementing some form of RTI, and all high school and middle school teachers will be participating in this initiative by 2016; many are already doing so (Allen, Alexander, Mellard, & Prewett, 2011; Duffy, n.d.; Fuchs, Fuchs, & Stecker, 2010; Hoover, Baca, Wexler-Love, & Saenz, 2008; James, 2010; Kame'enui, 2007; NASDSE, 2006; NHSC et al., 2010). In that sense, this innovation provides the opportunity for fertile discussions within leadership teams, as well as substantive school improvement opportunities.

The vast majority of states and provinces began their RTI efforts in the area of elementary reading, and the strongest research base for RTI is in that area (Berkeley, Bender, Peaster, & Saunders, 2009; Fuchs & Deshler, 2007; Fuchs & Fuchs, 2007). However, as early as 2007, educators across North America began to turn their attention to applications of RTI in middle and high schools and to develop various pilot programs (Allen et al., 2011; Duffy, n.d.; Gibbs, 2008; James, 2010; Johnson & Smith, 2008; NHSC et al., 2010; Protheroe, 2010; Rozalski, 2009). Since 2008, scholars have produced several books and white papers that include information on how middle and high schools are implementing RTI around the United States (Duffy, n.d.; Gibbs, 2008; NHSC et al., 2010). Since many high school or middle school faculty may not be familiar with RTI, I will begin with the basics.

> RTI has begun to restructure how middle and high school teachers teach in a profound and fundamental way.

What Is RTI?

RTI is a set of systematic, increasingly intensive educational interventions designed to target an individual student's specific learning challenges and to provide a supplementary intervention aimed directly at those learning challenges in order to assist the student in progressing (Boyer, 2008; Fuchs et al., 2010). Based on several changes in federal legislation, the U.S. federal government now allows schools to implement the RTI procedure as one component of the eligibility determination for students suspected of having a learning disability (Bradley, Danielson, & Doolittle, 2007; Fuchs et al., 2010; NASDSE, 2006). However, RTI has now transitioned beyond this eligibility function. Today, RTI is not primarily a tool for identification of students with learning problems, but rather is a general education initiative to assist all students in meeting their potential (NASDSE, 2006). In fact, few students are identified with learning disabilities in the upper grades, since most such learning problems are identified in the mid-elementary grades.

RTI is a set of systematic, increasingly intensive educational interventions designed to target an individual student's specific learning challenges and to provide supplementary interventions as necessary.

RTI has already widely impacted elementary education (Bradley et al., 2007; Fuchs et al., 2010; NASDSE, 2006). Since 2005, virtually every elementary teacher across the United States has modified his or her instruction to use RTI procedures to assist students with learning challenges (Fuchs & Deshler, 2007; Fuchs & Fuchs, 2007; National Center on Response to Intervention [NCRTI], n.d.a). As has been the case in the elementary grades, middle and high school classes are likely to use RTI, differentiated instruction, and instructional technologies together, since each of these supplement and support the others in many ways (Duffy, n.d.).

Before examining the separate catalysts, let's take a closer look at the tiers that make up RTI.

The RTI Pyramid of Intervention for Middle and High Schools

Typically, RTI models are described in terms of a pyramid of intervention divided into instructional tiers, and each tier represents a different level of intensity of instruction (Buffum, Mattos, & Weber, 2009; Fuchs et al., 2010; Kame'enui, 2007; Protheroe, 2010). Approximately 73 percent of U.S. states have adopted a three-tier pyramid model for their RTI efforts (Spectrum K–12 School Solutions, 2009). See figure 1.1.

Educators have widely applied the three-tier model in elementary schools, though few authors have attempted to describe the three-tier model in the context of middle and high schools. With that caveat in mind, the description that follows suggests how this model might look in the higher grade levels. Tier 1 is instruction that is provided for all students in the general education classes (Bender & Shores, 2007; Buffum et al., 2009; Fuchs et al., 2010). It appears at the bottom of the model to suggest that all students participate in instruction at the Tier 1 level. As the percentages within the

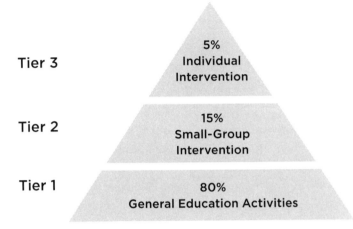

Figure 1.1: RTI pyramid.

model indicate, however, this level of instruction typically meets the educational needs of only 80 percent of the students in the class (Boyer, 2008; Bradley et al., 2007; Fuchs & Deshler, 2007), while the remaining 20 percent of the class needs more intensive supplemental instruction to meet educational goals. Those estimates are based on reading instruction in the elementary grades, specifically from research on primary reading in programs such as Reading First, and thus these general percentages may be somewhat inaccurate in other subjects or at higher grade levels (Bender, 2009a).

Some RTI proponents note that, over time, learning deficits compound and result in more students demonstrating increasing deficits in the higher grade levels; thus the percentages presented in the original RTI pyramid might be underestimates (Gibbs, 2008). This suggests that Tier 1 instruction in secondary schools may not be meeting as much as 30 or 35 percent of students' instructional needs (Gibbs, 2008). At a minimum, it seems clear that at least 20 percent of all students in the middle and higher grades will demonstrate academic deficits, thus more than 20 percent of secondary students might need to progress into the more intensive RTI tiers of instruction.

> Over time, learning deficits may compound and result in more students demonstrating increasing deficits in the higher grade levels; thus the percentages presented in the original RTI pyramid might be underestimates.

Tier 1

In the various discussions of Tier 1 instruction for RTI implementation in middle and high schools, researchers strongly recommend differentiated instruction as the essential basis for RTI efforts (Duffy, n.d.; Gibbs, 2008; NHSC et al., 2010). In fact, scholars now consider differentiated instruction the most effective basis for all instruction, and educators must implement the strongest instructional model available at the Tier 1 level as the basis for RTI (Duffy, n.d.; Gibbs, 2008). As a result, these authors have strongly encouraged all middle and high school teachers in every subject to implement differentiated instructional lessons in order to meet the needs of a maximum number of students in Tier 1.

Of course, at the Tier 1 level, the general education teacher provides all of the instruction in this RTI model. Thus the general education teachers must deliver differentiated instruction for large and small groups, as well as some individual assistance based on the individual needs of the students.

In addition, general education teachers (at least in the elementary grades) also have the responsibility to conduct universal screening assessments to identify students who are struggling (Boyer, 2008; Bradley et al., 2007; Fuchs & Deshler, 2007; Fuchs et al., 2010; Kame'enui, 2007). All students in the elementary class take these screening assessments, usually a minimum of three times each year. Based on those universal screening assessments, general education teachers must then identify students who may need more intensive supplemental instruction at the Tier 2 or Tier 3 levels of the RTI pyramid (Fuchs & Deshler, 2007; Fuchs et al., 2010; Kame'enui, 2007).

Universal screening measures assess basic skills, and schools usually conduct such screenings a minimum of three times each year.

While most schools have applied that universal screening procedure in elementary grades, it is not clear from the research literature if or how they will implement universal screening in the middle and upper grades (Duffy, n.d.; Johnson & Smith, 2008; NHSC, 2010). In fact, there is little research literature on screening procedures or other aspects of RTI implementation for middle or high schools (Johnson & Smith, 2008). Therefore this question of who is responsible for universal screening assessments at the Tier 1 level is, like many other questions, still open for the higher grade levels (Gibbs, 2008; NCRTI, n.d.a; NHSC et al., 2010).

Several pilot RTI implementation programs in secondary schools do, however, shed some light on how to manage this screening. Many model RTI programs use existing achievement scores or those scores coupled with teacher recommendations to help determine which students might benefit from a Tier 2 or Tier 3 intervention (Duffy, n.d.; Johnson & Smith, 2008; NHSC et al., 2010). Several of those model programs are described in detail later in chapter 2.

Tier 2

Tier 2 interventions provide supplemental, targeted intervention for a small group of students—perhaps 20 percent of the class—who are struggling (Boyer, 2008; Fuchs & Fuchs, 2007). Again, this percentage may not be accurate, and in the higher grade levels, it is probably somewhat low, since some proponents of RTI have suggested that many more students need assistance as grade levels increase (Gibbs, 2008). Using this figure as a basis, however, in a typical class of perhaps twenty-five students, one might expect that at least five or six students would be struggling enough to require a supplemental Tier 2 intervention. The good news is that Tier 2 interventions work for the majority of students, as shown by rather extensive research in the elementary years. In fact, a combination of Tier 1 instruction and Tier 2 intervention typically meets the needs of as much as 95 percent of students (Bender, 2009a).

In the elementary grades, the general education teacher delivers Tier 2 intensive instruction for small groups of struggling students (Fuchs & Fuchs, 2007). In middle and high schools, because students change classes frequently and periods may be only forty-five to ninety minutes long, Tier 2 interventions typically occur during separate instructional periods (Duffy, n.d.; Gibbs, 2008; Johnson & Smith, 2008; NHSC et al., 2010). The descriptions of middle and high school model programs in chapter 2 provide examples for a variety of ways to structure Tier 2 and Tier 3 interventions.

Tier 3

Educators frequently describe the Tier 3 level of intensive intervention as one-to-one instruction that attempts to meet the needs of the remaining 5 percent of the class (Fuchs et al., 2010; Fuchs & Fuchs, 2007). Given a class of twenty-five students, one might expect that only one or two students may require this level of intensive intervention, and research has shown that many of those students will respond positively to highly intensive instruction (Fuchs & Fuchs, 2007). When intensive Tier 3 interventions do not meet students' needs, faculty typically refer these students for consideration for special education services; the faculty may use RTI procedures to help determine eligibility for those programs. While such eligibility decisions become less frequent in the higher grades, faculty sometimes make such determinations in middle school and occasionally in high school.

That said, in some school districts, states, or provinces, this level of instruction takes place after the school identifies a child as needing special education services (Fuchs et al., 2010; Fuchs & Fuchs, 2007; Johnson & Smith, 2008). In other areas, however, the school must try Tier 3 intervention prior to any eligibility decision (Kame'enui, 2007; NASDSE, 2006), and educators should certainly check the eligibility regulations in their own regions and school districts to determine when students may participate in Tier 3 interventions.

> There is considerable disagreement in literature on RTI concerning who is responsible for Tier 2 or Tier 3 instruction; this may be an instance in which reality doesn't match stated intentions.

Because of the issue of teacher time in middle and high school classes, there is considerable disagreement in the literature on RTI concerning who is responsible for Tier 2 and Tier 3 interventions; indeed, this may be an instance in which reality doesn't match stated intentions. In the real-world examples, no middle or high school model program holds general education teachers responsible for the direct delivery of Tier 2 or Tier 3 interventions (Duffy, n.d.; Fuchs et al., 2010; Gibbs, 2008; Johnson & Smith, 2008), even though some state or provincial RTI plans indicate that general education teachers are responsible for such instruction across the grade levels (Bender, 2009a). In fact, various discussions of RTI in the literature suggest that other educators—perhaps special education teachers, reading coaches, or mathematics coaches—typically have the responsibility for Tier 2 and Tier 3 interventions in middle and high schools (Hoover & Patton, 2008; Johnson & Smith, 2008).

Common RTI Elements

At this point, it is quite clear that various states and provinces have implemented different types of RTI models. In spite of these regional differences, a number of elements are common to most if not all RTI procedures (Buffum et al., 2009; Kame'enui, 2007). These are presented in the following feature box.

Common Elements in Most RTI Models

- Emphasis on screening multiple times each year in Tier 1
- Emphasis on a set of increasingly intensive interventions, structured into intervention tiers or levels
- Emphasis on the use of research-based curricula in each tier
- Frequent progress monitoring of each individual's performance in each tier
- Data-based decision making
- Team-driven determinations on students' placement in the RTI tiers

---

First, all RTI models include an emphasis on screening of some type in order to identify students struggling in various subjects. This is typically the responsibility of the general education teacher, and most states and provinces—as mentioned previously—require universal screening at least three times each year in the elementary grades. In contrast, most middle and high school models have devised other screening techniques. All RTI models present some concept of increasingly intensive, supplemental education interventions that are referred to as *intervention tiers* (Boyer, 2008; Buffum et al., 2009; Kame'enui, 2007). In the literature, it is clear that proponents of RTI assume students will progress through these levels of intervention in numeric order: schools place struggling students in Tier 2 interventions prior to Tier 3 interventions (Berkeley et al., 2009; Buffum et al., 2009; Hoover et al., 2008; Kame'enui, 2007).

Most RTI models use research-based curricula as the basis for instruction within the various intervention tiers. Teachers must also perform frequent monitoring of each individual's performance in each tier to document the efficacy of the intervention for each student (Buffum et al., 2009; Kame'enui, 2007). This performance monitoring becomes critically important should various tiers not meet a child's needs and the school subsequently consider that child for special education. In addition, a collaborative team should use data-based decision making to interpret the child's progress relative to curricular standards (Buffum et al., 2009; Kame'enui, 2007).

Now we'll take a closer look at the importance of a leadership team.

Building an RTI Leadership Team

One major emphasis in this implementation model is the importance of building the leadership team for RTI. Most proponents of RTI indicate that it takes a minimum of three to five years to build an effective RTI intervention system (Bender, 2009a; Buffum et al., 2009; Canter, Klotz, & Cowan, 2008; Gibbs, 2008), and RTI implementation, like any instructional innovation, can fail to meet student needs unless it is placed in an ongoing, high-quality professional development context.

To emphasize this point, Orosco and Klingner (2010) reported on a schoolwide RTI failure, a situation in which RTI did not result in the anticipated improvements among students who were English learners. Using a qualitative research design, these researchers studied one RTI implementation effort in depth and demonstrated that several factors were critical in successful implementation of RTI, including:

- Strong support from the administration

- Provision of high-quality professional development for teachers

- Focus on developing positive teacher beliefs in efficacy of RTI

- Specific professional development in the team decision-making process

What that program lacked, a leadership team focused directly on RTI could explicitly address. As this list indicates, effective professional development in the context of a leadership team over the longer term will be essential for RTI to work effectively.

Once the leadership team is in place, team activities might cover a variety of issues such as resources available, discussion of scheduling that will facilitate Tier 2 and Tier 3 interventions, data-collection options, management of educational decision points, and any necessary administrative support. A list of possible topics for discussion by the leadership team is presented in the following feature box. Keep in mind that every RTI implementation effort is different, so this list of issues or tentative decisions is only a guide. Of course, all team decisions should refer to state/province and district RTI guidelines, and the team should present the decisions as recommendations to the school faculty as a whole.

RTI Issues and Decisions for the Leadership Team
1. Who is responsible for Tier 2 and Tier 3 interventions in various areas such as reading, language arts, and mathematics? Does our state, province, or district RTI guideline document provide guidance on this question for middle and high schools?
2. What is our overall goal for a pupil-teacher ratio in Tier 2 and Tier 3 intervention?

Continued➔

3. Do we plan to use doubling or intervention periods? If so, in which subject areas? What other scheduling mechanisms should we consider to make RTI a reality in our building?

4. What research-proven reading and language arts curricula will be implemented as Tier 2 and Tier 3 interventions? Do we wish to use specific curricula for specific intervention tiers? Do we wish to use specific supplemental curricula for specific subpopulations in our school?

5. How can we ensure instructional fidelity in the use of those supplemental curricula? Can we prepare various teachers in certain curricula and use those teachers for Tier 2 or Tier 3 interventions? Is professional development on the use of those selected curricula available?

6. What is the duration, frequency, and overall timing for each Tier 2 and Tier 3 intervention? Are these interventions to be done daily? How do we structure intervention length for our students—for example, one grading period or one semester?

7. Do we need to conduct universal screening? If so, how? Can we use previous assessment scores and teacher recommendations as our universal screening procedure? Is additional assessment necessary for all students or merely for some students? What state or district policies exist that might address that question? How often should we conduct universal screening—three times a year, twice a year, or once a year?

8. In Tier 2 and Tier 3 interventions, how frequently must we monitor performance (weekly, every other week, three times per semester, and so on)? What progress-monitoring tools do we currently have? What progress monitoring should we undertake? Should we standardize these to all our students or across the school or school district? Should faculty develop progress-monitoring tools, or should the school purchase a schoolwide system for progress monitoring?

9. When do we notify parents that students are participating in a Tier 2 or Tier 3 intervention? Whose responsibility is such notification?

Advocacy for RTI in Middle and High Schools

In addition to understanding how RTI works in model middle and high school programs, educators need more information on RTI during the implementation process within their school (Allen et al., 2011). For example, understanding the research supportive of RTI will allow educators to become effective advocates of RTI within their districts and schools. Likewise, understanding the planning process for RTI will help schools begin to implement this important innovation. This section addresses those aspects of RTI in the context of middle and high schools.

It has become clear that unless teachers buy into the RTI process, significant improvements in instruction will not be possible (Duffy, n.d.; Gibbs, 2008; Orosco & Klingner, 2010). In particular, members of the school leadership team must serve as advocates of RTI in order for it to become a meaningful school reform effort. Educational leaders must be prepared to address the question, "Why should we do RTI?"

Fortunately, the answer is simple: RTI works! Research has proven RTI in the lower grades to be one of the most effective instructional options available (Fuchs & Fuchs, 2007; Gibbs, 2008; Johnson & Smith, 2008).

Because much of the early research on RTI took place in elementary schools, those results are, of necessity, part of the rationale for implementation in middle and high schools. This section presents research results in several areas using available research across the grade levels, with a particular emphasis on the limited research on RTI or tiered interventions in middle schools.

RTI Works for Struggling Learners

First, research has consistently shown that RTI works for students who are struggling in reading and mathematics (Bender & Shores, 2007; Duffy, n.d.; Lolich et al., 2010). In the lower grades, between 20 and 25 percent of students struggle in reading, and that number is higher as grade levels increase (Bender & Larkin, 2009; Gibbs, 2008; Podhajski, Mather, Nathan, & Sammons, 2009). If schools do not address these reading difficulties, they are likely to increase over time and will persist into the middle and high school grades, resulting in many other achievement deficits across the subject areas (Podhajski et al., 2009).

For this reason, educators initially implemented RTI procedures in the elementary grades to address these reading deficits, and research has shown that RTI is extremely effective in curbing early reading problems (Hoover et al., 2008; Katz, Stone, Carlisle, Corey, & Zeng, 2008; Mahdavi & Beebe-Frankenberger, 2009; Vaughn et al., 2009). The limited anecdotal evidence on RTI in middle and high schools suggests similar success in the upper grade levels (Gibbs, 2008; Johnson & Smith, 2008; NCRTI, n.d.a; Rozalski, 2009). Research has shown that RTI works for almost all students struggling in reading and mathematics. Thus it seems clear that RTI represents best practice in 21st century schools across grade levels.

> Educators have undertaken the RTI initiative because research has shown that RTI works for almost all students struggling in reading and mathematics.

Research from 2006 and 2008 has shown that even short-term interventions have profound positive impact (Denton, Fletcher, Anthony, & Francis, 2006; Simmons et al., 2008). In some cases, computer-based Tier 2 or Tier 3 interventions lasting only six or eight weeks have resulted in reading gains of one, two, or even three years (Bender & Waller, 2011).

Additional research has demonstrated that many students who do not respond positively to a Tier 2 intervention will respond positively to a more intensive, Tier 3 intervention (Rozalski, 2009; Vaughn et al., 2009). Taken together, the available research suggests that providing multiple tiers of intervention in an RTI process seems to alleviate reading problems for between 75 and 95 percent of students who initially struggle in reading, depending on the individual study (Hughes & Dexter, 2008; Torgesen, 2007; Vaughn et al., 2009). In terms of what educators now face in middle and high school classes, this RTI process holds the potential to significantly reduce the number of students who function below grade level. Given that conclusion, what educator would not be committed to RTI?

> Aside from the fact that RTI is now legally mandated in many districts, the plain fact is that research has proven RTI to be one of the most effective instructional options available.

RTI Helps Schools Meet Adequate Yearly Progress Goals

Another important advantage of RTI implementation is that it helps schools meet and exceed their educational goals related to state or provincial standards. Specifically, RTI is highly effective for students who traditionally struggle in reading, such as students with disabilities or students who are English learners (Denton et al., 2006; Linan-Thompson, Vaughn, Prater, & Cirino, 2006; Lovett et al., 2008; Rinaldi & Samson, 2008; Simmons et al., 2008). For example, the teachers at Tigard High School in Oregon stated explicitly that RTI implementation allowed them to close the achievement gap between average and lower-functioning students in their school (Lolich et al., 2010). This research is critically important since in many schools, the English learners and students with special needs are the very subgroups who do not meet their educational goals.

At one RTI pilot school in Montana, only 49 percent of students were meeting yearly benchmarks in 2006, prior to the implementation of RTI. After only two years of RTI implementation, 76 percent of the children were meeting benchmarks in reading (Mahdavi & Beebe-Frankenberger, 2009). In short, if schools wish to meet and exceed adequate yearly progress for even the most challenged students, schools should rigorously implement RTI in each of the basic skill areas. For that reason, advocates present RTI as a school improvement effort, and many districts across North America have emphasized their RTI efforts under the overall umbrella of school reform.

RTI Reduces Bias in Educational Placements

Implementation of RTI also impacts a pressing and persistent problem in education. The term *disproportionality* has been used to describe how minority students have been more highly represented in special education classes than white students, suggesting some systematic bias in the educational placement decision-making process

(Artiles, Kozleski, Trent, Osher, & Ortiz, 2010). In some cases, a young African American student was almost twice as likely to be referred and placed in special education as a white student, and this problem has not adequately been addressed (Artiles et al., 2010). Anecdotal evidence now suggests that rigorous RTI procedures may eliminate that systemic bias (Abernathy, 2008; Donovan & Cross, 2002; Duffy, n.d.; NCRTI, n.d.b).

For example, in a pilot RTI study in North Carolina, Abernathy (2008) reports that prior to RTI implementation, an African American student was 1.7 times as likely to end up in special education classes, but that ratio decreased to 1.1 after only one year of RTI implementation. Duffy (n.d.) reports a similar finding for a school district in Michigan. While these reports are anecdotal in nature and are not based on controlled research designs, this is still a crucial finding. If RTI procedures can reduce or eliminate disproportionality, that alone is sufficient reason to implement this procedure throughout the grade levels.

> If RTI procedures can reduce or eliminate disproportionality, that alone is sufficient reason to implement this procedure throughout the grade levels.

RTI Empowers Teachers

Anecdotal evidence also suggests that many teachers have experienced a sense of empowerment through the RTI process (Allen et al., 2011; Lolich et al., 2010) and express themselves in terms of "owning" students' academic problems. Teachers feel empowered to provide enhanced supplemental instruction for students who may previously have fallen through the cracks in the educational system. Under an RTI system, those students receive meaningful educational assistance (Lolich et al., 2010).

This sense of empowerment is understandable given the realities of the middle and high school classrooms. Virtually every experienced classroom teacher has felt, at one time or another, a desire to provide a bit more time for a struggling student. However, those teachers, particularly in departmentalized schools, often feel they cannot provide that additional time because they have so many other students. RTI offers exactly that: a mechanism for providing supplemental assistance for struggling students. Educators recognize that RTI will require a reshuffling of resources at the school level (Duffy, n.d.; Gibbs, 2008); when that reorganization of resources occurs, they often feel empowered to assist struggling students more than ever before (Allen et al., 2011).

These research results can provide a strong position of advocacy for RTI and should motivate educators to spend the time necessary to implement this innovation across the grade levels. Schools should share these results with parents and students as educators develop their RTI procedures at the school level.

Overview of Research Results for Advocating RTI

- RTI works for struggling readers across the grade levels.
- RTI assists schools in meeting educational standards-based goals.
- RTI helps alleviate reading and mathematics problems among students with special needs and students whose primary language is not English.
- RTI helps reduce disproportionality and results in less bias in eligibility decisions.
- RTI empowers teachers to intervene early to assist struggling students.

Developing an Implementation Plan for RTI

As educators in middle and high schools plan the RTI interventions for their students, they need access to resources to assist with that planning as well as a firm understanding of the distinctions between the intervention tiers.

Resources for RTI Implementation

While research information on RTI implementation in middle and high schools is limited, several resources are available (Bender, 2009a; Gibbs, 2008; NHSC et al., 2010). Web-based resources are available to teachers embarking on their initial RTI efforts, and many of these apply to middle and high school grades. For example, the RTI Action Network compiled resources on middle school RTI implementation just as many middle schools were expanding their RTI initiatives (www.rtinetwork.org /middle-school#nogo). This set of resources is quite helpful for high school educators as well. It includes blueprints for various stages of RTI implementation as well as information and articles on a wide variety of topics including universal screening, progress monitoring, data-based decision making, RTI in mathematics and behavior, diversity in RTI, and many other areas.

Another resource to check is from the National Center on Response to Intervention (www.rti4success.org). This site presents a series of webinars, including one that focuses on RTI implementation in high schools, as recorded on May 12, 2010 (www.rti4success.org/webinars/video/902). This webinar, titled "The High School Tiered Interventions Initiative: Progress Monitoring," was created by the High School Tiered Interventions Initiative, a collaborative effort among the National Center on Response to Intervention, the National High School Center, and the Center on Instruction. It discusses using curriculum-based measurements to monitor student progress in reading, mathematics, and content areas at the high school level, focusing on a model RTI program from Walla Walla High School in Walla Walla, Washington.

The following feature box presents a series of additional websites that teachers should review when seeking assistance with RTI. Educators in middle and high schools should also investigate the references and resources at the end of this book (page 215), with particular attention to those presenting middle and high school RTI practices.

Helpful Websites in RTI Implementation

The Florida Center for Reading Research
www.fcrr.org

This site provides free lesson structures for differentiated reading instruction and information on core reading activities, student center reading activities for grades K–5, interventions for struggling readers, and reading assessment at the elementary, middle, and high school levels. It also provides information targeted to parents, teachers, administrators, literacy coaches, and researchers.

IES What Works Clearinghouse
http://ies.ed.gov/ncee/wwc/publications/intervention

This is a clearinghouse sponsored by the U.S. government that describes various research-based instructional curricula in reading and math. Unlike some of the websites dedicated to reporting only on scientifically supported reading curricula, this clearinghouse likewise reports on new mathematics curricula. While rigorous research standards prevent this site from reporting on some curricula, this site will clearly state the rationale and describe the curricula that are listed.

Kansas Institute for Positive Behavior Support
www.kipbsmodules.org

This website was developed by the University of Kansas in 2001 to assist educators and others concerned with behavioral problems in children and youth to move forward in developing an integrated, effective plan for behavioral change, based on involvement of all stakeholders in a student's life. The site explores wraparound planning, with a strong emphasis on person-centered planning, as well as various models for team-based decision making.

National Association of State Directors of Special Education
www.nasdse.org

This site presents a number of items that will assist educators in the implementation of RTI, including various lists of guidelines, position papers, and brief explanations. Continued➔

National Center on Response to Intervention
www.rti4success.org

The National Center on RTI provides an assortment of briefs, fact sheets, presentations, media, and training modules relevant to RTI that are divided into eighteen categories. Many of the current resources were created by other organizations, associations, state departments, or districts; center-authored resources are added on a regular basis. Visitors to the site can sign up to receive an online monthly newsletter, the *RTI Responder*.

National Center on Student Progress Monitoring
www.studentprogress.org

This website was established by the U.S. Office of Special Education Programs under funding for the National Center on Student Progress Monitoring. It is structured as a technical assistance center, working in conjunction with Vanderbilt University in Nashville, Tennessee. The site provides a wide array of resources including online discussions, newsletters, and web-based training on monitoring student performance.

National Wraparound Initiative
www.nwi.pdx.edu/

This website is the home of the National Wraparound Initiative, which provides information on the wraparound process, a widely implemented approach to community-based treatments for students with emotional and/or behavioral disorders.

OSEP Technical Assistance Center on Positive Behavioral Interventions and Supports
www.pbis.org

The OSEP Technical Assistance Center on Positive Behavioral Interventions and Supports was established to address the behavioral and discipline systems needed for successful learning and social development of students. Positive Behavior Support (PBS) aims to prevent inappropriate behavior through teaching and reinforcing appropriate behavior and social skills. The process is consistent with the core principles of RTI as it provides a comprehensive system of interventions based on the needs of all students. The site provides a significant number of planning and evaluation tools, research-based information on PBS, resource links, video links, and PowerPoint presentations. Visitors can also sign up to receive newsletters and new articles as they are added to the site.

RTI Action Network

www.rtinetwork.org

The RTI Action Network was created by the National Center for Learning Disabilities and is dedicated to the effective implementation of RTI in school districts throughout the United States. The site contains a variety of free resources for districts and other stakeholder groups, including webcasts, national online forums, implementation guidelines, and research summaries. Visitors can also sign up to participate in various webcasts or online workshops.

School-wide Information System

www.swis.org

School-wide Information System (SWIS) is a web-based information system developed to facilitate behavioral intervention planning. This system presents options for inputting behavioral data on the number of office referrals to allow school administrators to compile data in a variety of ways. Individual data may be used to support student behavior for particular students, but administrators may also compile data on specific time periods during the day, specific locations within the school, and so on, to analyze and solve behavioral problems throughout the school. According to the website, the system is currently used by more than 8,100 schools in various countries worldwide.

University of Oregon

http://reading.uoregon.edu

This site provides information on interventions used in RTI, including the essential components of reading instruction; assessment within a comprehensive schoolwide reading model; evaluating and selecting core, supplemental, and intervention reading programs; and links to other helpful reading resources.

Vaughn Gross Center for Reading and Language Arts

www.texasreading.org/utcrla/materials

The Vaughn Gross Center for Reading and Language Arts is dedicated to improving the educational outcomes of traditionally underrepresented student populations, such as English learners and students with learning difficulties. The Vaughn Center has more than sixty products related to effective research-based reading instruction for prekindergarten, primary, secondary, and special education students. The professional development guides, videos, CD-ROMs, and booklets address a range of reading topics, including phonological awareness, phonics, fluency, vocabulary, and comprehension. Many products and publications can be downloaded and can be explored digitally through an online database such as Searchlight.

Creating Intervention Tiers in Middle and High Schools

What, exactly, constitutes a Tier 2 intervention, and how is that different from the routine instructional supports that might be presented in Tier 1? For example, many schools provide a one-day-per-week homework support period, perhaps as an extended homeroom class period or even an after-school homework assistance period. While that is an excellent support for Tier 1 instruction, it is probably not wise to consider that type of support Tier 2 intervention, since it is neither systematic nor intensive enough.

Some state and provincial RTI guidelines define specific requirements for Tier 2 interventions, and educators should check their department of education websites for that information. Other regions do not provide such guidelines for middle and high schools, and those educators will need a place to begin their planning. The general guidelines presented in the following feature box stem from the synopsis of Tier 2 interventions in model programs at the middle and high school levels.

Schools should continue current academic support programs (such as tutoring in subject areas one period per week or afternoon support in homework) as valid Tier 1 differentiated support for students, but in many cases, such support programs are not intensive enough to be considered Tier 2 interventions in the RTI context.

Guidelines for Developing a Tier 2 RTI Intervention

1. Tier 2 interventions must be intensive, systematic, and targeted explicitly toward individual student achievement. Interventions should target precise academic deficit areas for each individual student. In short, merely adding a support mathematics class should not be considered a Tier 2 intervention unless that support class targets specific skill deficits for each student.

2. The school can document the intensity of an intervention using a number of factors.

   • The team can describe Tier 2 interventions in terms of minutes per day, days per week, and number of weeks. Few interventions in the model programs involve less than twenty minutes per day, three days per week, over six to nine weeks. Most involve more time (for example, thirty minutes daily, five days per week, for one or more grading periods).

   • Pupil-teacher ratio should be smaller than general education classes. Some states provide guidance of 6 : 1 as a maximum; some upper-grade Tier 2 interventions increase that to 12 : 1 or 15 : 1.

   • Most model programs continue supplemental instruction over one or several grading periods to help students catch up with peers.

   • All of these factors should result in clear indications that Tier 2 interventions in a given school are more intensive than Tier 1 instruction and that Tier 3 interventions are more intensive than Tier 2.

3. Some states and provinces require the use of designated, research-proven, supplemental curricula for Tier 2, and most of the research indicates that schools use specific curricula. However, some RTI programs use selected, targeted skills from the core curriculum rather than a separate curriculum.

4. Tier 2 (and Tier 3) interventions require frequent progress monitoring. Most schools perform this a minimum of every two weeks, and some model programs may require it every week. Frequent progress monitoring in Tier 2 and 3 is critical to document the impact of the intervention for a given student. Sometimes systems use curricular probes on specific skills in reading and mathematics.

Schools should continue current academic support programs (such as tutoring in subject areas one period per week or afternoon support in homework) as valid Tier 1 differentiated support for students, but in many cases, such support programs are not intensive enough to be considered Tier 2 interventions in the RTI context.

Restructuring an Existing Support Class or Creating One

RTI implementation in middle and high schools most frequently involves either restructuring an existing instructional support course in reading or mathematics or creating such a support course in those subjects to serve as the Tier 2 or Tier 3 intervention in those areas. Of course, the school may need to offer multiple sections of those support courses throughout the school day, depending on how many students need them. Thus the first question faculty must address is, do we have support courses in these areas that we can redevelop to meet the needs of Tier 2 or Tier 3 intervention, or do we need to create them?

When educational leaders choose among the options of restructuring an existing support class (typically a support class in reading or mathematics) or creating a new support class, they might consider a variety of questions in the development process. Figures 1.2 and 1.3 (pages 24–25) provide guidance for making those decisions. Figure 1.2 will help if a school leadership team decides to restructure an existing support course to make it an appropriate Tier 2 or Tier 3 intervention course. Figure 1.3 will help if the team decides to develop a new support class. Visit **go.solution-tree .com/rti** for reproducible versions of these figures.

While this discussion has focused on developing or refocusing support classes to make them appropriate Tier 2 interventions, educators can use the same process to develop Tier 3 interventions in middle and high schools. This text has focused on program development for Tier 2 simply because more students will progress into Tier 2 interventions than Tier 3 interventions, and the overall planning process is the same. In short, once a school has developed effective Tier 2 interventions, development of Tier 3 interventions will proceed much more smoothly and easily.

This worksheet might assist educational teams in middle and high schools in restructuring an existing academic support class to create Tier 2 and Tier 3 instructional options.

1. What supplemental reading and mathematics curricula programs, if any (reading support, math lab), currently exist in our school? Can we restructure these to provide Tier 2 or Tier 3 support in those core areas, or should we continue to consider them Tier 1 instructional supports?

2. How will we determine which students should be placed in Tier 2 or Tier 3 intervention support classes? What screening procedures should we use, and what group of students should we screen?

3. What assessments in mathematics might currently be available that we could adapt for progress monitoring in reading and mathematics once students are in Tier 2 or Tier 3 interventions? Have we heard about any tools in this workshop that we'd like more information on?

4. Will our current instructional arrangements in those support classes work as Tier 2 and Tier 3 interventions in reading and mathematics? Are general education teachers in language arts and algebra delivering those support classes? Should they undertake the Tier 2 and 3 interventions?

5. Do we need new supplemental intervention curricula in reading or mathematics? Can anyone recommend a curriculum? Should we seek a computer-driven intervention curriculum to save teachers' time?

6. How many intervention classes are we likely to need for Tier 2 interventions in reading and mathematics in our school? Who can deliver the Tier 2 and Tier 3 interventions for struggling students in those areas? Can our current staff in language arts and mathematics deliver those sections without assistance? What supports can we offer in order to make time available to assist in that regard?

7. Whose responsibility is this restructuring? Will the leadership team guide this process? Who will undertake scheduling these sections for the intervention support classes, and who will schedule students into them? Who will monitor it and ensure that it is undertaken?

8. What timeframe should we recommend for having our Tier 2 and Tier 3 RTI reading and mathematics intervention options in place?

9. Is professional development on RTI in reading or mathematics necessary for our faculty, and if so, what timeframe works for that?

Figure 1.2: Restructuring current support classes in reading and mathematics to become Tier 2 and 3 intervention classes.

This worksheet might assist educational teams in middle and high schools in creating new intervention classes for Tier 2 and Tier 3 instructional options.

1. We need a content-area reading support class and a mathematics support class. What curricula should we consider using?

2. How will we determine which students to place in Tier 2 or Tier 3 intervention support classes? What screening procedures should we use, and what group of students should we screen?

3. What assessments in mathematics might currently be available that we could use for progress monitoring in reading and mathematics once students are in Tier 2 or Tier 3 interventions? Have we heard about any tools in this workshop that we'd like more information on?

4. Who will teach these support classes? Can our general education teachers in language arts and algebra deliver those support classes? What support or additional personnel might they need?

5. Can anyone recommend a computer-driven intervention curriculum in reading or mathematics that might save teachers' time?

6. How many intervention classes are we likely to need for Tier 2 interventions in reading and mathematics in our school?

7. Whose responsibility is this restructuring? Will the leadership team guide this process? Who will undertake scheduling these sections for the intervention support classes, and who will schedule students into them? Who will monitor it and ensure that it is undertaken?

8. What timeframe should we recommend for having our Tier 2 and Tier 3 RTI reading and mathematics intervention options in place?

9. Is professional development on RTI in reading or mathematics necessary for our faculty, and if so, what timeframe works for that?

Figure 1.3: Creating a new support class as a Tier 2 intervention.

Tier 2 and 3 Support Classes for Double Dippers

As middle and high school faculty develop Tier 2 and Tier 3 intervention options, one additional issue has come to light: the need to develop support classes for students who need support in both reading and mathematics. In several instances, educators have informally utilized the phrase *double dippers* to mean that certain students require support in both of these core areas.

While few model programs have addressed this question, several schools have come up with a rather unique option: one support class that provides Tier 2 instructional support in both reading and mathematics. For example, if a student needs support in both areas, that student might enroll in a support class for one period (say a fifty-five-minute period) in which twenty minutes are spent on a supplemental mathematics curriculum and the other thirty-five minutes on a supplemental reading curriculum.

Supplemental Curricula Choices

RTI guidelines do not require that a supplemental curriculum be implemented for Tier 2 or 3; the guidelines merely state that a *research-proven* curriculum be utilized. Some districts have chosen to implement RTI based on the core curriculum, but most of the research on RTI assumes the use of different, supplemental curricula instead of the core curriculum.

Supplemental curricula come in two types: computer-delivered interventions and hard-copy curricula. Many middle and high schools have access to computerized curricula that are very appropriate for Tier 2 or 3 interventions. When using these programs, many students can work in a math lab, for example, and receive totally individualized intervention programs. In fact, use of computer-delivered interventions is strongly encouraged for the upper tiers (or even Tier 1 support) since research shows that many of these work well and save time. Computerized curricula frequently used include: Fast ForWord, Academy of READING, Academy of MATH, PLATO, SuccessMaker Math, Vmath, and Voyager Reading, among others. Of course, prior to utilizing any supplemental curricula, staff should explore research support for them; the What Works Clearinghouse website can help in that regard.

RTI literature has also monitored other curricula that are not primarily based on computerized instruction. Some of these specifically target middle or high school students, whereas others are useful across grade levels. These include Algebra Rescue!, Accelerated Math for Intervention, Read Well, Read Naturally, TransMath, and Corrective Reading. Educators should consider the academic needs of their students, since many of these curricula do not reach above grade 8. However, for struggling students behind by several grade levels, such curricula may be appropriate even in high school RTI efforts.

Developing an Implementation Plan

As middle and high schools move into RTI implementation, many issues will arise that go far beyond the format for a single student's RTI plan, and several authors have begun to address these issues at the secondary level (Duffy, n.d.; Gibbs, 2008; NHSC et al., 2010). The first step in the planning process should be to form a leadership team for RTI planning if such a group is not already active in your school.

Most proponents of RTI indicate that implementation will be a multiyear process (Duffy, n.d.; NCRTI, n.d.a), so each middle and high school faculty should certainly consider initiating a team dedicated exclusively to this task. The faculty at Cheyenne Mountain Junior High created such a leadership team and found that this group effectively guided the RTI process and enhanced the impact of that process in improving instruction across the curriculum (Johnson & Smith, 2008). Once such a team exists, that group will lead the school's RTI implementation efforts (Johnson & Smith, 2008). Within a multiyear plan, it may undertake a wide variety of activities to further the goal of RTI implementation. The following feature box presents some of these activities.

Activities for a Leadership Team Focused on RTI

RTI Goals for Toccoa Middle School and Toccoa High School: Academic Year 2011–2012

1. All teachers will receive three hours of in-service on each topic that follows:

   - RTI procedures for our state or province; in one faculty meeting, we will introduce an RTI planning grid as our primary planning mechanism. We will complete it during the first month of school, and an outside expert (perhaps from the state department of education) will introduce RTI to our faculty and discuss model middle and high school RTI programs around North America.

   - Various screening assessments and procedures for performance monitoring in reading and mathematics

   - Computerized interventions available in reading, math, and algebra I or algebra recovery

2. Members of the RTI leadership team will meet monthly and undertake various book studies and web reviews on model RTI programs in high schools and middle schools around North America.

3. During the second meeting during this academic year, the team will select specific professional development opportunities at various state or provincial and national conferences and identify members to attend them. They will bring back additional information on RTI implementation to share in the next scheduled faculty meeting. Attendees will make a thirty-minute presentation to the entire faculty.

4. The leadership team for RTI will develop and present an RTI implementation plan for reading, general mathematics, and algebra to the school faculty. Faculty will discuss it at one meeting, modify it as suggested, and adopt it at the next meeting. The leadership team then presents recommendations for the RTI implementation timeline.

Continued➜

5. The RTI team will work with the principal on necessary resources for RTI on an ongoing basis. These may include:

   • Additional professional or support staff for RTI interventions

   • Purchase of intervention curricula in various areas

   • Reallocation of job responsibilities for RTI implementation

   • Doubling certain instructional periods for struggling students, specifically in English, general mathematics, and algebra I

6. The RTI team will implement a needs assessment on RTI among the faculty.

7. The RTI team will conduct a school-based inventory to identify assessments, curricula, and specialized staff training currently available at the school that may assist in RTI implementation.

8. The RTI team will discuss items on the schoolwide planning grid at the end of the year to note any changes from the initial planning session.

9. The RTI team will collect data on student referrals to special education and data on school dropouts at the end of this year as a comparison measure on efficacy of RTI.

RTI Goals for Academic Year 2012–2013

1. Toccoa Middle School will implement universal screening in reading literacy and mathematics for all students twice each year. These screenings may rely on both state/provincial assessment data and/or additional assessments for students scoring below 35 percent on state- or provincewide tests.

2. Toccoa High School will undertake screenings for all incoming ninth graders and identify students who are performing two or more years below grade level in reading or mathematics. The school will place those students in a double English or mathematics period.

3. Toccoa Middle School will provide Tier 2 interventions in reading and mathematics for all students requiring more intensive instruction by providing a minimum of thirty minutes of small-group supplemental instruction four times each week. This will be conducted as after-school tutoring sessions when possible or scheduled as a "double English" or "double math" class when necessary.

4. By January of 2013, Toccoa Middle School will provide Tier 3 interventions in reading and mathematics for students requiring them. These will be provided five days per week for a minimum of thirty minutes per day. These will be provided at the same time and in the same manner as the Tier 2 interventions.

5. The RTI team at Toccoa High School will expand to include all former members as well as two representatives from Toccoa Middle School and all department chairs.

6. The RTI team will invite various teachers to attend professional development opportunities that address RTI implementation in reading, English, mathematics, and behavior.

7. Both schools will use the schoolwide planning grid again in May of this and each subsequent year to note any changes from the initial planning session.

8. The schools will collect data on student referrals to special education at the end of this and each subsequent year as a comparison measure on efficacy of RTI. Faculty will compare these data to data from the previous year to determine the impact of RTI in our schools.

RTI Goals for Academic Year 2013–2014

1. Toccoa Middle and Toccoa High Schools will continue universal screening in mathematics and reading for all students in the middle school and for all incoming students in grade 9 at the high school.

2. Toccoa Middle and High Schools will continue to provide Tier 2 interventions in mathematics and reading for all students requiring more intensive instruction by using the intervention models described previously.

3. By January of 2014, Toccoa Middle and High Schools will collect behavioral data on students recommended by teachers for supplemental behavioral interventions. Ultimately, the RTI team will identify and recommend one or more screening instruments in behavior to each school faculty. Each school has previously implemented a schoolwide positive behavioral support system, and the team will focus on articulating those efforts with the RTI process during the 2013–2014 academic year.

4. The schools will collect data on student referrals to special education and student dropouts at the end of this year as a comparison measure on the efficacy of RTI. Faculty will compare these data to data from previous years to determine the impact of RTI.

While some of these activities are professional development activities that initially focus on the members of the RTI leadership team itself, at some point the team will initiate a series of faculty meetings to begin to delineate RTI procedures with the school faculty. I developed a planning grid, presented in table 1.1 (page 31), that teams may use for those meetings (Bender, 2009a). This grid presents many of the questions that will arise during RTI implementation, and while the leadership team may initially discuss some of these issues in the initial structuring of RTI efforts, the whole faculty should also address these questions, as open discussion of these issues is likely to result in more faculty buy-in for the RTI process.

While some questions may be school specific, the general issues to address are presented across the top of the grid. Those issues cross-reference the individual instructional tiers, which appear down the side of the grid. Many schools have used this planning grid to focus faculty discussions of RTI. For a more detailed discussion of these issues, readers may wish to consult other sources (Bender, 2009a; Bender & Crane, 2011).

Formats for Individual RTIs

Several researchers have developed RTI formats that can help educators document the various interventions and the resulting data for a single student during the RTI process. In some cases, forms for RTI documentation are available from the school district or the state or provincial department of education website, and those forms may be required in specific areas. Educators should check those sources first to ascertain what may be required in the RTI process within a particular school or school district.

With that noted, some schools or school districts may leave the actual RTI documentation format up to the particular educators involved. Researchers have indicated the types of information that must be documented (Bender, 2009a; Bender & Shores, 2007; Vaughn & Roberts, 2007); these forms generally present a variety of areas on which information is needed, and educators should compile that information during the RTI process for every student whose learning needs necessitate a Tier 2 or Tier 3 intervention. The form typically includes six areas:

1. A description of Tier 1 instruction with evidence (data of some type) documenting a significant educational problem in Tier 1

2. A detailed description of a Tier 2 intervention plan

3. Observational notes of the Tier 2 intervention

4. A data chart coupled with a discussion of the data resulting from implementation of that Tier 2 intervention plan and recommended actions

5. A detailed description of a Tier 3 intervention plan if one is necessary

6. A data chart coupled with a discussion of the data resulting from implementation of that Tier 3 intervention plan and recommended actions

Table 1.1: An RTI Planning Grid

	Person Who Implements	Pupil-Teacher Ratio	Curriculum	Intervention Time and Duration	Frequency of Performance Monitoring	Treatment Fidelity Observation	Notifications
Refer for Special Education							
Tier 3 More Intensive Interventions							
Tier 2 Targeted Supplemental Interventions							
Tier 1 General Education							

Of course, teachers must supply detailed descriptions of the Tier 1 instruction and the Tier 2 and 3 interventions as well as high-quality progress monitoring of the student's performance. Faculty may use these data for subsequent discussion of the child's progress and may wish to develop a form based on these areas. While educators can address items 1, 3, and 5 in the list with a descriptive paragraph or written statement, items 2, 4, and 6 should be addressed via the development of data charts that actually show a student's performance over time. Following is a sample RTI that models this format, as do several more examples later in this book.

A Case Study: RTI in U.S. History

This section presents a sample RTI from a ninth-grade history class. In this scenario, a student named Tomás is struggling with U.S. history. His family moved to the United States two years ago, so Tomás did not have the opportunity to study U.S. history in elementary school; he completed grades 1 through 6 in Mexico City. While his English skills are considered good for conversational English, his academic command of the language is more limited. He is reading English at approximately a fourth-grade level but is participating in ninth-grade courses. A sample of an RTI documentation form for Tomás is presented in figure 1.4.

Most academic RTI efforts in middle and high schools involve supplemental reading instruction from the English or language arts teachers or supplemental mathematics instruction from the mathematics teachers. This example presents an RTI in content-area reading that might take place in the context of a high school subject-area class. Additional examples of middle and high school RTIs are presented in subsequent chapters.

Student: Tomás	Age: 15	Date: 11/05/2011
Initiating Teacher: Ms. Elly Runner	School: Trenton High School	Grade: 9

1. Student Difficulty and Summary of Tier 1 Instruction:

   Tomás is having difficulty reading the text in the U.S. history class. His assessment scores from last fall (at the end of eighth grade) indicate a reading level of approximately 4.3. While I used a learning center instructional approach that allows for considerable differentiation in lesson activities, Tomás seems to need even more assistance than I can provide. I have observed that Tomás has difficulties with the text, and I have been using peer buddies for many of the activities required in class. I have also provided individual tutoring assistance on his assignments in class as frequently as I could, but this did not help as much as I'd hoped. Although Tomás has good conversational English, his limited academic English does impair his reading skills, and that limits his achievement.

Ms. Elly Runner, 11/05/11

2. Tier 2 Intervention Plan:

As a Tier 2 intervention, Tomás will begin using a reading support curriculum in his U.S. history class. He will begin working on the computer-based program Study Island (www.studyisland.com). This curriculum presents multiple-choice reading comprehension questions related to specific content-area readings tied directly to the state standards in North Carolina (American Revolution, Federalist Period, and so forth).

Tomás will work on this curriculum every other day for at least fifteen minutes per session, for the next four weeks, during the next two units of study (American Revolution and the Federalist Period). Tomás will use his history text to seek answers as he moves through the questions presented on the computer program. Each week, I will print out a chart on how many comprehension questions he completed successfully, on average, that week. That will serve as a progress-monitoring tool for this Tier 2 intervention.

I presented this Tier 2 intervention plan to Mr. Strange, the chairperson of our student support team. He indicated that this intervention seemed appropriate and that I would be expected to present results of this intervention and a chart of data from this intervention to the student support team in five weeks to determine whether further intervention is necessary for Tomás.

Ms. Elly Runner, 11/07/11

3. Observational Notes of Student in Tier 2 Intervention:

I had the opportunity to observe Tomás working on his Study Island curricular assignment, and I noted that he appeared to truly enjoy his work in that curriculum. He was focused on the content and seemed motivated to perform correctly. It appeared he was still struggling with several of the questions, as he sought information from his textbook, but he was able to answer most of the comprehension questions correctly. He seemed excited when he got a question correct, and his awareness that there would be a weekly printout of his progress helped him stay focused on task and well motivated. In fact, he mentioned the data chart to me after his work was

Figure 1.4: RTI documentation form for Tomás in U.S. history.   Continued➔

completed, and he stated his desire to show progress. This curriculum is working for Tomás, in my opinion, and I look forward to reviewing the progress-monitoring data with Ms. Runner.

Mr. Jack Strange, student support team chair, 11/19/11

4. Tier 2 Intervention Summary and Recommendations:

Mr. Strange and I believe that Tomás has made some progress on the Tier 2 intervention over the last several weeks, but we believe that his progress will not allow him to catch up with his classmates in reading comprehension in the content area of U.S. history by the end of the year [see fig. 1.5, page 38]. While Tomás was able to work on the Study Island curriculum at least three times each week for the last four weeks, his progress in comprehending the history reading assignments was somewhat slow. At the end of four weeks, his reports showed some growth, but he was still not answering all of the questions correctly, even though this was essentially an open-book reading comprehension exercise. Thus his scores indicate continued reading comprehension problems.

Tomás's data chart shows that while his overall comprehension of main ideas was improving (from 41 percent to 70 percent), other areas were still far below proficiency [see fig. 1.5]. He went from answering 21.4 percent of his summarization questions correctly to answering 35 percent correctly, indicating poor comprehension skills in that area. Also, he only scored 45 percent on inferential comprehension. He is making progress, but it is not enough progress for Tomás to catch up to his classmates before the end of the year. These data suggest that Tomás will need more intensive intervention in reading comprehension in order to succeed in ninth-grade history. Mr. Strange and I requested a meeting of the student support team to discuss a Tier 3 intervention for Tomás.

Ms. Elly Runner, 01/03/12

5. Tier 3 Intervention Plan:

After reviewing Tomás's intervention data at the end of the four-week Tier 2 intervention, the student support team discussed providing a more intensive intervention program for Tomás. The student support team consisted of Ms. Runner, Tomás's history teacher; Mr. Jackson, the special education teacher; Mr. Strange, student support team chair; Ms. Snyder, another social studies teacher; and Ms. Luis, the department chair in social studies. During the meeting, the team agreed on several components of a Tier 3 intervention plan.

The team decided that Tomás would be assigned to a double period of U.S. history at the next grading period. Because a number of our ninth-grade students have required additional supplemental reading instruction in the content areas previously, several teachers have undertaken teaching "doubled" classes in various subjects, in which the first period is a general education class and the second period is a class only for those students struggling in reading in the first period. In those double-period classes, the second class has a much smaller pupil-teacher ratio, and teachers can deliver much more individual instructional assistance.

Ms. Snyder teaches such a double class in U.S. history, and the committee decided to place Tomás in that class at the end of the next grading period. Thus he will continue to take U.S. history in a doubled period and will continue to use the Study Island curriculum, though much more intensively than in the Tier 2 intervention.

During that second U.S. history period, Tomás will use the Study Island curriculum daily for forty-five minutes, and he will work with a small group of students on the study questions at the end of each chapter in the history text. This daily supplemental instruction on reading in the history text will continue for one grading period. Weekly printouts from that software will be utilized to track his content-area reading comprehension progress.

Mr. Jack Strange, student support team chair, 01/08/12

6. Tier 3 Intervention Summary and Recommendations:

After implementing the Tier 3 intervention for a nine-week grading period, the student support team (identified previously) met together again to discuss Tomás's progress. [Data from his Tier 3 intervention are presented in figure 1.6, page 39.] After reviewing the data, it was determined that Tomás was making significant gains in reading comprehension as well as in his knowledge of history during this Tier 3 intervention. We concluded that if that intervention were continued, he would continue to increase his reading and perhaps be able to achieve proficient reading in the content areas at some point. The committee instructed Ms. Snyder to have Tomás continue his work in the Tier 3 intervention (that is, a double period of U.S. history). The team will meet again as necessary to review Tomás's progress, at least once prior to the end of the current academic year.

Mr. Jack Strange, student support team chair, 03/18/12

Figure 1.4: RTI documentation form for Tomás in U.S. history.

Identifying a Need for Intervention

There are several important points to note in this RTI case study. First, the format used here provides an opportunity to document all phases of a complete RTI process, including documentation of Tier 1 instruction and Tier 2 and Tier 3 interventions. A form of this nature will be necessary to ensure that staff implement a complete RTI process; other resources discuss this particular format at length (Bender, 2009a; Bender & Shores, 2007).

In this example, the first section of the form presents information on the Tier 1 instruction. Ms. Runner was the ninth-grade teacher for U.S. history. She noticed that Tomás was having problems in the class, and both her observations and his recent state assessment scores indicated a need for assistance. Thus, in this example, the student support team used a combination of teacher recommendation and previous assessment scores to document the need for a Tier 2 intervention. Many middle and high school model programs use this combination to document the need for Tier 2 interventions (Bender, 2009a; Duffy, n.d.; Gibbs, 2008; James, 2010; Johnson & Smith, 2008; Rozalski, 2009).

Planning the Tier 2 Intervention

Ms. Runner sought a Tier 2 intervention that both addressed Tomás's reading comprehension in the subject matter and taught U.S. history. She selected the Study Island program because it could serve as a supplement in various content areas and was tied with state standards in Ms. Runner's home state of North Carolina. A program description of Study Island is presented in the following feature box.

The Study Island Supplemental Curriculum

Study Island is a web-based computerized instructional program tied specifically to each U.S. state's standards of learning as well as to each state's testing program. In general, teachers should select software programs specifically developed for their particular state, if possible. By basing this program exclusively on the web rather than on software presented only on the school's computers, the Study Island developers have made these instructional and assessment materials available to licensed users both at school and at home; this can be a significant advantage since middle and secondary students can complete these instructional activities as homework. Some students will undertake many of these instructional activities in the home environment, whereas a software-based program loaded exclusively on school computers does not present any home-study options.

In addition, because the program is tied to statewide instructional standards, instructional activities are available in a wide array of subject areas including mathematics, reading, science, and social studies. Teachers can either allow students to select topics on which to work, or they can assign topics tied to the specific unit of instruction, as shown in the case study example. The student will then receive various computer-based work or educational gaming activities on that specific topic. When using this program for individual students as opposed to the entire class, concrete goals and frequent progress monitoring are both critical in order to document exactly how a child is progressing.

Based on adaptive assessment technology within the program, the curriculum adjusts itself according to the learning curve of particular students, either moving students through the content faster or moving students into a slower track with more practice on various content items. Once students have mastered a particular lesson and assessment, they receive a blue ribbon and are able to move to the next lesson. However, should a student receive a low score, the program may prompt the student to continue working on the same skills until he or she develops proficiency, or it may prompt the student to discuss the lesson with the teacher. Through the software, students receive instructional feedback each time they answer a question.

The Study Island program can supplement Tomás's U.S. history textbook. Ms. Runner decided to utilize that software to increase Tomás's reading comprehension skills and his knowledge of U.S. history. This curriculum, like almost all modern software, allows the teacher to customize each lesson for each individual student. Furthermore, as noted, the available lessons within the program correlate with the state's reading standards and course of study. Given Tomás's trouble with reading the history text, Ms. Runner decided to focus on several comprehension strands tied to her state reading standards and Tomás's specific skill deficits, including finding the main idea, summarizing, and comprehending.

During each Tier 2 intervention session, Tomás logged into the computer, opened the correct lesson, and, using his history text as an additional information source, completed the lesson questions for the day. The weekly report the Study Island software generated detailed how many questions Tomás completed, the amount of time it took to complete each session, the percentage correct on that lesson, and his reading proficiency score for each type of question in the lesson (inferential, summarization, and so on).

Finally, note that Ms. Runner shared her Tier 2 intervention plan with the chair of the student support team, Mr. Strange, prior to implementing that intervention. Some degree of student support team involvement is always advisable prior to initiating a Tier 2 intervention, and in some areas, school district or state- or provincewide RTI implementation guidelines require involvement of the student support team.

Reviewing Tier 2 Data

At the end of four weeks, Ms. Runner reviewed the data collected from Tomás's assessments on Study Island. Those data are presented in figure 1.5 (page 38). She

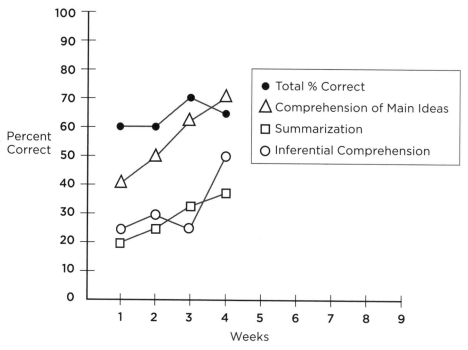

Figure 1.5: Tier 2 intervention data for Tomás.

then discussed Tomás's progress with Mr. Strange. Although Tomás was making some progress, he was still not progressing quickly enough to achieve grade-level status in reading comprehension by the end of the school year.

These data show that Tomás would still need a more intensive intervention in order to achieve grade-level status on content-area reading comprehension and master the content in U.S. history. Ms. Runner requested a meeting with the student support team to present her Tier 2 data and to plan a Tier 3 intervention.

Planning the Tier 3 Intervention

Using all of the available data, the student support team met to discuss an appropriate plan of action. The meeting began with a review of the Tier 2 intervention, and Ms. Runner began by explaining all the data she had collected from her informal classroom observations, previous assessment scores, and the Tier 2 data from Study Island. Using the data chart she had created during the Tier 2 intervention, she explained that Tomás was making some progress, particularly in comprehending the main idea, but not enough overall progress to achieve grade-level status by the end of the year. The team agreed that Tomás would need more intensive instruction and assessment, and they worked together to create a Tier 3 intervention plan.

In this example, the team deemed a double-period approach best for the Tier 3 intervention, since using it could address both reading comprehension skills and knowledge of U.S. history. Another social studies teacher, Ms. Snyder, was already teaching a double period of U.S. history, and like Ms. Runner, she was using the Study Island program. The student support team decided to place Tomás in that double period of U.S. history and continue his work, though more intensively, in Study Island. Thus Tomás would work with that curriculum on a daily basis for nine weeks, with his progress monitored weekly by Ms. Snyder. This would, therefore, be much more intensive than the previous Tier 2 intervention, and this level of intensity should help Tomás move toward grade-level reading skills by the end of the year.

Reviewing Tier 3 Data

At the end of nine weeks, the student support team met to discuss Tomás's progress throughout the Tier 3 intervention. Ms. Snyder provided the data she had collected from Study Island as documentation of Tomás's growth in reading comprehension. These data, presented in figure 1.6, demonstrate that, although Tomás was still not on grade level, he had made significant progress throughout the nine weeks.

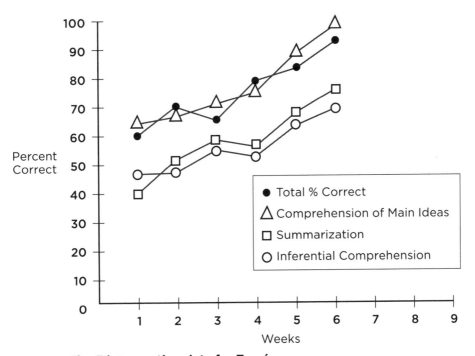

Figure 1.6: Tier 3 intervention data for Tomás.

The student support team decided that Tomás should remain in this Tier 3 intervention (a doubled class for U.S. history) for the next nine-week grading period. If he continued to be as successful, the team believed this intervention would move Tomás toward grade-level reading comprehension by the end of the year. Ms. Snyder agreed to monitor his progress each week and contact Mr. Strange immediately should she notice any decrease in Tomás's progress. The team also decided to meet at the end of the year to delineate any interventions that might be necessary for Tomás during the next school year.

Considering Issues From This Case Study

There are several issues to discuss in this case study. First, educators should consider the level of documentation presented here a minimum for RTI efforts in middle and high school programs. While the primary emphasis of the RTI initiative is provision of general education interventions for students in need, many states do use this documentation to determine whether a student who does not show progress in these intervention tiers has a disability, particularly in the middle school grades. When a teacher working with a student support team begins a Tier 2 intervention, he or she does not know if a disability eligibility determination might ultimately be necessary a few months later. Consequently, the teacher must develop and maintain complete descriptions of the interventions implemented and the progress-monitoring data from those interventions. Typically the general education teacher initially fills out the document, and after the Tier 2 intervention, the chair of the student support team completes it.

Note that the documentation describes the interventions very explicitly: how many days per week, how many minutes per day, and exactly what Tomás was required to do during the intervention. This level of description is critical in determining what interventions might work for that student if additional interventions become necessary.

I recommend creating a folder to maintain this information together as well as using a form such as that presented in figure 1.4 (page 32) to describe the complete RTI process for each student (Bender, 2009a). The support team should initiate that documentation prior to the beginning of every Tier 2 intervention. Schools might also consider using the first two sections of that documentation procedure as an "entry ticket." Prior to initiating a Tier 2 intervention or meeting with the team, general education teachers would document the learning problem using observations and some type of data and would design an intervention to alleviate that problem. That documentation would then become their introduction to the student's support team meeting.

Using computerized interventions such as the Study Island program makes conducting Tier 2 interventions much more possible for general education teachers in the middle and high school grades, because that software does most of the instruction. While most middle and high school RTI models involve holding Tier 2 and 3 interventions in a separate intervention period, some model RTI programs such as Berkeley Springs High School (a model described in chapter 2) involve having subject-area teachers conduct Tier 2 interventions.

In the Tier 2 intervention described here, Ms. Runner merely placed Tomás (and probably several other students) in the program for portions of the academic period on certain days. This is a very significant advantage of computer-based intervention programs at the Tier 2 and Tier 3 levels, and subsequent chapters will describe a variety of software or web-based intervention programs that middle and high schools may wish to obtain to facilitate their RTI efforts. While RTI is certainly possible without using technology support, such support greatly eases the time concerns associated with RTI.

Aside from time, however, there is a more pressing reason to utilize software or web-based instruction: by and large, these curricula work! There is even some evidence that these curricula work when other instructional approaches do not (see Bender & Waller, 2011, for a review). For that reason, if other instructional methods have not met struggling students' needs, it is absolutely essential to expose them to the most intensive computer- or web-based instruction possible that addresses their instructional needs. In fact, it may be a disservice to not use such technology-based programs for these students at some point during Tier 2 or Tier 3 interventions. Research has shown the efficacy of many of these programs (Bender & Waller, 2011; Cote, 2007; Elder-Hinshaw, Manset-Williamson, Nelson, & Dunn, 2006; Salend, 2009), and short of a single teacher working with a single student daily for a twenty- or thirty-minute Tier 2 intervention, nothing a teacher can do in the general education class provides the intensity of high-quality instructional software. Given modern software and technology options, every struggling student, and perhaps every child at the twenty-fifth percentile or lower in reading, must have the opportunity to benefit from exposure to such high-quality instructional software at some point during the RTI process.

Finally, this case study illustrates that some interventions work when others do not. Of course, the intensity of the intervention plays a role in that phenomenon; high-intensity, daily interventions are more likely to work than lower-intensity, two- or three-times-a-week interventions, and interventions that more closely align with specific student deficits are likely to be still more effective. While teachers should always plan an intervention they expect will succeed with a given student, they should also anticipate seeing some interventions fail. At that point, those teachers should be prepared to initiate another, more intensive intervention program. The student progress-monitoring data should be the overall arbiter of the efficacy of any intervention.

Conclusion

As this chapter indicates, the planning process for RTI implementation frequently takes more than a single year, and most proponents of RTI indicate the need for a three- to five-year implementation process. Initially, middle and high schools must understand the RTI process, initiate faculty discussion of the value of RTI, and determine whether to restructure current support classes as Tier 2 intervention classes or plan additional support classes in one or more subject areas (typically reading or mathematics). Furthermore, schools should develop a long-term plan for implementation, as this elevates the RTI process to a schoolwide reform initiative and is likely to result in improved RTI efforts over time.

With those RTI efforts in place, middle and high schools may then wish to consider their RTI efforts from the ground up. In short, RTI examples in virtually every state and province emphasize the necessity of building RTI interventions on the solid ground of differentiated instruction (Berkeley et al., 2009). Thus Tier 1 of RTI should be highly differentiated instruction in content-area classes. The next chapter provides several real-world examples of RTI implementation in middle and high schools.

Chapter 2

Existing RTI Structures in Middle and High Schools

The RTI effort holds the potential to significantly restructure most middle and high school programs (NASDSE, 2006), and such a restructuring effort is likely to involve all educators at these grade levels, though relatively few high school or middle school educators have been involved in RTI to date. In a 2008 survey of administrators of special education, 67 percent reported that implementation of RTI had already begun in the elementary grades, while only 27 percent indicated such implementation had begun for middle school, and 16 percent indicated such implementation in high school (Spectrum K–12 School Solutions/Council of Administrators of Special Education [CASE], 2008).

Still, a variety of middle and high school RTI initiatives have been described in the research (Allen et al., 2011; Duffy, n.d.; Gibbs, 2008; Johnson & Smith, 2008; NHSC et al., 2010; Rozalski, 2009), and these can help educators see the level of restructuring that may be necessary as well as how RTI procedures are already being implemented in middle or high schools. The model programs described in this chapter provide an initial point of departure for middle and high school RTI efforts. First, however, educators must consider one overriding question: how must RTI be structured within middle and high school schedules?

RTI in Departmentalized Schools

Deshler (NCRTI, n.d.a) notes several differences in the structure of departmentalized schools (that is, middle and high schools in which students change classes to take specific courses from teachers certified in specific subject areas) that might create implementation concerns.

For example, general education teachers in grades K–6 are typically expected to conduct Tier 1 instruction and universal screening for everyone as well as conduct Tier 2 interventions for some percentage of their class at some point during the school day. In those cases, the Tier 2 intervention is supplemental to the Tier 1 instruction, so teachers are not removing students from Tier 1 instruction with the whole class in order to receive their Tier 2 instruction. This is to say that Tier 2 and

Tier 3 interventions should be supplemental to the general education instruction, not a replacement for it.

However, middle and high school teachers teaching specific subject content areas (U.S. history, biology, algebra, and so on) usually have students for only one period per day (Protheroe, 2010). Those teachers will not typically have the option of providing supplemental instruction for a subset of students at the Tier 2 or 3 intervention levels during that single instructional period (Protheroe, 2010), and they certainly cannot remove a particular student from another teacher's class later in the day for supplemental instruction in their subject areas. This fairly rigid period structure of middle and high schools seems to be a major barrier to implementation of RTI unless options are forthcoming on how to implement RTI in that context (Lolich et al., 2010; NCRTI, n.d.a; NHSC, 2010).

Who would lead departmentalized Tier 2 or 3 interventions? In various middle and high school model programs around the United States, such interventions are undertaken not by general education teachers in content-area classes but by various instructional coaches or other educational personnel at the school (Gibbs, 2008; Hoover & Patton, 2008). Instructional coaches in reading or mathematics or special education teachers may undertake Tier 2 or Tier 3 instruction in the middle grades, whereas in the elementary grades, Tier 2 and in some cases Tier 3 interventions are led by the general education teacher.

It is frequently the case that the Tier 2 and Tier 3 interventions in middle and high schools are undertaken not by general education teachers in content-area classes but by various instructional coaches or other educational personnel at the school.

That is not to suggest that general education teachers will have no role in RTI. Quite the contrary. For example, the documentation of a learning problem in Tier 1 instruction will be the responsibility of all teachers, and that is a critical function in the RTI process (Gibbs, 2008; Johnson & Smith, 2008). All teachers will be expected not only to deliver high-quality differentiated instruction at the Tier 1 level but also to document the efficacy of that instruction (Gibbs, 2008).

In addition, some general education teachers in English, reading, or mathematics (for example, general mathematics or algebra I) may conduct the actual Tier 2 or Tier 3 interventions by teaching additional intervention-focused classes, as mentioned in chapter 1 (Johnson & Smith, 2008). Other teachers in special instructional roles may likewise provide some Tier 2 or Tier 3 interventions. For example, many Title I reading teachers are revamping their reading instruction to fit within RTI as a supplemental Tier 2 or Tier 3 reading intervention.

While RTI implementation in elementary grades can provide some information on what RTI involves, it seems clear that RTI implementation in middle and high schools will be different (Duffy, n.d.; Gibbs, 2008; King-Sears & Bowman-Kruhm, 2010; NCRTI, n.d.a; NHSC et al., 2010). The best guidance on implementation of

RTI in middle and high schools comes from actual implementation experiences, as these can help identify concerns and suggest solutions for addressing complex challenges during the RTI implementation process.

Real-World RTI Example: Berkeley Springs High School

While several articles illustrate interventions in middle and high schools (Gibbs, 2008; Johnson & Smith, 2008; NHSC et al., 2010), Rozalski (2009) describes RTI implementation focused on reading at a rural high school. Berkeley Springs High School in West Virginia has a relatively high percentage of students from a lower socioeconomic background (33 percent). A total of 750 students were enrolled in the school, and 11 percent of those students were receiving special education services. This school was selected as a test site for the West Virginia RTI implementation program and developed the RTI implementation plan that the following feature box describes.

RTI Implementation at Berkeley Springs High School

Resources Restructuring: Educators will frequently have to restructure school resources to facilitate RTI (Gibbs, 2008). At Berkeley Springs High School, the administration scheduled classes such that teachers had a common planning period. In addition, several teachers received specific training on the selected research-proven reading program, Corrective Reading (www.mcgraw-hill .co.uk./sra/correctivereading.htm), a curriculum designed to assist older readers who demonstrate a lack of reading skills. Teachers were requested to help identify students who, they believed, needed supplemental assistance, and a total of sixty-seven students were tentatively identified. Those students then received several reading assessments to document their specific reading problems. All of these activities represent RTI tasks that require some refocusing of resources at the school level.

Universal Screening and Progress Monitoring: Staff members used teacher recommendations to select students who needed assistance and gave only those students additional reading assessments. They undertook no universal screening beyond the statewide assessments. They did perform more frequent benchmarking assessments to monitor individual students' progress at the Tier 2 level.

The Tier 1 Instruction: Each general education teacher was responsible for Tier 1 instruction in his or her subject area. Each teacher was also expected to provide traditional reading instruction as appropriate, embedded within his or her specific instructional area. Some might suggest that this is no different from what general education high school teachers were doing previously. Given the school's increased focus on reading intervention, however, it is quite

Continued➜

likely that many general education teachers spent additional time on reading skills within their subject areas.

The Tier 2 Intervention: Students who needed a Tier 2 intervention received additional reading instruction embedded within their Tier 1 classes, as well as additional in-class resource assistance. While the general education teacher can provide such assistance, special education teachers, functioning as inclusion teachers, might also provide that additional reading instruction (Hoover & Patton, 2008). Students at the Tier 2 level also underwent benchmark assessments multiple times throughout the school year. Teachers therefore followed their progress in reading more closely than that of Tier 1 students.

The Tier 3 Intervention: For students whose reading skills did not progress using the Tier 2 intervention, teachers initiated a Tier 3 intervention. Students in Tier 3 continued to participate in all Tier 1 and Tier 2 interventions, but they also received an additional intervention scheduled at a different point in the school day, and that scheduling varied from one student to another. In that Tier 3 intervention, the instructor used the supplemental reading curriculum. Some students also used a computerized reading program in the Tier 3 intervention level. Reading coaches, special education teachers, and other educators provided this intervention, rather than the general education teachers.

Results: The educators at Berkeley Springs High School were very pleased with the results of this intervention after the first year. They noted reading improvement in all three tiers, though students in Tier 1, as one might expect, demonstrated the lowest rate of improvement. At the Tier 2 level, improvement in various reading skills ranged from a half-year in reading fluency to more than a year in comprehension. At the Tier 3 level, the improvements were even more dramatic, based on a year-long intervention. Reading fluency for those low-skill readers jumped from a 4.7 reading equivalency to 6.6: almost two full grade levels. Word identification moved more than two grade levels, from 3.8 to 5.9, and reading comprehension skills jumped from 3.5 to 5.4. The article did not report on other possible outcomes, such as how many students were ultimately referred for special education or how this intervention may have impacted the dropout rate at the school.

Taking a Different Approach to Screening

Berkeley Springs High School described limited screening as a function of the Tier 2 intervention rather than Tier 1 instruction (Rozalski, 2009). The screening effort in this example was not universal in that not every student in the high school received an individually administered screening instrument, as is the case in elementary grades. Students were initially selected by teacher nomination and then provided some individual follow-up assessment for participation in the RTI process. Also, in this model program, screening was undertaken less frequently than the three-times-per-year standard for universal screening in the elementary grades. The more limited, selective screening process (Rozalski, 2009) saved time and resources for other aspects of RTI implementation. While this teacher nomination process could potentially open the door for some teacher bias, such bias is much less likely when teacher nominations are coupled with hard data from individual screening devices, as was the case in this example.

With that said, certainly all of these high school students had participated in various statewide assessments, and thus some screening data were available to tentatively identify students functioning below grade level (Rozalski, 2009). This, of course, suggests one option for screening in middle and high school RTI programs. Perhaps schools should use statewide assessment data for this purpose rather than implementing a new layer of universal screening assessments.

While multiple universal screenings are critically important in each of the lower grades—particularly in the primary grades—where reading and math skills are initially developed, such numerous screenings may be less useful during the later years of school. Much of the same information may be gleaned merely from reviewing routine assessments (for example, state or provincial assessments, which are typically administered each year, or in-class assessments completed in each instructional unit).

Furthermore, the need for multiple screenings per year may not be as pronounced in the upper grades. A solid track record of student progress is typically available for each student, unlike in the earliest grades of school, and thus middle and high schools are not necessarily bound by the three-times-per-year expectation for universal screening assessment. For example, Allen and his colleagues (2011) report that 64 percent of the middle school RTI programs in their U.S. sample undertake screening three times each year, and model high school programs report screening as an annual effort (Gibbs, 2008).

In situations where yearly state or provincial assessment data are not available, middle and high school faculty should explore the option used at Berkeley Springs High—a combination of teacher nomination followed by subsequent individual testing to document the need for Tier 2 or Tier 3 RTI interventions. This procedure is much more cost effective than screening all students in middle and high schools with new assessments specifically for RTI. Finally, few educators would argue that students need to be tested more frequently than they already are.

> In situations where yearly state or provincial testing screening data are not available, middle and high school faculty should explore a combination of teacher nomination followed by subsequent individual testing to document the need for interventions.

Leading Tier 2 Interventions

Berkeley Springs provided Tier 2 interventions by offering additional instruction within the context of the general education class (Rozalski, 2009). This was described as a combination of in-class resource assistance (which might include informal assistance such as individual after-class tutoring, longer time for various assessments, and so forth), and increased progress monitoring for students in Tier 2 and

Tier 3 that involved benchmarking assessments in reading administered three times each year. To clarify, while the school did not perform universal screening for all students in Tier 1 three times per year in this example, it did do progress monitoring in Tiers 2 and 3 three times each year for the students needing instruction at those levels. In addition, the general education teachers undertook responsibility for the Tier 2 interventions, making this similar to the overall model described for elementary RTI programs. Clearly, this practice was effective since impressive gains in reading scores resulted from this intervention (Rozalski, 2009).

When a student's academic performance measures are improving, middle and high school educators are doing it right!

Many proponents of RTI wonder if it is realistic to believe that middle and high school teachers, who may face up to 160 students per day in six or seven different periods, can undertake meaningful, substantive Tier 2 interventions (Gibbs, 2008). In this example, little information was available on the level of intensity of this intervention (Rozalski, 2009). Did Tier 2 students receive in-class resource assistance for a specific time period each day (that is, twenty minutes each day), or was the Tier 2 instructional assistance more sporadic and informal? Furthermore, who delivered that instruction—a special education teacher, a reading coach, a paraprofessional, or someone else working within the general education class, as has been recommended (Hoover & Patton, 2008)? Was a research-proven reading curriculum implemented during that in-class resource assistance, or did the assistance involve merely tutorial assistance on the Tier 1 curriculum?

With little guidance from the literature, the best answers come from the data provided by a hard look at student progress. When students' academic performance measures are improving significantly, educators are doing it right. That is clearly the case at Berkeley Springs High School.

Real-World RTI Example: Long Beach Unified School District High School

A supplemental intervention program in the Long Beach Unified School District is considered by many to be a model RTI initiative (Duffy, n.d.; Gibbs, 2008). The district has been implementing supplementary interventions for students moving into high school since the 1980s. It does not specifically refer to its system as an RTI procedure because the district implemented this intervention system prior to the development of the U.S. RTI initiative. All high school instruction in the district is based on differentiated instruction coupled with a pre–high school assessment in reading, supplemental interventions when needed, and a data-driven decision-making process (Gibbs, 2008). A synopsis of this model is provided in the following feature box.

The Long Beach Unified School District Intervention Initiative

Resources Restructuring: The Long Beach Unified School District has long committed resources to assist students who are behind in their academic progress at the end of grade 8. In fact, the district has been doing this so long that little information is available on resources committed to this intervention model; for educators in that district, this is simply best teaching practice (Gibbs, 2008). With that noted, one can see some resource reallocations, including assignment of English/language teachers to double blocks of instruction with the same group of struggling learners and purchases of supplemental curricula for basic skills.

Universal Screening and Progress Monitoring: The school undertakes a universal screening procedure at the end of grade 8 based on a student's state assessment scores, course grades, and for some students, additional individual assessments as needed. The assessment used is a component of the LANGUAGE! curriculum (Greene, 1999), which is a research-proven reading and literacy curriculum adopted by the state and district (see a description of this curriculum in chapter 6 and also at www.sopriswest.com). Frequent progress monitoring within various intervention classes is based on the assessments within the LANGUAGE! curriculum (Greene, 1999).

In Tier 3, as described in the following sections, the various assessments from these two curricula are used multiple times throughout the year to monitor the students' progress after they are placed in supplemental interventions.

The Tier 1 Instruction: Each general education teacher in the high school is expected to differentiate instruction based on the needs of the individual students within the class. Furthermore, consistent with best practices, each teacher is expected to provide reading instruction embedded within his or her specific instructional area.

The Tier 2 Intervention: While the Long Beach Unified School District does not specifically differentiate between Tiers 2 and 3 (remember, this system predated the three-tier RTI model), it does make distinctions based on the initial assessments of the students. Students entering high school who are one to two years behind in reading receive Tier 1 instruction supplemented by an additional literacy workshop course. No specific curriculum is associated with that course, but students receive scaffolded instruction and other content enhancements related to the core curriculum

The Tier 3 Intervention: For students who enter high school two or more years behind in reading, a double block of English/language arts is provided that includes the same core language/English course all students take as well

Continued➜

as a parallel period of intensive reading and literacy instruction. This is the most intensive intervention tier and involves instruction based on one of the research-proven curricula mentioned earlier.

Note in this example that it is possible for students to enter this most intensive intervention without having been subjected to the Tier 2 intervention (Duffy, n.d.; Gibbs, 2008). However, this entire intervention system predated the current RTI models, so use caution concerning overinterpretation of this point.

Results: This program reports results in terms of the percentage of students who are referred for special education services (that is, students for whom these interventions were not successful) rather than in reading score gains, as in the previous example. Data show a marked reduction in the number of students referred for special education services in this school (Duffy, n.d.; Gibbs, 2008). In the United States, 12 to 14 percent of students are ultimately referred for special education, whereas in Long Beach, the comparable percentage is only 7 percent, suggesting a 50 percent reduction in special education referrals resulting from this multitiered intervention system. Clearly educators in the Long Beach Unified School District are successfully addressing learning problems within the general education curriculum (Duffy, n.d.; Gibbs, 2008).

Doubling the Instructional Period for RTI Interventions

As mentioned previously, a major issue in implementation of RTI in middle and high schools involves deciding when to implement Tier 2 or Tier 3 interventions. In the Long Beach example, the faculty doubled the instructional period for struggling students (Duffy, n.d.; Gibbs, 2008). As mentioned in chapter 1, doubling involves identifying the basic skill area in which students are struggling and then doubling their instruction in that area, a process also referred to as *parallel periods* (Gibbs, 2008). In this example, students who entered high school two or more years below grade level in reading on their statewide assessment exams were placed in a double block of English/language arts (Duffy, n.d.; Gibbs, 2008), and the second language arts period was considered a Tier 2 intervention period. Typically, the second period in each doubled block involves fewer students than the usual classes, so the students received more intensive instruction based on the smaller pupil-teacher ratio. Note also that this screening procedure involves use of existing student scores rather than universal screening.

Other anecdotal reports indicate that various middle and high schools are doubling the instruction periods in math or language arts for struggling students (James, 2010; Stefanoni, 2009). For example, James (2010) reported that the faculty at Stewardson-Strasburg High School in Illinois also implemented this doubling idea, though they doubled the students' time in algebra I rather than in reading or language arts. In that instance, struggling students spent two consecutive instructional periods in algebra I, with the second period serving as a Tier 2 intervention.

Other proponents of RTI have advocated using an intervention period as one way to implement Tier 2 and Tier 3 interventions in middle and secondary schools (Gibbs, 2008; James, 2010), and doubling is one way to do that. Doubling, however, involves more than merely an extra period of English or mathematics. In this example, double periods in algebra I, English, or language arts were scheduled as back-to-back periods in which the same general education teacher taught both the initial class and the smaller second class. This ensured continuity such that the teacher could focus the second class directly on specific difficulties he or she had noted for each student.

Doubling involves identifying the basic skill area in which students are struggling and then doubling their instruction in that area.

Within the context of the second period, the essential requirements of RTI must be addressed. For example, teachers must implement regular progress monitoring. In a doubled language arts instructional period, the teacher should assess each student in decoding and comprehension skills every two to three weeks and generate a data chart tracking each student's progress in the Tier 2 intervention. In addition, the size of the doubled class must be kept small in order to ensure a more intensive supplemental instructional opportunity, as is typically required for Tier 2 interventions. For the second period of the doubled class, class sizes of ten to twelve students seem appropriate, since students in those classes could then receive considerable individual attention, and such class sizes allow time for the teacher to address individual problems and undertake the additional progress monitoring necessary. Doubling is certainly a model for RTI implementation that middle and high schools should consider for students struggling in basic skill areas of reading, language arts, or mathematics (Duffy, n.d.; Gibbs, 2008).

Using Differentiation and Research-Proven Curricula

Like most of the research literature supportive of RTI (see Bender, 2009a, for a review), the Long Beach Unified School District implementation practices stressed high-quality instruction as the basis for RTI. The district identified differentiated instruction in all secondary classes as the essential basis for Tier 1 instruction (Gibbs, 2008). Note that both the Long Beach and the Berkeley Springs models stipulated utilization of specific research-proven instructional curricula, particularly for Tier 3 (Duffy, n.d.; Gibbs, 2008). Most of the research on RTI (see Bender, 2009a, for a review) stipulates use of research-proven curricula for the targeted instruction in the RTI model, and instructional programs such as those mentioned in these case studies (LANGUAGE!, LiPS, and Corrective Reading) should certainly be considered for use in Tier 2 and Tier 3 interventions. In mathematics, research-proven curricula are fewer, but a number are available (SuccessMaker Math, Vmath; see Bender & Crane, 2011, for a discussion of RTI procedures in mathematics).

With that noted, not all RTI models involve implementation of specific, research-proven supplemental curricula. For example, the Heartland RTI model described in Tilly (2003) does not specify a separate curriculum for Tier 2 or 3 interventions. In those cases, Tier 2 or 3 may involve increasingly intensive instruction on the core curriculum the school adopts. Most RTI models, however, like those described herein, do involve implementation of specific supplemental curricula.

Measuring RTI Outcomes

Educators should note the various outcome measures they can use to gauge the effectiveness of the RTI procedures. The Long Beach Unified School District reported the positive outcomes in terms of reduction of the number of students referred to and placed in special education (Duffy, n.d.; Gibbs, 2008), whereas the outcome variables at Berkeley Springs High School involved actual academic improvements in various reading skills (Rozalski, 2009).

Gibbs (2008) mentions another possible measure of RTI outcomes at the high school level—dropout prevention. Research indicates that 30 percent of students drop out of school prior to graduation, and preventing dropouts can be a strong indicator of the overall success of a secondary RTI program (Gibbs, 2008). While one may consider any of these measures appropriate outcome variables for measuring success of the RTI program at the secondary level, the major focus of the RTI literature has been progress monitoring of individual academic success in either reading or mathematics. That is why the literature stresses highly detailed progress monitoring in those two subjects. Still, as Gibbs (2008) notes, measures of overall program success are available for secondary schools that are not available in the lower grades (dropout rates, for example), and schools should use all of these measures.

In fact, these different outcome measures really address different purposes. Individual student success measures must serve as the basis for determining the outcomes of the RTI interventions for individual students. In contrast, measures such as a reduction in dropouts or reduction in referrals to or placements in special education will not present a repeated assessment of an individual student's progress over time, but these can certainly serve as appropriate indicators of overall RTI program success.

Reallocating Resources for RTI

As both of the examples presented thus far indicate, a restructuring of resources is necessary to make RTI work in middle and high schools (NCRTI, n.d.a). In the Berkeley Springs High School example, both the formation of a common planning period and the opportunity for several teachers to undertake professional development on new curricula suggest that the administration was willing to reallocate resources (Rozalski, 2009). The same types of resource reallocations are apparent in the Long Beach example. In that district, administrators implemented doubled classes (Gibbs, 2008), showing a willingness to restructure resources and teacher instructional time to implement an effective RTI program.

Real-World RTI Example: Cheyenne Mountain Junior High

The faculty at Cheyenne Mountain Junior High began the RTI process in 2006 (Johnson & Smith, 2008). The school population at Cheyenne Mountain is mostly Caucasian, with small representation of certain minority groups, including 2 percent African American, 8 percent Hispanic, and 5 percent Asian. Approximately 10 percent of the students in the school are English learners. Prior to 2006, the faculty noted a growing number of failures in grades 7 and 8 and chose to implement RTI to improve the intervention system for those struggling students (Johnson & Smith, 2008). More information on the particulars of that implementation is presented in the following feature box.

RTI Implementation at Cheyenne Mountain Junior High

Resources Restructuring: Cheyenne Mountain Junior High had previously implemented a multitiered intervention system for schoolwide behavioral support, and building on that multitiered system proved to be the best approach to RTI implementation for this faculty (Johnson & Smith, 2008). Because of that background, the entire faculty was already aware of and, to some degree practicing, a three-tier, increasingly intensive intervention system for reducing behavior problems, so it was merely a matter of extending that same concept to academic problems (Johnson & Smith, 2008).

The faculty chose to build a bank of academic interventions to address students' individual needs in reading, and the faculty decided to use the existing problem-solving team at the school to assist teachers in selecting the appropriate academic intervention for each struggling student. Finally, the school had already implemented a professional development plan based on professional learning communities as a school improvement approach (DuFour, DuFour, & Eaker, 2008). That professional learning community dedicated itself to effective RTI implementation over a period of several years.

Universal Screening and Progress Monitoring: No universal screening measures were available when Cheyenne Mountain faculty implemented RTI (Johnson & Smith, 2008), so as in the previous examples, students were initially identified for supportive services through teacher referrals, parent referrals, and scores on state assessments. The school faculty set a goal of developing curriculum-based measures in the basic skill areas of reading, mathematics, and writing, as well as establishing a data-based decision-making process for inclusion in the more intensive Tier 2 and Tier 3 interventions. The school faculty also chose to undertake universal screening three times per year, as is generally recommended for elementary grades (Bender, 2009a; Johnson & Smith, 2008). During the first year, the school also implemented a commercially available individual screening measure in both reading and mathematics, and those data were compiled on a data sheet for each student in the RTI process.

Continued➜

The Tier 1 Instruction: Educators stressed differentiated instruction in each class at the school in order to ensure that the general education classes continued to meet the needs of 80 percent or more of the student body (Johnson & Smith, 2008). Teachers in the English classes, for example, differentiated instruction by offering a range of options for completing various assignments. Options for completing a book report included writing an essay, developing a scrapbook, writing a newspaper article, or creating a video production. The faculty noted that completion of these assignments increased considerably when students were offered a variety of choices for the format for their work (Johnson & Smith, 2008).

The Tier 2 Intervention: Because of limited resources, this school chose to aim the initial efforts exclusively at reading. Supplemental help in the general education class provided Tier 2 interventions, including options such as enhanced instruction, differentiated assignments, modifications of assignments, and various other accommodations. Targeted, small-group instruction was also emphasized.

To provide further Tier 2 instruction, the faculty developed or redesigned various elective courses, including the school's literacy lab, which was taught by the school's reading specialist. That program uses the LANGUAGE! curriculum (Greene, 1999), which is described in chapter 6. The school has a long-term goal of developing similar lab electives in both mathematics and writing (Johnson & Smith, 2008).

The Tier 3 Intervention: At Cheyenne Mountain Junior High, Tier 3 interventions were generally synonymous with special education services (Johnson & Smith, 2008). Thus students in Tier 3 would receive inclusive special education services in the general education classroom consisting of additional tutoring by the special education teacher and/or other small-group or individual educational assistance.

Results: The educators at Cheyenne Mountain Junior High note that approximately 50 percent of the students receiving Tier 2 intervention in the literacy lab have made significant gains in reading comprehension and have substantially improved their grades in other courses (Johnson & Smith, 2008). As in many middle and high schools that have implemented RTI, this faculty found that the number of students requiring special education services has substantially declined (Johnson & Smith, 2008).

One of the most profound results noted by this faculty, however, was the change in school culture that resulted from a collaborative effort to develop an effective RTI procedure to assist struggling students. The teachers themselves state this best: "Without the interventions of RTI and the focus of developing a professional learning community, the school would not have seen the concerted effort on implementation of such instructional practices as differentiation across the entire school" (Johnson & Smith, 2008, p. 49).

Scheduling Tier 3 Interventions

As the Cheyenne Mountain example illustrates, one issue schools and districts may have to determine is exactly when Tier 3 interventions should occur. Should Tier 3 interventions take place before or after a student is determined to be eligible for special education services? In the Cheyenne Mountain model, Tier 3 interventions generally took place after a student was placed in special education (Johnson & Smith, 2008), making this unlike the previous examples.

While most schools have developed a three-tier model in which all three tiers are functions of general education, other schools have implemented a three-tier model in which Tier 3 comes after placement in special education (Bender, 2009a). Of course, the state or provincial department of education often answers this question, and educators should check their department of education website about specific policies. Some states and provinces leave this question to the determination of districts or individual schools, however, and implementation may involve a determination of what is most appropriate for that particular school. Several researchers have discussed advantages and disadvantages of making Tier 3 a post-special-education-placement tier (Bender, 2009a; Fuchs & Fuchs, 2007), and readers should check those sources if this question arises in a particular school's planning process.

Another question involves exactly when Tier 3 interventions should be made available to students. As indicated in discussion of the RTI pyramid, most proponents of RTI assume that struggling students will receive a Tier 2 intervention prior to moving into a more intensive Tier 3 intervention (Berkeley et al., 2009; Hoover et al., 2008; Kame'enui, 2007). However, such a rigid tier structure may be somewhat less warranted in middle and high schools (Duffy, n.d.). By the upper grades, students have established track records of academic performance that faculty use to move students directly into Tier 3 interventions, in some cases without previously exposing them to less intensive Tier 2 interventions (Duffy, n.d.; Gibbs, 2008). For example, in the Long Beach program, students moved directly into the most intensive intervention if their reading scores were two or more years behind grade level, and this ensured they would get the most intensive intervention available in general education without having to fail in a less intensive intervention.

> As a general principle, educators decide which tier to implement with the best interest of the individual student in mind, as demonstrated by the student's assessment scores.

Gibbs (2008) recommended a similar approach, suggesting that educators apply certain cutoff scores as bases for decision making. In that approach, schools would place students scoring between 11 percent and 25 percent on screening assessments in reading in Tier 2 and students scoring lower than 11 percent directly in Tier 3 (Gibbs, 2008). Thus students could move directly into a Tier 3 intervention without exposure to a Tier 2 intervention and receive the level of assistance they needed sooner.

It would seem that a less rigid structure of applying RTI would better serve our struggling middle and high school students. As a general principle, educators must decide which tier of intervention to implement with the best interest of the individual student in mind, as demonstrated by the student's assessment scores. For students who are extremely deficient, rigidly requiring a Tier 2 intervention prior to placement in Tier 3 may be a disservice, and perhaps a move directly into a highly intensive Tier 3 intervention is warranted.

Exploring Universal-Screening and Progress-Monitoring Options

Like many schools, the faculty at Cheyenne Mountain Junior High was concerned with the lack of available basic-skill assessments that were grade appropriate (Johnson & Smith, 2008). While assessments for universal screening and benchmarking in reading and mathematics are available for middle and high school grades, these have typically not been widely utilized, and this faculty had to do some exploration prior to selecting appropriate assessment devices (Johnson & Smith, 2008).

In this example, the faculty chose to emphasize reading as a first priority, given the fact that reading skills tended to cut across all curricular areas, and strengthening those skills among the struggling students was likely to have the maximum impact. This faculty selected and purchased screening and progress-monitoring measures in that area first. However, middle and high school faculties implementing RTI should certainly designate a subgroup of the faculty to seek out and evaluate appropriate screening and progress-monitoring measures in reading, mathematics, and perhaps writing. Alternatively, many schools implement curriculum-based measures they can develop through reading or mathematics intervention teachers, and this can provide a lower-cost alternative than purchase of large numbers of screening assessments.

Real-World RTI Example: Tigard High School

Tigard High School has successfully implemented RTI for several years (Lolich et al., 2010). This school has a student body of 1,875, and of those, approximately 25 percent are on free and reduced-price lunch programs, indicating a lower socioeconomic level for that percentage of the student population. Information on this model program is available in the form of a ten-minute video, which can be located at www.rtinetwork.org/professional/virtualvisits. A summary of this program is presented in the following feature box.

The RTI Model From Tigard High School

Resources Restructuring: Tigard High School in Tigard, Oregon, operates on a block schedule for course credit (Lolich et al., 2010). In this RTI implementation example, the block scheduling allowed the faculty to restructure the school schedule to allow for instructional interventions within the context of English classes and various math classes. The faculty at that school saw the

---

school schedule as one of the barriers to implementation of RTI, but they were able to create a more fluid schedule within the large block-schedule framework (Lolich et al., 2010). They created time for meetings that allowed teacher teams to evaluate student performance data. They also restructured scheduling in order to offer a wider variety of options for students, including:

- Taking a class every day for a full semester, resulting in one course credit

- Taking a class every other day for a year resulting in one course credit

- Taking a class every other day for a semester resulting in ½ of a course credit

Universal Screening and Progress Monitoring: Prior to entering the ninth grade, students undergo a universal screening that consists of either direct screening or investigation of existing assessment scores. Those data determine if a student needs the general education curriculum by itself or the more intensive RTI program (Lolich et al., 2010). More frequent progress monitoring is built in for students in the Tier 2 intervention. The authors note that they used student performance data to make all placement decisions and that they could modify a student's program quarterly if needed. They described this RTI procedure as much more responsive to student needs than waiting to obtain end-of-the-year grades to make changes (Lolich et al., 2010).

The Tier 1 Instruction: This school operates on the model that 80 percent of students should have their educational needs met with no supportive services (Lolich et al., 2010). All teachers were expected to modify instruction and make adaptations to achieve that level of student success.

The Tier 2 and Tier 3 Interventions: Tigard High School faculty restructured various classes to provide Tier 2 and Tier 3 support within the context of specific general education classes (Lolich et al., 2010). With some of the general education English classes meeting on only certain days each week, the school was able to adapt the schedule such that, for students needing a Tier 2 intervention, the student could take the English class on several days each week and the supplemental intervention class on the other weekdays. Interventions were directed at basic skill areas of reading and mathematics, so English teachers and mathematics teachers undertook most of the Tier 2 and Tier 3 instruction for students that needed those intensive levels of support.

Thus while all students took an English class, the 20 percent of students who needed additional supplemental reading instruction were placed in an intensive decoding reading curriculum for either two or three days per week in addition to their English class. On other weekdays, they continued their Tier 1 English class activities with all other class members. Faculty implemented a research-proven reading curriculum (which was not named in the video) on

Continued➜

those days for the struggling students. Those students were also provided extensive scaffolded instruction related to the core English curriculum.

Results: The results described in this video indicate that the data showed many more students succeeding in the high school curriculum than previously, though the video did not specifically share numeric data (Lolich et al., 2010). The video did, however, share student responses to RTI that were quite moving, as several students discussed the assistance they received through the RTI English classes. The teachers' comments about the RTI initiative were also quite supportive:

- "Teachers feel empowered, and students are optimistic!"
- "Kids' lives are changed dramatically."
- "When you hear the success stories, there's no other way to go!"

I strongly recommend a review of this video by every middle and high school teacher prior to RTI implementation; this will do more to get teachers on board with RTI than almost any other activity imaginable.

Finding Instructional Time for RTI

In this example, like in the previous model programs, restructuring of resources was necessary (Lolich et al., 2010). Embedded within that is the issue of teacher time to implement RTI; when will middle and high school teachers make or find the time to do screening, Tier 2 instruction, and frequent progress monitoring in Tier 2 and still conduct high-quality Tier 1 instruction for all of the students in the class? In addition, who is responsible for delivering Tier 2 and 3 interventions in these model RTI programs?

In the Tigard High School example, the general education teachers teaching those adapted English/reading intervention classes also delivered the Tier 2 intervention, and in this case, that approach worked very well (Lolich et al., 2010). Some students took the traditional English class that met only two or three times weekly, but students in the Tier 2 intervention took that same class, supplemented by Tier 2 support interventions on the other days each week. The fact that students were already in block schedules allowed some flexibility in providing reading instructional support at the Tier 2 level. Many proponents of RTI have discussed the issue of teacher time for implementation (Fuchs & Fuchs, 2007; Gibbs, 2008; NCRTI, n.d.a), and various recommendations have been provided. Suggestions for helping general education teachers find or make the time for conducting RTI procedures are presented in the following feature box.

Strategies for Making Time for Tier 2 and Tier 3 RTI Instruction

Modify Instructional Roles: Many teachers' instructional roles will be modified to some degree during RTI implementation (Hoover & Patton, 2008). Special education teachers, math or reading coaches, school psychologists, speech-language pathologists, mentor teachers, and other educators may all find their roles modified somewhat to allow time for them to implement Tier 2 or Tier 3 RTI interventions (Bender, 2009a).

Modify Student Schedules: In several of the examples (see Tigard High School and Cheyenne Mountain Junior High), faculty were able to modify student schedules to place students in intervention classes. Block schedules, because of the longer times for individual classes, may allow for more flexibility in this regard, and actual changes in schedules are typically done only at the end of grading periods or semesters, when students change classes anyway.

After-School Interventions: Some middle and high schools have implemented Tier 2 and Tier 3 interventions as after-school interventions (Bender, 2009a) and used current personnel to conduct that instruction. When transportation can be arranged via school resources or when parents can assist with transportation for an after-school program, this intervention option can work. This option was implemented at Hilsman Middle School in Athens, Georgia, as well as in other middle and high schools around the country. However, other options must be implemented for students who must receive their Tier 2 or Tier 3 instruction during school hours.

Computer-Based Interventions: High-quality educational software can deliver Tier 2 and Tier 3 options within the context of the class (Bender & Waller, 2011). For example, if a teacher has five computers and appropriate reading or mathematics software, that teacher can place students requiring a Tier 2 or Tier 3 intervention on that software while simultaneously conducting the other class activities, and that is a real advantage in terms of how to allocate and manage teachers' instructional time (Bender, 2009a). I strongly recommend implementation of Tier 2 and Tier 3 interventions using research-proven computerized software whenever possible because of the saved time (Bender & Waller, 2011). One report suggests that high school students could gain as much as 1.1 year in average reading skill based on only thirty days of computerized reading instruction (Kolonay & Kelly-Garris, 2009), and those types of achievement gains certainly command attention. Subsequent chapters include more information on research-proven, software- or web-based instructional curricula currently being used in the RTI process.

Continued➔

Paraprofessionals to Conduct Interventions: In some cases, schools have hired or reassigned paraprofessionals to specific classes in which Tier 2 or Tier 3 instruction was implemented. In some schools, students requiring a Tier 2 or Tier 3 intervention are assigned to particular teachers who have received paraprofessional support. Those students would then receive Tier 2 or Tier 3 instruction from that teacher, supported by and sometimes also delivered by the paraprofessional. This has been done in middle schools by assigning paraprofessionals to the English and language arts teachers to enable them to deliver Tier 2 instruction while the paraprofessional monitors instructional activities of other class members.

Doubling: As discussed previously, double periods or parallel classes for struggling students provide one option for making Tier 2 or Tier 3 interventions available. Middle and high schools cited in the literature frequently use this option (Duffy, n.d.; Gibbs, 2008; James, 2010; Lolich et al., 2010).

With those suggestions noted, all of these case studies seem to indicate that departmentalized schools most frequently address the teacher time issue in terms of changes to the schedule for struggling students (Gibbs, 2008; Lolich et al., 2010). Most of these models either adapted an existing support program (such as math lab or reading support class) to work as a Tier 2 or Tier 3 intervention, or added an intervention class to the class schedule to serve as a Tier 2 and Tier 3 intervention period (such as doubled periods). In the synopsis of middle school RTI practices, Allen and his coworkers indicate that many Tier 2 interventions were scheduled as supplemental elective classes, whereas many Tier 3 interventions actually replaced the existing core class in either language arts, reading, or mathematics (Allen et al., 2011). Of course, any administrator will probably agree that restructuring the schedule is no small matter, but such a change can address the needs of many students for Tier 2 or Tier 3 interventions. Furthermore, these model programs suggest that this may be exactly the type of resource reallocation necessary for RTI to succeed.

Choosing Between Supplemental and Replacement Instruction

In most of the RTI literature, interventions at the Tier 2 and Tier 3 levels are described as supplemental to Tier 1 instruction (Bender & Shores, 2007; Boyer, 2008; Bradley et al., 2007; Buffum et al., 2009; Fuchs & Deshler, 2007; Kame'enui, 2007). Thus students should not be taken out of the general education instruction in a subject area to receive Tier 2 or Tier 3 interventions. This has certainly been the accepted practice for RTI implementation in elementary schools (Bender & Shores, 2007).

In the higher grades, however, some schools have chosen to implement RTI a bit differently. For example, in some cases in my experience, students in a block-schedule English class were presented with Tier 2 instructional activities for two or three days per week during that block time, which may be more justified in middle and high school grade levels, particularly if the school is using a block schedule. Block schedules are quite flexible and may allow time for teachers to work with small groups of students in intensive Tier 2 interventions, while other students might participate in small-group project work or even homework completion. In short, block schedules were designed and intended to provide instructional flexibility, and using that flexibility to facilitate effective Tier 2 or Tier 3 interventions is perfectly reasonable.

Allen and his colleagues (2011) also report another option. A large number of the forty-two programs they studied actually use Tier 3 intervention courses as replacement courses for the Tier 1 core instruction. This might be justified on the basis that students requiring a Tier 3 intervention are, typically, many years below grade level in mathematics and reading and may therefore be somewhat less likely to benefit from core instruction in the typical language arts and mathematics classes.

Using Data-Based Decision Making to Modify Instruction

The teachers involved in RTI at Tigard High School, as in the previous examples, were strongly supportive of data-based decision making (Lolich et al., 2010). Furthermore, using actual student performance data made the educational program highly responsive to student needs, as noted by several of those teachers. In the case of Tigard High School, one teacher noted that the committee could modify a student's instruction each quarter rather than at the end of the year (Lolich et al., 2010). While more frequent instructional modification certainly took place within the supplemental reading program, modification of a class schedule in a departmentalized school is a big issue in middle and high schools. As in the Tigard High example, the best solution seems to be to standardize those modifications, with actual course rescheduling taking place at the end of quarters, grading periods, or semesters (Lolich et al., 2010).

The best class rescheduling option seems to be standardization of schedule modifications, with actual course rescheduling taking place at the end of quarters, grading periods, or semesters.

While elementary schools can and should be in a position to change a student's schedule whenever data indicate a need for a change, such modifications in middle and high schools are unrealistic. If scheduling changes were permitted in the middle of a grading period, such changes would result in students leaving classes prior to earning a partial course credit or beginning classes in the middle of grading periods.

A Synthesis of RTI Models in Middle and High Schools

In addition to these examples, the National High School Center, the National Center on Response to Intervention, and Center on Instruction (2010) completed a summary of various middle and high school tiered-instructional models. This synthesis of programs, coupled with the model programs described in this chapter, suggests certain tentative conclusions relative to how middle and high schools are implementing RTI. These conclusions are not research based but do represent a summary of the various model programs and, thus, might suggest where middle and high schools could begin to implement RTI in the higher grade levels. These are presented in the following feature box.

Synthesis of Ideas on RTI Implementation in Middle and High Schools

A. Virtually all RTI models in middle and high schools are maintaining the three-tier pyramid of intervention as the basis for their RTI.

B. Virtually all descriptions of RTI models in middle and high schools stress highly differentiated instruction as the basis for all Tier 1 instruction.

C. Virtually all Tier 1 descriptions of RTI models in middle and high schools implemented screening differently from the elementary model. The elementary RTI model stressed individual screening for all students at least three times each year. Instead of that type of universal screening, most middle and high school models used existing data for screening. These data may come from existing scores, teacher nomination, students' grades, or individually administered screenings given to selected students rather than all students. There are three reasons for this difference in screening:

   1. By the time a student reaches middle or high school, schools have a catalogue of that student's academic performance. Some programs have used teacher nomination in conjunction with state- or provincewide assessment scores to place students in Tier 2 interventions.

   2. Screening all students in the upper grades using individually administered screening assessments is probably a waste of resources (particularly for students scoring above 30 percent or 50 percent on group-administered state- or provincewide assessments).

   3. Multiple screenings are probably more important in early reading and math than in later grades. A four-month deficit in math in grade 1 is much more devastating for long-term academic growth than a four-month deficit in grade 9 mathematics.

D. There seem to be two approaches to providing Tier 2 and Tier 3 interventions: (1) modification of existing support programs (for example, reading support programs or math labs) and (2) creating a new intervention period.

E. More than 50 percent of Tier 2 intervention descriptions in middle and high schools involve some type of additional intervention period during the day for supplemental instruction in core areas.

F. One variation of the intervention period idea is doubling the class. Some programs have doubled the mathematics period. They hold struggling students in that class for an additional period with a reduced pupil-teacher ratio and the same teacher rather than an intervention period taught by a different mathematics teacher.

G. Virtually all Tier 2 intervention descriptions in middle and high schools provide RTI interventions in reading (provided by the language arts faculty) and in mathematics (typically algebra I or general mathematics provided by the mathematics faculty).

H. In most middle and high school RTI programs, while Tier 1 instruction may stress tutorial assistance in various subject areas, all Tier 2 and Tier 3 RTI models described to date stress reading, mathematics, or behavior.

Conclusion

As shown repeatedly in this chapter, the RTI process promises to restructure instructional practices in middle and high school classrooms in a significant, perhaps profound manner. This theme is repeated by those who have actually been involved in implementing the RTI process in the higher grades (Johnson & Smith, 2008; Lolich et al., 2010; Rozalski, 2009).

The impact of RTI, when coupled with differentiated lesson activities for all Tier 1 instruction supported by up-to-date instructional technologies, is likely to refocus instruction in middle and high school classes rather drastically. For that reason, these instructional innovations must be discussed together in order to appreciate their impact. The next chapter introduces the differentiated instruction initiative in the context of Tier 1 instruction.

Chapter 3

Differentiating Instruction in Middle and High School Classes

As indicated in chapters 1 and 2, differentiated instruction is the basis on which schools should build effective RTI procedures. In that sense, differentiated instruction *is* Tier 1 instruction, and should thus characterize virtually every content-area class in middle and high schools. In fact, the concept of differentiated instruction predates the RTI initiative.

Origins of Differentiated Instruction

Tomlinson first defined and described differentiated instruction in 1999 as a way to provide an increased set of different instructional activities to address the increasingly diverse learning needs of modern students (Sousa & Tomlinson, 2011; Tomlinson, 1999, 2001; Tomlinson & McTighe, 2006).

From this perspective, provision of a single set of educational activities is no longer sufficient to provide adequate learning experiences for all students, since the academic diversity of the students in most general-education classes is much greater than in previous years. Present-day insight into the varied learning styles of these highly diverse students also allows teachers to target specific instructional tactics toward their varied learning styles from kindergarten through high school (Gregory & Kuzmich, 2005; Smutny & von Fremd, 2010; Sousa & Tomlinson, 2011). Marzano (2010) refers to this concept using the phrase *nonlinguistic representations of knowledge*. Under that overall category, he included teaching ideas such as imagining a picture of the content, role-playing, using graphic organizers, or discussing photographs of the content.

Tomlinson initially developed the differentiated instruction concept based on several different areas of instructional theory and research, including learning styles and brain-compatible instructional techniques (Caine & Caine, 2006; Sousa, 2005; Sousa & Tomlinson, 2011; Tomlinson, 1999). Each of these areas continues to play a role in the development of various differentiated instructional techniques for all grade levels,

> Differentiated instruction involves providing an increasing set of different instructional activities to address the increasingly diverse learning needs of modern students.

though differentiation has been more widely implemented in elementary classes than at the high school level (Gregory, 2008; Gregory & Kuzmich, 2005).

To practice differentiated instruction, teachers must know the learners in the class, understanding not only such things about each learner as the learning style and learning preferences but also relating those differences to a wide array of instructional activities and procedures tailored to meet the needs of each individual student (Sousa & Tomlinson, 2011; Tomlinson, Brimijoin, & Narvaez, 2008). In short, the wider academic diversity in modern classrooms requires a wider array of learning activities to reach each learner, and the teacher's job in middle and high school classrooms is to design and provide that set of different learning activities based on the individual needs, strengths, and preferences of the students.

Wider academic diversity in modern classrooms requires a wider array of learning activities.

Various proponents of differentiated instruction have recommended that a wider array of instructional activities be included in the middle and high school curriculum (Connor & Lagares, 2007; Gregory, 2008; King & Gurian, 2006; Sousa & Tomlinson, 2011; Tomlinson et al., 2008), and research has indicated that more modifications within the curriculum do result in higher student engagement and fewer behavior problems among high school students (Lee, Wehmeyer, Soukup, & Palmer, 2010). Furthermore, some evidence has demonstrated that differentiated instruction increases student achievement (King & Gurian, 2006; Tomlinson et al., 2008). For example, Tomlinson and her colleagues (2008) presented evidence from an elementary school and a high school on the number of students achieving proficiency on statewide, norm-based assessments for three years prior to implementing differentiated instruction and for three years after such implementation. The data from both schools showed significant increases in students reaching proficiency in reading, language arts, and mathematics (increases of 17 percent, 15 percent, and 17 percent, respectively). Thus differentiation is recommended as one way to improve student achievement.

Tomlinson's Recommendations for Differentiation in the Higher Grades

Tomlinson (1999) originally identified three possible ways to modify instruction in order to develop differentiated lesson activities—modification of *content*, instructional *process*, and instructional *product*—and since 2000, these have become the foundation for most differentiation efforts (Smutny & von Fremd, 2010; Sousa & Tomlinson, 2011; Tomlinson et al., 2008).

Learning content is almost always delineated by and within state-approved curriculum standards, and teachers typically do not control the specific content students must learn. Teachers do, however, have options on how and to what depth they present the curricular standards. That is, teachers can modify content for presentation based on the learning styles of the students, and in that modification process, they may emphasize some content more than others for certain groups of students (Tomlinson, 1999; Tomlinson et al., 2008). For example, in learning about the American Revolution, some students might need the causal events emphasized, whereas others need to see the complex relationships between the causes of the war and the long-term results. Assignments could differentiate along those lines based on the learning needs of the students.

In differentiation based on the learning process, some students with a visual/spatial learning preference might draw pictures of critical battles or events, while others with a linguistic strength might delineate reasons for or results of that war in an outline. Students who seem to learn best through physical activity might act out one of the major battles. Again, such differentiation should depend on the learning styles and strengths of the students (Sternberg, 2006). Creative teachers can develop a wide array of instructional activities based on the varied learning processes and styles of their students.

Finally, the learning product may vary according to the needs of the various learners in the class, because varied demonstrations of learning allow the teacher to determine which students have mastered the material and which may need more time or continued instruction (Sousa & Tomlinson, 2011; Tomlinson, 1999; Tomlinson et al., 2008). In the differen-

> Creative teachers can develop an array of instructional activities based on the varied learning processes and styles of their students.

tiated classroom at the middle or high school level, it would not be uncommon for a given unit of instruction to have three or four different types of culminating projects, and students should have some choice in how they wish to demonstrate their knowledge of the topic. Some students may choose art projects, whereas others may develop role plays or mini dramas. Library or web-based research projects and development of multimedia presentations all represent legitimate products that demonstrate knowledge of the subject content.

Learning Styles: One Foundation of Differentiation

Students learn in different ways, and those differences are typically referred to as *learning styles* or *learning preferences* (Gregory, 2008; Silver & Perini, 2010; Sousa & Tomlinson, 2011). Many proponents of differentiated instruction suggest that different instructional activities aimed at those different learning styles and learning preferences in general will increase students' achievement overall (Marzano, 2010; Silver & Perini; 2010; Sousa & Tomlinson, 2011; Sternberg, 2006). The literature on differentiated instruction emphasizes research on brain functioning coupled with instruction targeted at different learning styles (Silver & Perini, 2010; Sousa, 2010; Sousa & Tomlinson, 2011).

Many activities currently used in high school classes are founded, in part, on learning-styles instruction. For example, in middle and high school mathematics instructors' manuals, it is not at all uncommon to see instructional recommendations for the "spatial" learner, or the "bodily/kinesthetic" learner. These terms, and the concept that different instructional activities may be directed at learners with varying learning styles or preferences, stem largely from the emphasis on differentiated instruction (Sousa & Tomlinson, 2011; Tomlinson et al., 2008).

Research discusses a number of learning styles (Silver & Perini; 2010; Sousa & Tomlinson, 2011), and the following feature box presents some of the most commonly mentioned learning styles. As these descriptions indicate, learning styles can hold implications for learning.

A List of Commonly Mentioned Learning Styles and Learning Preferences

Analytical: Stresses seeing how parts relate to the whole when contemplating a concept or construct; sometimes referred to as the "understanding" learning style

Linguistic: Highlights the ability to understand and use spoken and written communications, abstract reasoning, symbolic thinking, and conceptual patterning

Contextual: Stresses recognition of how ideas work in the context of real-world situations and developing practical solutions to actual problems

Mastery: Involves practical step-by-step consideration of a problem

Musical: Shows the ability to understand and demonstrate such concepts as rhythm, pitch, melody, and harmony and to use these to aid memory

Creative: Focuses on shaping concepts in ways that fit or result in innovative solutions to problems

Spatial: Shows the ability to cognitively understand, orient within, and manipulate three-dimensional space

Bodily/kinesthetic: Stresses the ability to coordinate and control physical movement and to use the body to express learning and understanding

Interpersonal: Features the ability to learn socially and understand, interpret, and interact well with others

---

Adapted from Silver & Perini, 2010; Sousa & Tomlinson, 2011; and Sternberg, 1985, 2006.

If a student has a relative weakness in analytical/linguistic learning but a strength in interpreting information spatially, perhaps that student should be shown how to take notes in the form of graphic organizers that he can develop while the teacher and other class members discuss new material. Alternatively, some students might grasp content more quickly when seeing concepts presented in spatial relationships with each other, and for those students, concept maps or semantic organizers might be much more effective in teaching content (Marzano, 2010). Other students might grasp the content more quickly when they are allowed to represent it spatially on the floor and "move through" the content under study (Marzano, 2010; Sousa, 2010). For example, having a 2 × 5 foot map of one's state outlined on the floor would allow students to move around the state when discussing distances between different cities or geographic features such as rivers, beaches, or mountain ranges.

Implementing instruction aimed at learning styles and learning preferences involves planning lessons that present instructional opportunities for students in several ways during the course of an instructional unit (Gregory, 2008; Smutny & von Fremd, 2010; Sousa & Tomlinson, 2011; Tomlinson & McTighe, 2006). Planning instructional activities with learning styles in mind results in a wider array of educational activities in the classroom and will increase academic engagement of more students (Moran, Kornhaber, & Gardner, 2006; Silver & Perini, 2010; Sternberg, 2006; Tomlinson et al., 2008).

However, questions have been raised based on a lack of research support for the learning-styles instructional approach (Silver & Perini, 2010; Sousa, 2010). Some caution is in order when considering using this approach in isolation. There are, however, several points on which almost all educators agree (Moran et al., 2006; Silver & Perini, 2010). First, students do seem to learn in highly diverse ways, and knowledge of these different ways of learning can offer teachers the opportunity to create more varied instructional tactics (Silver & Perini, 2010; Sousa & Tomlinson, 2011; Sternberg, 2006). Second, expanding the range of educational activities in the classroom is likely to enhance engagement of students, since novelty seems to increase attention and academic performance in and of itself (Silver & Perini, 2010; Sousa, 2010). For these reasons, many practitioners have advocated use of various learning styles approaches for differentiating instruction in middle and high schools (Gregory & Kuzmich, 2005; Silver & Perini, 2010; Sousa & Tomlinson, 2011; Sternberg, 2006; Tomlinson et al., 2008).

How Can Teachers Use Learning Styles in Content-Area Instruction?

Many instructors' manuals include teaching suggestions for various learning styles and preferences (such as for analytical learners or bodily/kinesthetic learners). The following feature box provides sample suggestions one might use in an eighth- or ninth-grade social studies class as it focuses on a U.S. history unit dealing with westward expansion and manifest destiny. In a six- to ten-day instructional unit on that topic, teachers should be able to implement each of these instructional ideas as either individual or small-group work.

Learning Style Instructional Ideas for Teaching Manifest Destiny

Analytical: Have some students with this strength develop an outline of the specific sequence of events that resulted in westward expansion (for example, emigrants seeking new land in the 1840s, the California Gold Rush of 1849, building the transcontinental railroad, the end of the Civil War in 1865, and displaced young men resulting from that).

Mathematical: Using a map of the United States, students with a strength in mathematics might document, describe, and evaluate the numbers of westward emigrants throughout each decade from 1810 through 1890.

Contextual/Spatial: Students who focus on real-world experiences and tend to learn through spatial representations of content might develop a map of the U.S. territories, with pictures showing various westward routes and numbers of emigrants that traveled each.

Bodily/kinesthetic and Interpersonal: Students with these learning strengths might select two or three main scenes from the text on different routes and develop a one-act play about each (such as a family on the Oregon Trail or a "forty-niner" moving west to lower California). These students could then present those plays to the class.

While planning activities to address these varied learning preferences and strengths is certainly a major component of differentiated instruction (Silver & Perini, 2010), many educators have moved beyond this initial focus, and some have recommended that educators actually teach these different learning style preferences to their students as a way to empower the students with knowledge of how they might learn more effectively (Willis, 2010). This can result in students having a better understanding of their own learning strengths. Middle and high school teachers might invite their students to consider their own learning styles and preferences with statements such as, "Think about your own learning style, and based on that, decide how you might need to complete this particular assignment."

Some of the brain research to date has supported instruction that focuses on learning style preferences (Sousa, 2010; Willis, 2010). For example, researchers have consistently recommended using bodily/kinesthetic learning tactics for struggling students (Druyan, 1997; Dwyer, Sallis, Blizzard, Lazarus, & Dean, 2001; King & Gurian, 2006; Marzano, 2010; Sousa, 2010). This might involve having students role-play a section of a chapter in history or a great discovery in science. Research has shown that having students move through representations of the content actually increases academic achievement for many (Aubusson, Fogwill, Barr, & Perkovic, 1997; Druyan, 1997; Dwyer et al., 2001; King & Gurian, 2006). Evidence from ongoing brain research has shown that movement leads to increased production of neurotrophins within the brain; these neurotransmitters increase the connections between brain cells, and in that fashion, movement enhances learning (Hannaford, 1995). Movement also increases students' energy, and this is likely to increase their arousal and their engagement with the content overall (Dwyer et al., 2001; Silver & Perini, 2010).

Finally, researchers recommend giving students limited choices about their assignments based on their varied learning styles and preferences, which is likely to increase their motivation to participate and will typically result in students taking more responsibility for their work (Caine & Caine, 2006; Gregory & Kuzmich, 2005; Silver & Perini, 2010; Sternberg, 2006).

> **Having students begin to think about their own learning strengths will typically result in more effort on learning tasks.**

Brain-Compatible Differentiation

Another area of research has provided a basis for differentiated instruction: the growing body of neuroscience research on brain functioning in learning environments (Doidge, 2007; Merzenich, 2001; Merzenich, Tallal, Peterson, Miller, & Jenkins, 1999; Sousa, 2010; Sousa & Tomlinson, 2011; Tomlinson, 2001; Tomlinson et al., 2008). This body of research is often referred to as brain-compatible instruction, because many proponents emphasize making classrooms compatible with what we now know about how brains learn. While scientists have undertaken studies of human brain functioning in learning tasks for the past several decades, only since 1995 or so has this emerging biomedical research progressed enough to inform teachers on effective instructional strategies for middle and high school classrooms (Caine & Caine, 2006; Sousa, 2005, 2010; Sousa & Tomlinson, 2011).

How Adolescent Brains Function

Much of our growing understanding of brain functioning has come from the development of the functional magnetic resonance imaging (fMRI), a technique dating from the late 1980s (Doidge, 2007; Merzenich, 2001; Merzenich et al., 1999). An fMRI is a nonradiological—and thus relatively safe—brain-scanning technique that has allowed scientists to study the performance of human brains while the subjects concentrate on different types of learning tasks (Caine & Caine, 2006; Sousa, 2010).

Specifically, the fMRI measures the brain's use of oxygen and sugar during the thinking process, and from that information, psychologists have determined very precisely which brain areas are most active during various types of cognitive tasks (Sousa, 2010). They have also noted that the more involved brains are in a specific learning process, the more those two nutrients are consumed in specific brain areas. In short, this brain-imaging technique can show the degree to which specific areas of the brain are optimally engaged in learning.

> **The more involved brain areas are in a task, the more likely that long-term learning results.**

Researchers have now used this and other brain-scanning techniques to identify brain regions that are specifically associated with various thinking activities such as language, reading, math, motor learning, music appreciation, or verbal response to questions in a classroom discussion (Sousa, 2010). In the vast majority of cognitive tasks, multiple brain areas are involved, and as a general guideline, the more brain regions that are actively involved during a learning task, the more likely long-term learning becomes. Brains do, however, become more efficient in completing specific cognitive tasks over time (Sousa, 2010), so the results of extensive involvement of different brain areas in learning are more complex than the previous statement indicates. Perhaps an example can illustrate this best.

The Walkthrough

Here is an example of a brain-compatible instructional idea for middle and high school biology and health classes. Imagine a tenth-grade student completing a worksheet on the topic of blood circulation through the heart and the body. In such a language-based, pencil-and-paper task, the student is likely to be utilizing only a limited number of brain regions, including several cerebral areas associated with understanding and interpreting written language, reading, and visual scanning. In such a "language only" learning task, only the cerebrum—essentially the top two inches of the brain—is highly involved, since language is based in that area. Depending on the student's level of motivation and overall concentration, that task will result in a somewhat limited level of recall for that content.

In contrast, imagine that same content taught using a walkthrough. The walkthrough is a movement-based instructional technique that is very appropriate for all middle and high school subject areas (King & Gurian, 2006; Sousa, 2010; Tate, 2005), and research has shown that moving through representations of the academic content will enhance learning (Aubusson et al., 1997; Druyan, 1997; Sousa, 2010). In this instructional idea, students would be required to actually experience this content by "walking through" a representation of it. Prior to class, a middle or high school teacher would use masking tape to create a large outline of the four heart chambers on the floor, along with the lungs and the major blood vessels. Alternatively, teachers might direct a group of students to prepare this outline on the floor.

Once the heart diagram is on the floor, the students' task would be to read a brief section of the chapter describing how and where blood flows—through the various chambers in order, out to the lungs to retrieve oxygen, back to the other heart chambers, and then out to the body. During that reading, the students would also walk through those sections of the heart and body as delineated by the masking tape. After the students complete the reading and walkthrough, the teacher should pointedly emphasize the relationship between the walkthrough activity and the content in the text in order to stress the representation of the content (Aubusson et al., 1997; Druyan, 1997; Dwyer et al., 2001; King & Gurian, 2006).

In that type of movement-based instruction, many brain areas are actively involved in learning the content. All of the brain regions involved in the pencil-and-paper task—the linguistic brain areas—would still be involved in the learning, but numerous additional brain areas would also be actively involved, including brain areas dealing with motor nerves throughout the body and the visual-motor cortex within the brain itself (Aubusson et al., 1997; Druyan, 1997; Sousa, 2010). In short, the latter teaching example is much more likely to result in long-term retention for that content because much more brain processing is involved when teachers use bodily movement to represent the content under study (Aubusson et al., 1997; Druyan, 1997; King & Gurian, 2006). Additional examples of this instructional approach for the higher grades are presented throughout this chapter.

Songs and Rhythms

The use of songs, chants, and rhythms to teach middle and high school content represents another example of brain-compatible teaching that researchers now recommend across the grade levels (Glassman, 1999; Tate, 2005). A research study by Stein, Hardy, and Totten (1984) indicates increased memory for vocabulary terms when the students were allowed to study while listening to music. Music has been shown to activate nearly the entire cerebrum as well as to enhance long-term memory (Stein et al., 1984; Webb & Webb, 1990; Weinberger, 1998). As a result, many learners have experienced instructional approaches that involve music already. For example, having students verbally rehearse the letters of the alphabet in sequential order will activate many brain cells in certain brain regions, but having students sing the alphabet, as do almost all primary teachers, activates many more brain regions, including those areas associated with letter sounds and memory for letter shapes as well as memory for the tune, musical understanding, and a variety of other brain areas (Glassman, 1999; Weinberger, 1998). This results in increased retention for that content (Stein et al., 1984; Weinberger, 1998).

Certainly teachers in middle and high school subjects, where the content load is so much greater, are well advised to use songs and chants in their teaching in order to help students rehearse and remember complex content. Even in the higher grades, teachers should not let a period go by without a song, rhythm, or chant that teaches the critical elements of the instructional content for that unit.

Using songs, chants, and raps is not a never-ending process of creation. Rather, the instructor should sum up the essential content from an instructional unit in eight to sixteen lines and then put it into a song or rhythm. That same song, rap, rhythm, or chant should then be repeated each day during the instructional unit, since repetition of that critically important content will lead to long-term learning.

> Teachers in higher grades should not let a single instructional period go by without a song, rhythm, or chant to teach the critical elements of the instructional content for that unit.

The walkthrough strategy and the songs or chants strategy present only two of the numerous instructional techniques researchers now recommend for middle and high school instruction. Additional techniques are discussed later in this chapter. Caine and Caine (2006) also identified a number of general guidelines for instruction that stem from this emerging research in the neurosciences, as presented in the following feature box.

Instructional Activities Suggested by Brain-Compatible Research

Based on the emerging brain-compatible research, students should:

- Undergo sensory and emotional experiences tied to the content, because sensory and emotional tags associated with content enhance memory and help students make associations with previous knowledge

- Articulate questions and develop a focus that leads to planning their activities on the content

- Perform an action or actions (movement, song, chant) related to understanding the content

- Produce a product associated with content to reinforce critical points

- Meet challenges in high-quality curricula that are more difficult than tasks the student can perform independently

---

Adapted from Bender, 2008; Caine & Caine, 2006; and Tate, 2005.

Preadolescent, Adolescent, and Adult Brains in the Classroom

A number of additional conclusions resulting from brain research should inform how we teach in middle and high schools. First, teachers must understand that brains function differently at different phases of life (Sousa, 2010), and teachers in middle and high schools are well advised to become aware of the general information on adolescent brains. Such insight will better prepare teachers to understand their students, note their differences in learning styles, and prepare lessons rich in content that engage students more concretely.

Of course, the overall structure of the human brain is constant throughout life, and that structure has not changed in scores of thousands of years. Still, students' brains do function somewhat differently than many teachers' brains, depending on the age of the teacher, and teachers should be aware of that fact when creating instructional activities.

For example, cell-to-cell communication in different brains may vary considerably among individuals at different ages (Sousa, 2010). Neurons are the brain cells associated with learning and thinking, and neurons communicate with each other through dendrites. Dendrites are the parts of the neuron that branch out specifically to communicate with other neurons, and as dendrites communicate with other brain cells nearby, they develop a consistent set of connections, which one may think of as a pattern of communication representing learning of particular content. When such dendritic connections are extensive enough and repeated often enough, learning takes place. Thus one can define learning as neurons communicating with each other in a predictable way that they have established over repeated practice and that they associate with particular stimuli in the environment. One popular phrase in brain-functioning research sums up this concept: "cells that fire together wire together" (Doidge, 2007; Sousa, 2010). As cells repeatedly activate each other, learning takes place.

Since dendritic connections emerge from repeated learning experiences, and learning experiences may be different between persons of different ages, students' brains may not function exactly like teachers' brains. Understanding that point can be critical in teaching adolescents. To illustrate this idea, one need only consider the learning experiences creating dendritic connections in our students' brains that did not even exist thirty years ago. Neuroscience has shown that brains mature quite extensively from prebirth through the age of twenty-four, and thus brains are most ripe for learning (that is, making long-lasting dendritic connections) between the ages of zero and seven, with some increased learning capacity up through the age of twenty-four years (Doidge, 2007; Sousa, 2010). Thus educators are well advised to ask what modern students' brains have been exposed to during those years that their own brains were not exposed to. Here is an example.

When my brain was in those formative childhood, preadolescent, and adolescent years (admittedly some forty to fifty odd years ago), the video-game culture that drastically impacts most students' brains today did not even exist. One public broadcasting news show reported in 2010 that adolescents are "wired" or online nearly fifty hours each week through activities including texting, social networking, using smartphones, doing online learning, web surfing, and so forth (Dretzin, 2010). That telecast posed the question of how this might impact students' brains.

We know that brains that are repeatedly and frequently exposed to video-gaming experience during those early formative years are much more likely to learn the types of skills required for success in those games, including enhanced eye-hand coordination, immediate—near instantaneous—visual interpretation, quicker reaction time, and increased reactivity to novel, moving stimuli (Willis, 2010). Research has shown that when a student succeeds in video gaming, the brain generates increased dopamine—another neurotransmitter associated with pleasure (Willis, 2010). Thus playing such games or engaging in pleasurable social networking in an online format can be quite reinforcing, and such increased online activities actually "rewire" the students' brains to some degree (Willis, 2010). In fact, research has shown that it doesn't take very long to develop strong dendritic connections of this nature, and even minimal training can restructure a brain's dendritic connections (Doidge, 2007; Merzenich, 2001; Merzenich et al., 1999; Willis, 2010).

Of course, the same is true for educational tasks. Research has demonstrated that when a student experiences success on an educational intervention, even interventions lasting as few as eight weeks (for example, two hours daily for eight weeks), there will be measurable changes in brain activity (Simos et al., 2007; Temple et al., 2003). Thus making extensive dendritic connections may take only a limited time of fairly extensive practice.

Adolescents' brains, by virtue of the highly interactive world in which they developed, have dendritic connections that mature brains could never and will never develop.

These preteen and adolescent brains may have learning strengths that focus on the specific types of learning skills associated with a media-rich, simulation-gaming, online, social networking environment (Willis, 2010). Those brains, by virtue of that highly interactive, quickly changing, visually rich, and novel digital environment, will probably have dendritic connections that mature brains do not have. Younger brains may also have certain learning deficits that result from the same early learning experiences, however. Because those learning experiences foster quick interpretation and immediate attention to highly stimulating visual movement, those brains may be less responsive to lower levels of visual stimulation. This may result, among some younger learners, in a somewhat limited attention span for many low-stimulation learning tasks, and those types of learning deficits do seem to be showing up more frequently in modern classrooms (Dretzin, 2010).

Just to complicate matters a bit more, research has shown that brains can and do establish new dendritic connections throughout life, much more so than was previously thought (Doidge, 2007; Merzenich, 2001; Merzenich et al., 1999; Sousa, 2010). While younger brains are exposed to a different, more instantaneous, and more digital world than older brains, neural pathways of intricate dendritic connections continue to develop throughout life—a concept referred to as *plasticity* in brain development (Doidge, 2007; Merzenich, 2001; Merzenich et al., 1999).

Of course, video gaming is merely one example of the intense, media-rich environments in which today's students engage. Television viewing, communications through social networking sites, and instant messaging all probably have an impact on the learning capabilities of students' brains and all may result in dendritic connections that either foster greater learning or limit attention in some learning processes (Dretzin, 2010).

Teachers in middle and high schools must realize that our instructional efforts must compete favorably in that modern, highly digital world that so commands our students' attention. This is one reason why so very many teachers are using high-stimulation instructional activities (computer-based simulation games or webquests). These types of activities are more likely to engage students' brains than are traditional pencil-and-paper, worksheet-based learning tasks (Dretzin, 2010; Tate, 2005). There are now instructional programs based on this exciting, emerging knowledge of how brains function, and researchers recommend some of those curricula for middle and high school learners (Doidge, 2007; Temple et al., 2003).

Gender Differences in Learning

Brain research has highlighted gender differences among students at various age levels, and while some of these differences are more strongly associated with younger learners, other differences persist into the middle and high school years (King & Gurian, 2006; Sousa, 2005; Sternberg, 2006). For example, research has shown that boys have certain predictable deficits in reading when compared to girls (King & Gurian, 2006; Robelen, 2010), and this may be related to the types of curricula used in schools. When presented with an array of reading materials, males and females will choose different types of material (King & Gurian, 2006). Males will typically choose to read topics with more conflict between characters and very clear role distinctions between heroes and villains. They often choose topics with a hint of danger and aggression and stories that involve clear winners and losers, including material on topics such as NASCAR, football, atomic bombs, battles, or animals fighting (Bender & Waller, 2011; King & Gurian, 2006). In contrast, females tend to avoid reading material that represents high levels of overt conflict, preferring topics such as deep friendships, relationships, or fantasy, such as mermaids and unicorns. It is not known if this is an innate preference or the result of socialization, but these preferences seem quite well established (King & Gurian, 2006).

> Males frequently choose to read topics with clear role distinctions between heroes and villains. In contrast, females tend to choose topics such as friendships or relationships.

Scientists have now documented other gender differences in brain functioning as well (Sousa, 2005). For example, King and Gurian (2006) also note that elementary-aged males tend to be more active generally than young females and attend to visually novel stimuli in different ways. Males attend to learning stimuli suggestive of movement, whereas females attend to color differences in novel stimuli. This brain research on gender differences is now explaining behaviors that teachers frequently note in classroom performance (King & Gurian, 2006; Robelen, 2010; Sousa, 2005; Sternberg, 2006). More on these particular gender differences is presented in the following feature box.

Gender Differences That Impact Learning

Cross-talk between brain hemispheres: Females may be somewhat better at multitasking than males, because structural differences in females' brains generate more cross-talk between the brain hemispheres. Males' brains, on the other hand, tend to lateralize and compartmentalize brain activity much more so than do those of females. School-aged male brains do not seem to process language as effectively, and thus the modality preference of boys may have more impact on their learning than is the case with girls (Williams, 2010). Females tend to pay attention to more information on more subjects at any given time, whereas males tend to concentrate best when they follow specific steps while focusing on a single task (King & Gurian, 2006).

Continued➔

Males' natural aggression: For a number of neural and biochemical reasons, males are more naturally aggressive and competitive than females, and as a result, females gravitate less toward competitive learning activities than do males (Sousa, 2010). Males also tend toward greater impulsivity and more aggression and have less desire than females to comply with instructions or to please others (including pleasing teachers!). This suggests teachers may enhance males' engagement through competitive gaming simulation activities focused on the learning content.

Frontal-lobe differences: The prefrontal cortex is generally more active and develops more quickly in females than in males. That area of the brain is associated with reasoning and efficient decision making as well as reading and word production. This may account for the fact that females tend to be slightly less impulsive than males in the primary grades. King and Gurian (2006) suggest that when teachers are unaware of these brain differences, normal males may be misdiagnosed as having learning disabilities or conduct disorders.

Visual system differences: The visual system of males tends to rely more heavily on type M ganglion cells (the visual cells that detect movement) than do females' visual systems (King & Gurian, 2006). In contrast, females generally have more type P ganglion cells (cells that are sensitive to color variety). Consequently, males rely more on pictures and moving objects in their learning, whereas females tend to focus more on color, picture detail, and other color-based sensory information. Novel visual material (novel in color-coded material) and movement of the visual stimuli can be quite effective in teaching but are likely to be differentially effective for males and females based on these differences in the visual system.

Neural rest states: Males' brains lapse into what neurologists refer to as a "neural rest state" more frequently than do those of young females. Males may seem more likely to "zone out" in class. Some males attempt to arrest these natural rest states by engaging in self-stimulation activities that might include moving around the classroom, tapping their pencils, playing, or engaging others in conversation. In short, when the male brain gets bored, some of the brain functioning shuts down, which, of course, negates the possibility of effective learning. However, when the female brain gets bored, more of the brain functioning remains active, and thus even when a girl is bored, she is more likely to retain the ability to participate in relatively passive instructional activities in class such as taking notes or listening. This seems to suggest that movement that keeps students actively involved in learning may be more effective for males than for females.

> **Verbal/spatial brain differences:** The brains of young males have more cortical areas dedicated to spatial-mechanical functioning than those of females (King & Gurian, 2006). This difference may play a role in the higher mathematics achievement, on average, among boys in middle and high schools. In contrast, young females' brains generally have greater cortical emphasis on verbal-emotive processing. This shows up in classroom behavior because females use more words on average than males do, and females tend to think more verbally in the elementary grades.

Of course, middle and high school teachers are not expected to become brain experts, but having some insight into this emerging information on brain functioning is advisable (Gregory, 2008; Gregory & Kuzmich, 2005). In fact, some schools have found that differentiated instruction based on these brain-compatible teaching approaches can make a difference in how students perform academically. For example, King and Gurian (2006) report on one school in Colorado that chose to develop supplemental-reading curricular materials that addressed the needs and interest areas of males in the elementary and upper elementary grades based on the gender differences in brain functioning noted earlier.

In that example, the faculty had noted that males were falling behind females in overall reading skill at their school, and when they surveyed the school's reading curriculum, the faculty concluded that the story content did not match the interests of males as well as those of females. The faculty then collectively determined to supplement their reading curriculum with additional stories that were of more interest to males (King & Gurian, 2006). In addition, after studying the brain-compatible instructional literature, teachers began to teach with more attention to novel stimuli, conflict, and movement-based instruction. As a result of these modifications, the school was able to close the reading achievement gap between males and females in only one year.

While this is merely an anecdotal example, that result does indicate the potential for highly differentiated brain-compatible instruction in meeting the specific needs of all of the students in the class (King & Gurian, 2006). In short, understanding that males and females are interested in different types of content can assist teachers across the grade levels in capturing the attention of our students. In this example, differentiating instruction based on these gender differences resulted in keeping the males on track for higher levels of academic success (King & Gurian, 2006).

> When teachers began to teach with more attention to novel stimuli, conflict, and movement-based instruction, the school was able to close a reading achievement gap between males and females in one year.

Conclusions About Brains and Learning

While brain research is ongoing and will continue to contribute instructional tactics for middle and high school classes, teachers for those grades can draw several conclusions from it. First, engaging brains in active, involved, in-depth thought on the content is the key to higher levels of conceptual learning (Doidge, 2007; Merzenich, 2001; Merzenich et al., 1999; Sousa, 2010; Tate, 2005; Weinberger, 1998). Active cognitive engagement with the content is more critical than "content coverage" for overall mastery, so the idea of teaching less content but teaching it more thoroughly is a sound teaching principle across the middle and high school grades.

Effective teaching involves creating exciting, innovative learning activities that will actively engage today's brains with the content in a rich, meaningful, highly involved manner (Bender, 2008, 2009a; Doidge, 2007; Tomlinson & McTighe, 2006). Modern brains expect and respond to nothing less than the stimulation they have grown used to in a media-rich, highly interactive world. Researchers now recommend using modern technologies (smartphones, iPods, social networking sites) to engage today's brains in middle and high school classes (Davis, 2010; Manzo, 2010a). Examples of these technologies in use are presented in subsequent chapters in this book. Instruction is likely to be more effective when teachers can create learning activities that emulate our students' high-tech world (Connor & Lagares, 2007; Gregory, 2008; Lee et al., 2010; Manzo, 2010a, 2010b). To the degree possible, teachers should create "authentic" learning environments in which students actually experience the content rather than merely read about it, discuss it, or study it. Interactive activities such as role play, debates, or creation of newspaper articles that are actually published in a local newspaper or on the school website are likely to enhance learning much more than traditional instructional approaches. Such experiential learning will result in deeper understanding and longer-term learning of the content (Moran et al., 2006; Sternberg, 2006). These brain-compatible instructional practices are designed and intended to have exactly that effect.

SHEMR: A Tool for Summarizing Brain-Compatible Instruction in Upper Grades

In 2009, I developed the acronym SHEMR to summarize the instructional guidelines for effective differentiation that stem from the research on brain-compatible instruction. Each middle and high school teacher should consider using SHEMR as a self-check memory tool when planning differentiated instructional units. This acronym is intended to remind teachers to develop an array of differentiated activities for the unit and to check that each instruction unit has one or more instructional activities designed to address each of the various learning styles. The letters in the SHEMR acronym represent the following types of activities, which experts now recommend for all middle and high school classes:

Songs, chants, rhythms for learning essential content

Humor to teach content

Emotional ties to the content

Movement-based content instruction

Repetition of activities daily

Songs, Chants, and Rhythms for Learning Essential Content

Songs, chants, and rhythms have long been used as effective memory-enhancing tools (Stein et al., 1984; Webb & Webb, 1990; Weinberger, 1998). They can greatly assist middle and high school students in memorizing content, and teachers can generate them for almost any subject area. However, teachers should not develop songs or chants for every single fact but, rather, should use this high-impact teaching idea only for the most important content in the instructional unit. When planning each instructional unit, teachers should identify the most critical concepts or instructional points and write a short sentence about each. These become the essential core concepts to be taught. Teachers should then have several students write a song or chant emphasizing each of those essential points (Bender, 2009b). Alternatively, teachers may develop songs or chants themselves or select such activities from other sources (such as www.teachersworkshop.com) and then have the students sing them each day to reinforce those critical concepts.

Once the class has prepared a content-rich song, students should then sing that song or do that chant each day during the instructional unit to teach and reinforce those critical concepts. It is critical to develop only one song or chant per instructional unit, since development of more than one can get confusing and will lessen the impact of this teaching idea. Such teaching is quite likely to lead to lifelong learning of that content. Teachers should manage this as a fun, engaging, yet relatively quick learning activity each day; after the first day, it should take no more than three to five minutes for students to sing the song and for the teacher to discuss each major point within it.

This strategy is particularly effective for teaching critical vocabulary in middle and high school classes (Glassman, 1999; Stein et al., 1984). With a list of critical vocabulary terms and their definitions serving as the content of the song or chant, students should practice singing or chanting every day. When the vocabulary list for a chapter is too long, the teacher should pare it down to only the most critical terms.

> Once the class has prepared a content-rich song, students should sing that song each day during the instructional unit to teach and reinforce those critical concepts.

Finally, the song or chant should not be too long. Chanting a more restricted list of terms and definitions is always easier to master. Of course, students can learn longer songs and chants, including singing the entire Declaration of Independence or a list of elements within the periodic table. Teachers across the grade range are now using this technique with great success, since this type of activity makes learning more interesting, and students typically enjoy this instructional innovation (Bender, 2009b).

Humor to Teach Content

A humorous story can often help summarize the important aspects of the unit content, and humor always makes learning more fun. Humor activates regions of the human brain that may not otherwise be involved in learning, and because more dendrites are involved when humor is used, humor is likely to increase retention for the content (Tate, 2005). In fact, neuroscience has shown that laughter increases the production of neurotransmitters associated with alertness and memory (Fry, 1997); thus humor indirectly impacts learning. If the teacher can associate humor with particular aspects of the reading content, students are more likely to understand it quickly and remember it longer.

One idea is for teachers at virtually any grade level to supply six to ten main points from a text to a group of students and have those students compose a humorous story or poem that includes each of those main points. In turn, that story or poem can become a teaching tool for the rest of the class.

Emotional Ties to the Content

Emotional intensity and response are highly involved in the learning process, because emotional intensity can dictate the level of cognitive involvement of various brain regions, and this can either interfere with or enhance learning (Sousa, 2010). Based on current brain research, we now know that negative emotional states or even negative emotional associations with particular learning tasks can become impediments to successful completion of those tasks (Sousa, 2005).

Positive emotional ties to the content can strengthen both motivation to learn and longer-term retention for the material.

For example, if a student is asked to read aloud in front of his peers when the reading level is too high for the student, emotional mechanisms within the brain become quite active, and that may, in turn, prohibit maximum cerebral functioning. In such an instance, when one associates extremely negative emotions with particular learning tasks, the emotional regions in the mid-brain become active while the higher-cognition regions in the cerebrum become somewhat less active. This is a particular concern in subject areas that make students unusually nervous such as mathematics or some of the higher-level sciences, since some students may have fears associated with those subjects. In these cases, students can often overcome such negative emotional responses to learning tasks with additional individual support and encouragement from the teacher.

Fortunately, the opposite is also true. Positive emotional ties to the content can strengthen both interest in the task (motivation to cognitively engage with the task) and longer-term retention (Caine & Caine, 2006; Fry, 1997; Sousa, 2010). Teachers are well advised to associate positive emotional experiences with learning content whenever possible. For example, diaries of scientists as they seek to make new discoveries can make study of those discoveries much more interesting. Notes of mathematicians as they solve new formulas can enhance both interest in and achievement in mathematics.

Of course, certain types of content lend themselves to more emotional connections than others; history or social sciences are typically more easily "connected" to students' emotional interests than, say conjugations of verbs. Still, teachers should use emotional tie-ins whenever possible to enhance memory for the content students read (Bender, 2008). Personal stories of individuals involved in the content often provide the most effective way to help capture students' emotional interest.

Movement-Based Content Instruction

As discussed previously, the research on human brain functioning has demonstrated that movement is one of the most powerful teaching tools we have, and thus we should use it to teach content across the grade levels (Aubusson et al., 1997; Druyan, 1997; King & Gurian, 2006; Sousa, 2010). Because the survival of our species was tied to movement (chasing prey for food or running from larger species), our brains seem to prioritize movement as a survival skill. For that reason, instructional content that is consistently associated with specific movements will be learned more quickly and retained over a much longer period of time.

There are two ways to create content-based instructional movement: (a) use an individual student pointing to body parts to represent content, or (b) use groups of students to represent the content, perhaps as a diagram or a graphic organizer (like the example of blood flowing through the heart, page 72). In using the individual's body as a learning tool, teachers must ask, can we logically represent the content by associating it with specific parts of a student's body? If so, the student should touch those body parts, such as the chest or the elbow, and do the chant at the same time. This movement and chant combination can help teach almost any content, as long as that content can be presented in spatial relationships (Aubusson et al., 1997; Druyan, 1997).

For example, several teachers in Ohio taught about the major cities and regions within that state by associating certain actions, such as raising hands, with particular geographic areas. While facing an unlabeled map of Ohio, students might do the following movement and chant.

Movement	Statement to Chant
Raise right hand	Cleveland: Industrial center and port city
Raise left hand	Toledo: Port city below Detroit
Touch center of chest	Columbus: Capital of our state
Extend left hand down to the side	Cincinnati: Gateway to Kentucky
Extend right hand down to the side	Farm region: Flowing into the mountains

Teachers throughout North America have used this idea for many content areas. As another example, teachers in Texas developed a way to teach the early history of that state by using their arms to picture the four major rivers in Texas, which formed the basis of that early history. The only limits on this teaching idea are the content and the creativity of the teacher (or the students).

The easiest way to develop movement for instructional content is to use overheads or diagrams that are probably already in use in content-area classes. Overheads and videos are already effective teaching techniques, but teachers can make them much more effective by adding a movement activity. One can easily do so by using students to form the basic concept depicted on the overhead. In short, let students "become" that overhead diagram by standing them in positions representing that diagram (Aubusson et al., 1997; Druyan, 1997; Sousa, 2010). The blood-in-the-heart example illustrates this type of movement.

These two ways to use movement (individual body or groups of students) can each enhance the novelty associated with specific content and thus enhance learning. Again, as with many brain-compatible techniques, students should complete these movements every day during the instructional unit in order to continually reinforce the essential content. In most instances, this will take very little instructional time—frequently less than two or three minutes.

Repetition of Activities Daily

While schools have used repetition throughout the ages, brain research has suggested that repetition is much more effective for learning some types of activities than others (Bender, 2009b; Bender & Waller, 2011). Traditionally, students completed repetitive exercises using a worksheet type of activity, but worksheets are merely linguistically based activities and don't usually provide maximum stimulation to the brain. Repetition of problem completion on a mathematics worksheet is not likely to involve as many brain regions or as many dendritic connections as repetition exercises in which students act out the solution to a math problem; having students repetitively practice addition and subtraction of positive and negative integers on a worksheet is not nearly as effective as having them practice that task by moving along a number line on the floor. The latter activity will activate their learning much more than a pencil-and-paper task and is also much more fun.

Students should repeat a mnemonic a minimum of three times each day for ten to fifteen days to foster long-term learning.

As a general guideline, if a mnemonic such as a content-rich song, chant, poem, or movement is available and is not too time-consuming, students should repeat that mnemonic a minimum of three times each time they are exposed to it. Students should keep up that level of repetition every day for ten to fifteen days to foster long-term learning. Repetition of fun activities such as these is much more interesting and fun for students in middle and high school than repetition based on pencil-and-paper tasks. Students in all grade levels enjoy this type of learning activity and are, therefore, much more likely to actively participate.

Using SHEMR can assist middle and high school teachers in developing exciting, content-rich instructional activities that will enhance learning. The following feature box provides additional guidelines and examples on how teachers may use SHEMR in their instructional planning.

Middle and High School Brain-Compatible Teaching Guidelines and Examples

Write out the critical content when you plan the instructional unit. Teachers should seek eight to ten points, terms, or concepts that students should learn for life, and those become the content for the high-impact brain-compatible instructional tactics. These may be considered the power standards for that unit of instruction.

Arrange these points in some logical order. Can you identify an order or relationship that is a core component of the reading content? Perhaps a causal order, a temporal order, or a spatial relationship that makes sense and aids in memory? Describe the basis for that order in some fashion (perhaps a picture representation, causal, time-ordered relationship?). Can that order assist the students in learning the content? Can a group of students establish a logical order for the power standards?

Create a visual aid (such as a graph or chart) to represent that content. Can you depict the logically ordered content in a chart, graph, or overhead? Can you use novel visual enhancements (color coding, movement-based examples) to increase the efficacy of that graph or overhead for learning purposes? Either teachers or students may create that representation.

Use humor. Have students develop a humorous story or poem on the content. If you have humorous ideas about representing the content, jot them down and have groups of students develop them. Take care to summarize each important aspect of the content if possible.

Are negative emotional experiences associated with the content? If so, the teacher or other students must provide some additional emotional support for those students having negative experiences. Perhaps this could take the form of teacher support or peer-partner instruction.

Can you provide positive emotional, engaging examples of the content? Can a personal story from a community member help teach the material or help focus students' attention on the content? Could several class members conduct an interview with that community person if he or she cannot come into class?

Continued➔

Does the content itself suggest a song that can be used for teaching? Is there a piece of music or a popular song that represents a similar theme to that of the reading content? Students with a learning style preference for musical instruction may rewrite the content points, fitting them to the music and timing of the song or chant.

Create a movement to represent the subject-area content. Develop or have a group of students develop a movement that teaches the essential concepts in the instructional unit. Couple that movement with a chant or song that stresses the important content, and repeat that movement, song, or chant activity daily throughout the unit. This is high-impact learning and will result in increased achievement for that content.

Adapted from Bender, 2008; Bender & Waller, 2011; Sousa, 2010; Tate, 2005; and Williams, 2010.

Conclusion

Differentiated instruction is already having a drastic impact on instruction in elementary grades and has been widely applied in many middle and high school classrooms as well. Many state department of education guidelines for RTI specifically emphasize differentiated instruction as the Tier 1 basis for RTI (Berkeley et al., 2009). Overall, differentiated instruction does assist struggling students and tends to lead to a rather drastic decrease in the types of lectures and whole-group discussions that characterized many middle and high school classrooms in past decades. Researchers encourage highly differentiated instruction in core content classes because it is quite likely to lead to fewer students needing Tier 2 or Tier 3 academic interventions in middle and high schools.

Lecture, round-robin, oral reading, or whole-group discussion activities will never again characterize middle and high school instruction.

Because modern classes include students with a wide range of academic skills and needs, as well as a wide range of learning strengths and weaknesses, teachers simply must provide a wider range of instructional activities in order to provide appropriate instruction for all students, and traditional instructional methods clearly do not meet that need. To state the matter plainly, effective middle and high school teaching will, now and in the future, require highly differentiated and interactive instructional activities, tied to specific learning needs and preferences of the students. Toward that end, middle and high school teachers across North America are ramping up their differentiated instruction skills in order to better meet the needs of all students.

Chapter 4

Developing Tier 1 Differentiated Instructional Lessons for Middle and High School Classes

With a wide range of researchers and practitioners working on implementation of differentiated instruction since 2000, it should come as no surprise that educators have promoted many different approaches for differentiated instruction (Lee et al., 2010; Tomlinson, 2001; Tomlinson et al., 2008; Tomlinson & McTighe, 2006), including various suggestions for research-proven instructional tactics and strategies across the grade levels (Connor & Lagares, 2007; Gregory, 2008; Gregory & Kuzmich, 2005; Tomlinson et al., 2008).

Of course, this text cannot present all of these instructional strategies and approaches to differentiation, but it does offer two, both of which are highly recommended for middle and high school classrooms. One is based on modification of the traditional lesson plan format, and the other is based on learning centers in the middle or high school classroom. Of course, there is no single correct model of differentiation, and all teachers should feel free to use all of their expertise and the various resources available to develop their own differentiated instructional practices that meet the diverse needs of their students as well as their own instructional styles.

There is no one correct model of differentiation, and all teachers should develop their own differentiated instructional practices that meet the diverse needs of their students as well as their own instructional styles.

One final point: within the context of differentiated instruction, teachers have the possibility of working with small groups of students for more intensive Tier 2 instruction. When classrooms predominately contain smaller groups of students doing various projects and other differentiated tasks, it is somewhat easier for the general education teacher to spend fifteen minutes working with a group of students that needs intensive instruction on a particular topic. In that sense, RTI is much more possible in the context of a differentiated class than in one taught in the traditional, whole-group fashion.

Differentiation Modifications of the Traditional Lesson Plan

Most of the instructors' manuals for middle and high school classes present a traditional lesson plan format similar to that presented on the left-hand side of the following feature box. Based on that traditional lesson format, I recommend an approach for a differentiated lesson that is applicable in most middle and high school classes (Bender, 2008, 2009b). The example of such a modified lesson plan should help students master content in an introductory lesson on the American Revolution in the middle or high school grades. This lesson presents instruction for the first day of a two-week unit on that topic as an example of how teachers might begin with a traditional lesson plan and modify it to more appropriately differentiate for various students in the class.

An Outdated Lesson Plan

On the left-hand side, the traditional lesson plan format is presented. As surprising as it may seem, this lesson-planning format for group instruction has not changed substantively since at least 1970 (Bender, 2008)! In fact, these phases of instruction (introduction, teacher-led instruction, teacher-guided practice, and so on) are very familiar to almost all middle and high school teachers, and they are very comfortable leading students through each step in that type of traditional lesson plan. This lesson delivery format has been so common for so long that some teachers recall writing lesson plans based on it in their education classes! Almost all public school textbooks include some version of this traditional lesson plan model in their instructors' manuals.

This traditional lesson plan offers few options for differentiated activities, since all activities are intended as whole-class activities. In understanding the need for differentiation in middle and high school classes, one need only reflect on this traditional lesson plan and the assumptions on which it is based, such as that all the students in the class:

- Are functioning at about the same academic level
- Have the same level of knowledge of the content
- Will progress through this single set of activities at about the same time
- Learn in a similar fashion

While some of those assumptions (specifically the first two or three) may have been valid in the late 1960s and early 1970s when the traditional lesson plan for whole-group instruction was developed, these assumptions are clearly not valid for the highly diverse groups of students in modern classrooms because of the increased diversity in those classrooms (Bender, 2009b; Bender & Waller, 2011). The academic range in modern classes is much larger since inclusion of students with significant learning problems is now the norm (and it wasn't in the early 1970s). Modern classes also include more English learners, and that adds to the diversity. Thus the lesson plan assumptions are not valid for most modern classes in middle and high schools. In spite of that fact, most teachers' manuals still present the traditional lesson plan as the basis for instruction.

Traditional Lesson Plan and Differentiated Modifications

Traditional Phases/ Mainline Instruction Group	Modifications for Differentiated Groups
A. Introduction/Orientation Activity (Ten minutes) Use roll paper and photos to create a timeline for events in the American Revolution. Students pick pictures in text and then suggest why they should go on the timeline (importance in history and so forth). They then put a dot on the timeline where that event should show up.	
B. Teacher-Led Instruction (Twenty minutes) Go to the beginning of the chapter and discuss early causes of the war with the class.	Form Group A (linguistic students who can work independently) and have them locate and list two reasons why each picture should be on the timeline.
C. Teacher-Guided Practice (Fifteen minutes) Provide a worksheet on events leading to the war and have the class begin that work while you circulate, assisting students.	Form Group B (spatial learners or bodily/kinesthetic learners) and have them draw pictures for each event on the timeline.
D. Independent Practice (Fifteen to twenty minutes) Have the mainline instruction group work with peer buddies to exchange and check partially completed worksheets, using the text and Internet.	Form Group C (musical learners) and have them develop a song or chant to summarize one important fact about each of the five preceding events (causes) of the war.
E. Check and Reteach As groups complete their work, have them rejoin the mainline instruction group. As a review, have groups A, B, and C report on their work to the entire class.	

Modifying the Traditional Lesson Plan
for Differentiated Lessons

I recommend beginning with this lesson plan and developing modifications that facilitate differentiated instruction for targeted groups of students (Bender, 2008). This allows teachers to manage highly diverse groups of students. Such modifications are shown on the right-hand side of the feature box on page 89.

Note that in this modification approach to differentiated instruction, no modifications are recommended for the orientation phase of the traditional lesson (Bender, 2008). Teachers typically structure those introductory activities to be high-interest activities (Bender, 2009b), and most students can and will pay attention to the lesson for a few minutes during an introductory activity. Even students challenged with a reading problem or a behavioral abnormality such as hyperactivity can remain involved in most lessons during a high-interest introduction or orientation to the lesson.

Once teachers move from the high-interest introduction activity into the teacher-led instruction phase of the traditional lesson, however, some students begin to drift into inattention. This is when differentiated activities should begin, and this is exactly why differentiation in middle and high school classes is so important; when differentiation is done well, it increases rather drastically the time students remain engaged with the lesson content (Bender, 2008, 2009b).

Differentiation drastically increases the time students remain engaged with the lesson content. Rather than merely following the traditional whole-group lesson format as presented on the left-hand side of the feature box on page 89, teachers should begin to introduce differentiated activities for small groups of students, as shown on the right-hand side of the feature box, after the introduction activity. This modified lesson plan provides a variety of differentiated lesson activities. In this example, during the introduction, the history teacher wanted students to scan through the chapter on the American Revolution and find interesting pictures that are important enough to be considered critical events, which they will then select for inclusion on the class timeline. It should certainly include events such as passage of the Stamp Act, the Boston Tea Party, the Battle of Concord, the Battle of Bunker Hill, Washington crossing the Delaware River, the camp at Valley Forge, the Battle of Yorktown, and perhaps others.

During the introduction, all students in the class would search for interesting pictures in the text, read the captions, and if they are critically important, present these to the teacher while stating why they are important. Teachers would then help students identify the appropriate spot on the timeline, and the students place a dot at the approximate position on the timeline when the event took place and list the name of that event under the dot.

After eight to ten minutes on that introductory activity, the teacher would probably move into the next phase of the traditional lesson, teacher-led instruction. In this example, that might be a discussion of the causes of the war (the Stamp Act, taxation without representation), and in an ideal world, the entire class would actively participate in that discussion as they had in the introductory activity. In reality, the advanced or gifted students may mentally withdraw at that point, and some of the more challenged students may just stop paying attention altogether! The teacher may have lost the attention of 25 to 35 percent of the class.

In contrast, a lesson with differentiated instructional modifications offers an opportunity to keep all students cognitively involved with the lesson content by providing differentiated activities to various students at various points in the class after the introduction is completed. In the feature box on page 89, prior to the teacher actually beginning the teacher-led instruction phase of the lesson, he or she formed a differentiated group (called Group A in this example) for small-group work. Group A might consist of three or four gifted or advanced students with a linguistic learning strength who are likely to know something about the content and two or three students who are less likely to know the content. Their assignment is to search the text for at least two reasons each event identified in the introduction should be on the timeline. They should jot down those reasons for each event on a notepad, present them to the teacher, and upon approval, write them on the timeline.

During the teacher-led instruction phase of the lesson, the teacher will be working with most of the class following the main line of the traditional lesson plan while a subgroup of the class (Group A) is doing a differentiated activity. Several advantages of differentiation become obvious at this point. First, the attention of the advanced and more challenged students is more likely to remain focused on the learning content in a differentiated group such as Group A than in whole-class instruction. Next, as more students work in differentiated groups, the size of the mainline instructional group working with the teacher decreases. For that reason, the efficacy of the teacher's instruction is likely to go up! In fact, almost all teachers can monitor students' understandings in groups of eleven to fifteen students more effectively than in a whole-class activity with twenty-five students. In the smaller mainline group, teachers can make better eye contact with students, assess their understanding and insight more quickly, and immediately reteach any particular point as necessary.

> Differentiated lessons offer an opportunity to keep all students cognitively involved with the lesson content by providing differentiated activities to various students at various points in the class.

Another advantage of this type of differentiated lesson is the targeted activities that address a wide variety of learning styles. In this example, all of the differentiated groups are targeted to include students with various learning strengths (a musical, analytical, spatial, or bodily/kinesthetic learning style). In fact, it even targets an interpersonal learning style, because students have been instructed to work in small groups. These small-group activities targeted to students' strengths are likely to increase both attention and retention.

Taken together, the importance of these several advantages of differentiation cannot be overstated. As pointed out earlier, in a differentiated lesson:

- Attention levels increase as students participate in fun, novel differentiated activities.

- Teaching efficacy increases for students in the mainline instruction group.

- Activities aimed at specific learning styles are likely to increase student engagement and, thus, student learning.

As more students work in differentiated groups, the size of the mainline instruction group decreases, and the efficacy of the teacher's instruction goes up!

All of these advantages of differentiated instruction tend to increase students' involvement with the academic content, and modifications of this nature will increase academic achievement overall (Gregory, 2008; Gregory & Kuzmich, 2005; Lee et al., 2010; Tomlinson et al., 2008).

When the time comes for the teacher to move from the teacher-led instruction phase to the teacher-guided practice phase, he or she should once again form a differentiated instruction group, which is identified as Group B in this example. Group B, including four or five spatial learners, might draw pictures on the timeline for each event. While these students may use pictures from the text, they should add at least some informational items to their drawings based on important material from the text. When students address either of these assignments, they are more likely to remain cognitively involved with the lesson content than to drift into inattention.

These are interesting small-group tasks (working on the floor on the timeline or meeting in a small group to discuss why an event is important) and should increase attention to the content of the chapter. In each case, reading and study of the chapter content are likely to take place in the context of a student needing information from the text. After each phase of the traditional lesson, teachers should form a differentiated group for a specific, content-focused task, as indicated by Groups A, B, and C (page 89). As differentiated groups complete their tasks, they should merely be instructed to rejoin the mainline whole-class instruction.

Of course, teachers should not consider their teaching task completed merely by forming these groups. Sometimes small groups will not function properly, as some students get off task or become aggressive over a disagreement. Teachers will need to carefully monitor these small groups to ensure learning is taking place and the assigned task is being accomplished. The following feature box provides additional guidelines concerning how to make this type of differentiated lesson work in almost every middle and high school classroom.

Practical Suggestions for Differentiating Within a Traditional Lesson Plan

Take care in group selection. Generally, most students from grade 3 and higher can work in less-supervised small groups, so such work in middle and high school should be undertaken routinely. However, teachers must take care in group selection, only placing students with serious behavioral challenges in these groups after careful consideration. While teachers can form groups based on relatively homogeneous ability level, they can also use heterogeneous groups in which some students have a good grasp of the content and the task and others may be less adept. In that case, students are likely to learn from each other.

Move furniture around. In forming groups for various activities, teachers may send students to open spaces in the room or move desks to create such open space. The timeline described previously should be six to eight feet long to give appropriate space for the work, and that will require floor or table space. However, the teacher must visually monitor those groups while he or she teaches the mainline instructional group. Thus teachers should have students move desks around so that (a) the teacher can teach the mainline instructional group directly and still visually monitor the differentiated groups, and (b) students in the mainline group have their backs to the differentiated groups so as not to be drawn off task.

Empower the students who do not know the content. In heterogeneous groups, there will be a natural tendency for students who know the content best to merely do the task. By empowering the students who are less sure of the content, however, the teacher can encourage (or essentially force) the group to work as a more cohesive whole. How a teacher empowers less-sure students will vary from one activity to the next, but this does ensure that the students who know the content will be working with those who don't in order to complete the activity.

Coach and negotiate with students with behavioral challenges. Some students in middle and high school may not have acquired the social skills to work in less-supervised small groups. These students may become angry when they grasp the content before other group members, or they may wish to avoid any work. Generally, with a private discussion, teachers can negotiate with students who have behavioral challenges in various ways, requesting improved behavior or empowering them with specific tasks.

In some cases, teachers have these students participate for the first five minutes of the small-group activity and then rejoin the mainline group. In other cases, teachers develop a private sign that a behaviorally challenged student might use if she feels she is about to lose control while working in the differentiated group. Should a teacher see that student give the sign, the teacher could then call that student back into the mainline group to assist the teacher with a demonstration of a concept. In that way, the student with the behavioral challenge can escape the differentiated group prior to creating a behavioral disturbance.

Continued➜

Couple differentiated lessons with inclusion. In some middle and high schools, inclusive practices involve having a general education teacher and a special education teacher teach in the same class. Having two certified teachers in the room is a great opportunity for differentiated activities, as both adults are available to supervise the various groups. Of course, any general education teacher can (and frequently does) manage small-group instruction for multiple groups, but having another adult in the room facilitates differentiated activities.

Differentiate two or three days per week in middle and high schools. In many middle and high schools, teachers might face 120 to 150 students per day (that is, six or seven classes of twenty to thirty students each). Teachers in that situation may feel they cannot plan enough differentiated instructional activities to differentiate effectively. Those teachers can take heart based on the following supports. First, the teachers' manual presents many activities for differentiated instruction, so teachers don't typically have to generate these ideas themselves. Next, in most subject-area classes, teachers might consider planning for differentiated lessons only two or three times each week. On other days, teachers should continue various whole-class activities that have worked in the past and have kept most of the students engaged with the lesson content.

Many proponents of differentiation recommend that teachers establish learning centers and use those as a basis for differentiated instruction (Gregory, 2008; Smutny & von Fremd, 2010). While learning centers have been implemented more frequently in the lower grades, various learning centers can also be used in middle and high schools as bases for differentiated instruction (Gregory & Kuzmich, 2005). The example that follows presents a learning center differentiation approach for the same basic content as the previous lesson example, a two-week unit in a ninth-grade U.S. history class studying the American Revolution. Of course, the same learning center ideas would certainly work in almost any of the core academic subjects in middle or high schools (such as health, biology, mathematics, consumer sciences, vocational education, and so forth).

Learning Centers

For each learning center assignment, the teacher must develop a rubric that delineates assignment requirements and the grading scale for that assignment, since rubrics are the most effective way to communicate assignment expectations to students.

To create a learning center in a subject-area class, the teacher needs a table placed along a wall that can be dedicated to that specific learning center. The teacher would then label each learning center with a large sign on the wall behind the table. It's important to keep the name and general focus of the learning centers constant throughout the semester or academic year. For example, a U.S. or world history teacher might establish three or four learning centers focused in the following areas: maps and geography, governance and societies' accomplishments, and peoples and culture. The teacher could use those titles in virtually all instructional units.

In addition to those topical areas, middle and high school teachers should create a center for computer-based or web-based instruction. It is ideal to have an area in the classroom that houses four to six computers with Internet access and subject-appropriate software. While this does present some budgetary concerns, the department may acquire computers and software over several years and may share them with others in the same subject area. Teachers could then label that center the "computer learning center." Finally, each learning center should hold various instructional materials, simulations, games, photographs, and other hands-on activities necessary for that semester. These may include:

- Bold markers
- Blank transparency sheets
- Assignment boxes
- Copies of maps
- Poster paper
- Storage bins
- Small whiteboards
- Historic diagrams
- Large roll paper
- Relevant magazines and books
- Copies of various texts
- Photograph collections

Each learning center should also include a description of specific daily or unit assignments students will do when they work in that center. Whereas the names of the centers and the necessary materials do not change from one instructional unit to the next, the assignments change with each instructional unit. The teacher might write assignments on a small whiteboard in the learning center or delineate them on a one-page set of instructions. He could also place assignment folders describing specific tasks within that unit in assignment boxes.

For each assignment in each learning center, the teacher should develop a rubric that delineates assignment requirements and the grading scale for that assignment, since rubrics are generally accepted as the most effective way to communicate assignment expectations to students (Larmer, Ross, & Mergendollar, 2009; see table 4.1, page 97).

Structuring the Content Assignments

Given the learning center structure, teachers may adapt the content of the learning centers from one instructional unit to another. For a unit on the American Revolution, a teacher might structure two different types of assignments for the unit:

1. A unit-long assignment (taking three to five days to complete) for a small group of five to seven students

2. A number of individual assignments students can complete in only one or two instructional periods

The description of the various learning centers that follows fleshes out these various types of assignments.

Maps and Geography Learning Center

Maps and geography are critical for understanding history; Valley Forge could not have happened along the coast of Georgia, since that region was simply not cold enough to nearly destroy General Washington's army, and one can only understand the early battles of 1775 and 1776 near Boston (such as Lexington Green and Bunker Hill) with a map of that region in hand, since geography played a role in each. Thus the maps and geography center should present an array of maps of the United States (and individual states if possible) along with various map-based instructional activities. In terms of a unit-long assignment for this unit on the American Revolution, the teacher might provide two options:

1. Using one or more maps of the Boston area, depict the various battles in the first two years of the war and note how the geography of that area affected those battles. Develop a PowerPoint presentation.

This type of assignment is particularly effective for students with a spatial learning preference, and a rubric for this unit-long small-group assignment appears in table 4.1.

2. Using a map of the Southeastern states as they existed in 1775 to 1783, hold a debate about the various battles stemming from the British "Southern strategy" from 1777 to 1781. Each group member should represent and advocate for the importance of each battle selected, and the group must discuss at least four of the battles from the following areas: Camden, Cowpens, King's Mountain, Guilford Courthouse, Savannah, or Yorktown. Focus primarily on the relationships between these battles and their relative importance in the war, addressing the question "Why was the American Revolution won in the South?"

This type of assignment would be highly useful for students with linguistic learning strengths. Again, provide a rubric for this assignment and all assignments in the unit.

Governance and Societies' Accomplishments Learning Center

This learning center may be somewhat less active during the unit on the American Revolution itself, since constitutional government was not established during the war. However, the teacher could still develop a unit-long group assignment similar to the unit-long assignment described previously.

With that noted, all of the learning centers should have a variety of individual, single-period assignments that address various aspects of the instructional unit. Here are several examples:

• Write a twenty-five-line rap describing the relationship between General Washington and Congress during the war, from Washington's perspective. This assignment is particularly effective for learners with musical skills.

Table 4.1: Assignment Rubric for Boston-Area Battles

	Required Information	Evaluation Criteria
Adequate	1. On one slide for each of two major events (Lexington Green, Bunker Hill), present two paragraphs of information in written form with bullet points summarizing each. 2. Describe how geography affected each event (such as Revere's ride and the "neck" near Bunker Hill). 3. Present at least two visuals for each of those events.	1. Meets assignment requirements 2. Students agree to a grade of C, C+, or B– depending on overall quality
Very Good	1. Meet all assignment requirements for three major events (include the two previous and Dorchester Heights). 2. Describe how geography affected each event. 3. Present at least two visuals for each of those events. 4. Present overall summary of action in Boston area.	1. Meets assignment requirements 2. Students agree to a grade of B, B+, or A– depending on overall quality
Excellent	1. Meet all previous assignment requirements except 4. 2. Present dialogue for a one-act play (of at least twenty-five verbal exchanges) of either the British leader or a colonial leader summarizing these fights and events.	1. Meets assignment requirements 2. Students strive for a grade of A or A+

Source: Adapted from Larmer et al., 2009.

- Develop a brief comparison chart on the types of commerce in the Southern states compared to the types of commerce in Boston and New York and how those differences may have affected history.

- American arms manufacturing was more primitive than manufacturing in Great Britain, but the Patriots at King's Mountain fought with much better rifles than the Tories. Develop a podcast focused on the impact that the Kentucky rifle had on that battle.

Peoples and Culture Learning Center

The role of various cultures and peoples is critical in understanding the American Revolution. For example, the Cherokee declared war on frontier settlers in the uplands of the rural South during the American Revolution, and that relatively small war occurred within the broader American Revolution. The English ultimately viewed the American Revolution as only a small manifestation of England's ongoing conflict with France. In that sense, various wars or conflicts are frequently embedded within other conflicts. On that basis, discussion of any of these cultures is relevant to the American Revolution. Assignments in this center may include:

- Write a letter from the French king to General Washington describing the French view of the importance of Washington's success at the Battle of Trenton.

- Conduct a webquest (a search of the Internet) to find statements by Cherokee leaders made during the American Revolution that indicate why they fought with the British. Present a summary of these to the class.

Teaching a Center-Based Instructional Unit

A teacher can conduct a two-week instructional unit with the three centers and activities described earlier coupled with considerable student choice among the various assignments. The teacher would expect all students to complete at least two individual assignments in two different learning centers as well as a unit-long assignment working with a small group.

While either students or teachers may determine which small-group assignments to undertake, student choice in differentiated educational settings is encouraged, because offering students choices generally results in higher motivation to complete assignments (Bender, 2009b). In differentiated instructional units, students should select assignments based on consideration of their interests and their learning strengths. Learners who learn best through bodily/kinesthetic tasks should select individual and unit-long projects that involve some physical movement, whereas learners with strength in spatial learning might select more art- or map-based activities. Of course, teachers should limit student choice as necessary, particularly if students' behavior is a concern or to make certain that students attempt an array of educational tasks.

I do not recommend highly differentiated activities every day in most middle and high school classes.

I do not recommend highly differentiated activities every day in most middle and high school classes, since planning that many activities in departmentalized schools can be quite time-consuming. In the unit described here, the teacher could implement center-based instruction for perhaps six or seven days of a two-week instructional unit. In other words, teachers should plan a mix of whole-group and differentiated, center-based assignments in each instructional unit. A schedule for this unit is presented in the following feature box.

Note that this instructional unit does not include a unit test as the culminating activity. While unit tests can certainly be the final activity of an instructional unit, teachers can also assign grades for other tasks and average them in some fashion to provide a unit grade. In this example, each student would complete a unit-long small-group project, for which each student would receive the same grade. As shown in the unit schedule, each student would also complete two individual assignments for individual grades. Teachers may choose to assign weights to these various grades or give students the option to select the relative weight of each grade in computing the overall unit grade or the overall quarter or semester grade.

Schedule for a Two-Week, Learning Center–Based Instructional Unit	
Day 1	Whole-class video (on American Revolution) coupled with a participatory organizer for students to complete and a discussion of the causes and results.
Day 2	Students select a unit-long project and begin work. Teacher oversees division of tasks and responsibilities and works with small groups of students needing individual assistance.
Day 3	Students complete one individual assignment of their own choosing from one learning center and then work on their unit-long project for the rest of the period.
Day 4	Whole-class discussion of some of the individual assignments with students presenting their individual work.
Day 5	Students work on unit-long project, and teacher works with small groups of students needing individual assistance.
Day 6	Students work on unit-long project, and teacher works with small groups of students needing individual assistance.
Day 7	Students complete a second individual assignment of their own choosing and then work on their unit-long project.
Day 8	Whole-class discussion of some of the individual assignments with some students presenting their work.
Day 9	Three presentations of unit-long projects to the entire class.
Day 10	Whole-class discussion with participatory organizer summarizing causes of the war, important military phases of the war, cultural involvement of various groups, and results of the war.

Summary of Differentiation Instructional Options

In both approaches to differentiation—modification of the traditional lesson plan or center-based instruction—effective differentiation will change the students' and the teachers' experience of the classroom. Students will become more invested in their learning as their choices go up and as the modification options increase (Gregory & Kuzmich, 2005; Lee et al., 2010). Students are also more likely to engage meaningfully with the instructional content in these types of learning activities than in more traditional teacher presentations or lecture-based instruction. In this manner, differentiated instruction does have the effect of re-energizing traditionally taught middle and high school classes, and evidence on differentiation implementation in high schools documents that student achievement will increase (Tomlinson et al., 2008).

Students are more likely to engage meaningfully with the instructional content in these types of learning activities than in more traditional teacher presentations or lecture-based instruction.

Furthermore, the differentiated classes of today are much more fluid, with students participating in a variety of individual and small-group activities and then rejoining the whole class for other activities. Teaching in this fashion results in increased attention to the learning content overall, and both students and teachers enjoy the freedom inherent in this lesson format.

RTI Within the Differentiated Class

With these differentiated instructional options in mind for middle and secondary classes, educators might well ask how RTI fits into the picture. Of course, the answer to that question will be as varied as the schools implementing these innovations. While current models of RTI in middle and high schools almost always involve a supplementary instructional period in reading or mathematics (Duffy, n.d.; Gibbs, 2008; James, 2010; Johnson & Smith, 2008; Rozalski, 2009), highly differentiated instruction in general education content classes can present additional options for Tier 2 instruction within the context of general education classes. Here are several possibilities.

For example, in the learning center instructional unit previously discussed, four or five students in that history class who require supplemental Tier 2 intervention might receive their intervention in the form of reading instruction from reading content that focuses on the unit under study via software instructional programs on that particular topic. If high-quality reading instructional software on the American Revolution is available that allows the teacher to adjust the reading level to a grade 4 or 5 level, that curriculum might be an appropriate Tier 2 intervention for some of the students.

In that case, instead of working on a unit-long group project, those students could move to the computer center and work on that reading software during the two-week unit described earlier. They could likewise continue that computerized instruction in subsequent units as necessary. Of course, almost all modern software presents numerous opportunities for daily or weekly progress monitoring, so teachers can use both the instructional software and the assessment tools to facilitate Tier 2 interventions. Finding software appropriate to the topic is the key. This type of RTI example was presented in chapter 1, wherein a social studies teacher undertook a Tier 2 RTI intervention using the Study Island software during the history class itself.

Should appropriate computer software not be available, another RTI option might have students requiring a Tier 2 intervention work with the history teacher while other class members complete their unit-long small-group project assignments. As shown in the previous feature box (page 99), students work for some portion of the instructional period on their unit-long projects on five different days during that unit (days 2, 3, 5, 6, and 7). In a U.S. history class of twenty-five students, if two groups of seven students are working in the learning centers on those days, the teacher could work with the other eleven students who might require a Tier 2 intervention focused on reading in the content areas. Thus a differentiated instructional approach based on learning centers fosters increased opportunities for undertaking Tier 2 instructional interventions.

While most models of RTI in middle and high school classes do not involve having the general education teacher provide Tier 2 interventions, increased differentiation in those classes may well involve that opportunity.

Conclusion

As is apparent from this discussion, planning a differentiated instructional lesson is and should be quite different from merely following the traditional whole-group lesson plan as described in various instructors' manuals. In order to foster high-quality differentiated instruction as well as response to intervention opportunities, teachers will, of necessity, have to restructure lessons somewhat. Such restructuring can likewise facilitate RTI by making time for various Tier 2 interventions in the context of general education classes. Of course, many middle and high school teachers have already undertaken these differentiated instructional procedures, and those teachers will find the growing emphasis on RTI to be an easier transition.

Supporting RTI and Differentiated Instruction With Modern Instructional Technologies

As discussed previously, technology and modern instructional software have revolutionized middle and high school instruction, and these modern technology-based teaching tools can greatly facilitate both RTI and differentiated instruction (Ash, 2010; Busch, 2010; Cote, 2007; Dretzin, 2010; Mann, Shakeshaft, Becker, & Kottkamp, 1999; McCoy, 1996; Partnership for 21st Century Skills, 2007, 2009; Wood, Mackiewicz, Norman, & Cooke, 2007). These technologies, as applied in various classrooms, will greatly enhance every teacher's opportunity to implement differentiated instruction in the various content-area classes, which, in turn, will assist students in meeting state educational standards (Dretzin, 2010). Furthermore, technology can assist in providing supplementary Tier 2 and 3 interventions, as well as facilitate progress monitoring of struggling students. For these reasons, the use of modern technologies in middle and high school classes is now widely recommended (Ash, 2010; Biancarosa & Snow, 2006; Dretzin, 2010; Elder-Hinshaw et al., 2006; Salend, 2009; Waller, 2011).

Technology Options for RTI and Differentiated Instruction

The wide array of available, research-proven software-based curricula can help differentiate middle and high school lessons in ways that were not possible previously (Cote, 2007; McCoy, 1996; Salend, 2009; Wood et al., 2007). Beyond educational software, the newly developed digital communications options available to teachers are nearly endless, and educators can integrate these options into virtually every subject area in the middle and upper grades in highly creative and exciting ways to facilitate differentiated instruction or intervention within the upper RTI tiers (Ash, 2010; Biancarosa & Snow, 2006; Dretzin, 2010; Elder-Hinshaw et al., 2006). In fact, today's middle and high school students are demonstrating a desire for increased technology through their increased use of social networking sites and other technologies in their daily lives.

It is not an overstatement to suggest that modern students' daily experience involves a connected, networked, highly digital world. Some estimates indicate that adolescents today spend fifty hours or more each week engaged with digital media (Dretzin, 2010); this alone seems to suggest the importance of modern networking and communications technologies. Dretzin (2010) postulates that students engaged with the digital world who walk into a classroom that is not implementing these instructional approaches would feel as if they were walking into a desert. Because most students have fairly extensive experience with these various technologies in nonschool settings, middle and high schools must adapt by implementing instruction using these modern technologies as much as possible to hold the interests of preteens and adolescents (Dretzin, 2010).

Technology-based teaching has now gone far beyond computerized instructional programs as a mechanism to deliver information. These instructional options provide actual opportunities for students to collaboratively create content using webquests, iPads, smartphones, BlackBerrys, Facebook, MySpace, Ning, Twitter, and many other innovations, and then publish that information to a worldwide audience (Ash, 2010; Dretzin, 2010). In this media-rich, high-technology world, effective teachers must embrace a wide array of technology innovations in order to reach students at all (Cote, 2007; Dretzin, 2010; Partnership for 21st Century Skills, 2007, 2009; Salend, 2009). Fortunately, many middle and high school teachers have already begun to embrace these options to facilitate high levels of differentiation in their classes.

Middle and high school teachers simply must embrace these instructional innovations to reach students.

With the implementation of these new technologies, effective middle and high school instruction in the coming years will look drastically different from instruction in 2010 (Ash, 2010; Dretzin, 2010). Specifically, one may well anticipate that virtually all teachers will soon be using class blogs, Moodle, smartphones, webquests, and other technological innovations for instruction (Cote, 2007; Waller, 2011). Teachers in middle and high schools must be prepared for these coming changes in instruction.

While this chapter cannot present a full discussion of all of these options, it does present a selected set of hardware and software, web-based tools, and curricula and progress-monitoring options currently in use. These examples indicate how increased use of technology can facilitate increased differentiation in middle and high school classes.

Hardware and Software for Differentiation

While instructional technologies and curricula are rapidly developing, classrooms should involve application of some of the most basic types (Biancarosa & Snow, 2006; Elder-Hinshaw et al., 2006; Partnership for 21st Century Skills, 2007; Salend, 2009). While few schools provide all of these technologies in every middle and high school classroom, the hardware and software discussed here represent the most basic options for schools, and school districts should build financing into their budgets for this type of hardware.

Computer Stations With Internet Access

Every middle and high school class should have access to four to six computers with Internet access. This can be accomplished either by placing that number of computers in each class or having mobile computers (sometimes called COWs or computers on wheels: five or six computers on a mobile table, which two or three teachers might share between classrooms). School budgets are often quite limited, but over time, schools can generally acquire these items by purchasing a few each year. As shown in the discussion in chapter 4, a computer center with five or six computers in each classroom will facilitate highly differentiated instruction through learning centers and can provide many Tier 2 intervention options as well. Computer availability along these lines can be a great boost for struggling learners across the middle and high school grades and can be effective in helping all students meet and exceed adequate yearly progress toward their educational goals.

Some educators suggest that computers should not be housed in computer labs but dispersed throughout the classrooms, since integration of these computer technologies throughout the curriculum results in improved academic performance of students (Mann et al., 1999). Almost every school administrator has, at one time or another, noted expensive computers loaded with software sitting unused in the back of one classroom or another, and by placing computers in labs specifically identified for computer usage, many administrators felt they increased the use of the technology. While such an assumption may have been valid in the early 2000s, it is probably no longer valid, since teachers today are much more computer fluent.

At this point, preservice teachers are extensively trained in using software-based instructional options, and to facilitate modern instruction, computers in all classrooms are preferable to separate computer centers. I prefer the option of placing computers in every teacher's class and providing training to all faculty on how to use them to provide differentiated instructional options. Research indicates that classroom use of instructional software is more effective for increasing student mathematics achievement than software use in computer labs (Mann et al., 1999), and this would suggest that it might be time to disperse computers into classrooms rather than gather them into computer labs. Of course, in the transition phase as schools increase the number of computers in each classroom, they should place them with teachers who are most likely to utilize them optimally.

> Teachers should have access to four to six computers with Internet access in every middle and high school classroom.

As computers become more available for student use in general education classrooms, Internet access will become a critical issue. The Internet presents a vast array of information that can enhance instruction in every subject in the curriculum

(Okolo, Englert, Bouck, & Heutsche, 2007; Skylar, Higgins, & Boone, 2007). However, schools should also carefully control the content to which students are exposed and use firewalls and student honor-based commitments to report accidental access of any inappropriate content. Schools across North America have already established such monitoring procedures and policies, so the coming increase in Internet usage will not require the development of new policies for most school districts.

Laptops for All

Since 2000, some states, provinces, and school districts have established a goal of providing a one-to-one ratio of students and laptop computers (Ash, 2010; Busch, 2010; Dretzin, 2010); this is often referred to as a one-to-one initiative. Essentially, districts instituting this initiative have stated the goal that either schools or parents should purchase and provide a laptop for every student in the classroom (Partnership for 21st Century Skills, 2009). For example, faculty at Sarah Banks Middle School in Michigan have been implementing a one-to-one laptop program since 2000. At Sarah Banks, parents are encouraged to purchase laptops for their own students, and students without that option are provided laptop access at school via mobile computer carts (Ash, 2010). To date, approximately 33 percent of parents have purchased laptop computers. In other states or districts, the schools have provided laptop computers for each student or each student in certain grades.

Advocates of this initiative anecdotally report many positive effects (Ash, 2010; Dretzin, 2010; Manzo, 2010a). For example, as reported on the public broadcasting television show *Frontline* (Dretzin, 2010), Jason Levy, principal at a South Bronx Middle School (IS 339), needed to make a change. That school was a lower-achieving school in a rough area of New York City, characterized by violence, poor attendance, and little academic success. Mr. Levy and his faculty implemented a one-to-one laptop initiative in 2004 and soon found that they could reengage nearly all students in meaningful learning. Schoolwide achievement increased 30 percent in reading and 40 percent in mathematics on nationally normed assessments, and teachers credited the laptop initiative as the basis for those increased scores. Other positive benefits reported included increased motivation to learn, increased participation in class activities, improved attendance, decreased school violence, and reduced discipline problems (Dretzin, 2010). Similar results have been reported elsewhere, though more research is needed before firm conclusions can be drawn (Manzo, 2010a). Still, this initiative seems to hold tremendous promise for improving academic performance in schools rather drastically in the same way that modern technologies have improved performance in the workplace.

Of course, this one-to-one laptop initiative is founded on current practices in the workplace. In many, if not most, workplace environments, every worker is provided a computer or access to a computer to facilitate better job performance. In this view, schools would be remiss if educators failed to emulate that workforce reality in the classroom (Manzo, 2010a; Partnership for 21st Century Skills, 2009).

While laptops and Internet capability for every student in the middle and secondary grades are worthy goals, there may soon be less expensive options. Educators might well consider exactly how much computing power every student really needs. Renaissance Learning, for example (the publishers of the widely utilized Accelerated Reader curriculum, www.renlearn.com), has launched a student laptop/desktop portable word processing device with some computer capability. The NEO 2 is available for $149 per student (www.renlearn.com/neo/NEO2/default.aspx). It includes wireless capability with limited Internet access and connection options for classwide sharing of papers and projects. It is possible that devices such as this, rather than laptop computers, can provide advantages for differentiation and RTI across the grade levels at a reduced cost.

Mobile Devices

Laptop computers aside, a bewildering array of mobile Internet devices, most with some computing power, are currently available (Manzo, 2010a). Educators are currently experimenting with devices such as iPads, smartphones, gaming platforms, MP3 players, and a seemingly endless array of other gadgets as teaching tools in middle and high school classrooms across North America (Ash, 2010; Davis, 2010; Manzo, 2010a). For example, in one North Carolina high school, when a student has difficulty on a homework assignment in algebra I, the student uses a school-issued smartphone to text the teacher or another student for help. That student can also use the smartphone to post a question about the problem on the school math blog (Davis, 2010). In Roswell High School in Roswell, Georgia, teachers and students are using their iPods to access enriched academic content in various science and history classes. These communication devices place a variety of very rich curriculum resources at the students' fingertips.

Clearly changes are taking place in middle and high schools, resulting from the use of these noneducational technologies in the educational setting (Manzo, 2010b), and educators are struggling to interpret these rather dramatic instructional innovations. Various teachers and proponents of technology believe that these mobile devices alone are creating a revolution in the teaching-learning process (Christensen, Horn, & Johnson, 2008; Ferriter, 2010). Middle and high schools are experimenting with high levels of connectivity based on this new generation of mobile, Internet-capable devices, and the initial applications of these tools in teaching look quite promising (Ferriter, 2010; Manzo, 2010a, 2010b).

In one sense, use of these mobile communication devices in education is somewhat difficult to manage because they change very frequently. New mobile devices seem to emerge with each passing month. As one example, during the writing of this chapter in early 2010, Apple introduced the iPad with great fanfare, and less than a year later, the iPad 2 became available. These devices offer Internet connectivity, email options, iBooks, and a range of other applications that can be used in the classroom. iPads sell for between $499 and $699 on the open market, which is somewhat less than state-of-the-art laptop computers, and again, this may ultimately offer an option that is somewhat cheaper than one-to-one laptop initiatives.

Mobile learning devices are drastically transforming education, and these instructional options make increased differentiation much more possible in the middle and upper grades.

While use of these mobile devices as educational tools in schools is still under study, the anecdotal support for them seems quite strong (Manzo, 2010a). Early research has indicated that achievement does increase as more and more students gain access to mobile learning capabilities and as teachers embrace the use of these devices in classes across the curriculum (Ash, 2010; Davis, 2010; Ferriter, 2010; Manzo, 2010a, 2010b). Other educators report the same types of positive results for these devices as were noted for the one-to-one laptop initiative, including increased student engagement, increased motivation, improved attendance, and reduction in both discipline problems and school dropout rates (Manzo, 2010a). Again, this research is still sporadic and quite tentative, since much of it is anecdotal in nature or based on self-reported data. Still, as smaller, less expensive mobile devices become more common, perhaps this type of device, rather than a laptop computer, will be the option of choice for students.

Whiteboards

Interactivity can be greatly enhanced in the classroom by use of a whiteboard (sometimes referred to as a smartboard). Middle and high school classrooms should include a whiteboard or some type of interactive technology that allows teachers to display the contents of their computer screen for the entire class to see (Bender & Waller, 2011; Marzano, 2009; Marzano & Haystead, 2009; Salend, 2009). These technologies also allow the instruction to be more interactive, as teachers and students can make display choices on the whiteboard itself. For example, when a high school class is reading about the Civil War, the teacher might be able to download a short video about the war or early photography, including some of the first battlefield pictures in history. He or she could then use the whiteboard to display the video segment or photos to the entire class; this will engage students and lead to increased academic performance. Marzano's research has documented significant increases in academic achievement, ranging from 13 to 17 percent, when teachers used whiteboards as interactive instructional media (Marzano, 2009; Marzano & Haystead, 2009).

Presentation Software

Each computer in the class should have some presentation software such as PowerPoint available for student use (Elder-Hinshaw et al., 2006). In modern instruction, both teachers and students should be routinely developing various presentations using such software to aid comprehension of the material. Once either a teacher or student group has developed an effective presentation, the instructor can easily store it in digital form for future use. Modern presentation software is designed in a user-friendly fashion to allow for use by all middle and high school students; in fact, students as young as grades 1 or 2 are developing PowerPoint presentations (Bender & Waller, 2011), and such media-savvy skills will clearly be in demand in almost all 21st century jobs (Partnership for 21st Century Skills, 2007; Salend, 2009). Therefore schools must teach these presentation development skills routinely in all content-area classes.

Classroom Response Systems

Classroom response systems assist in fostering class interactivity. Salend (2009) recommends using them for instructional purposes in middle and high school classes during whole-group activities. Classroom response systems (sometimes called "counters" or "clickers") allow each student in the class to immediately respond to a content question or other point made by the teacher. Each student would have access to a clicker at his or her desk that uses either a wireless or an infrared or radio frequency to connect to the teacher's computer. Students can then respond to questions using that clicker, and the teacher's computer synthesizes the data from the class or instructional group. The software typically produces a chart or picture displaying those responses in the aggregate, which can then be printed out or shared with the class via a whiteboard. Such presentations may picture each individual student's answer or a synthesis of the answers from the whole class or subgroups.

The clickers allow each student to respond to simple yes-or-no questions on the content, answer multiple-choice questions, predict the outcomes of reading selections, or address specific content questions. This immediate-response option typically results in higher levels of attention during whole-class activities, since students feel more connected with what is happening in the classroom (Salend, 2009). Another advantage is that by using these devices, students can respond in a less embarrassing manner should they be unsure of their answers.

Course and Instructional Management Systems

Moodle is a course management system designed to help teachers and students develop and formulate their own Internet-based courses and websites (http://moodle .org/about), and this is a great way to involve students in writing projects that ultimately end up online. The term *Moodle* was originally an acronym for *modular object-oriented dynamic learning environment*, but most teachers merely use the acronym. There is a reasonable site-based fee for Moodle services for teachers who wish to create web-based content associated with their courses. Over the years, many teachers have developed instructional content using Moodle (anyone who Moodles is a Moodler!).

There are presently more than 35 million users at more than 50,000 locations around the world, and these numbers have continued to grow rather dramatically since January of 2005. A demonstration site allows teachers to explore this Internet-based location to see if it is right for them. Moodle 2.0 was launched in July of 2010 and incorporates many more features that teachers using the original Moodle requested.

Choosing Hardware and Software

Researchers can state with assurance that these technologies are and will be drastically transforming education over the next decade (Christensen et al., 2008; Ferriter, 2010). These instructional options make increased differentiation much more possible in the middle and upper grades, and teachers will need to remain abreast of the potential uses of these emerging teaching tools (Manzo, 2010a, 2010b).

Educators should carefully consider all of the technology tools described here, including the new mobile devices, for classroom use (Ash, 2010; Cote, 2007; Elder-Hinshaw et al., 2006; Manzo, 2010a; Salend, 2009). Moreover, every teacher should expect that utilization of these hardware and software options will only increase in the coming years, and educators will need to undertake professional development activities to prepare themselves for this new world of teaching. A variety of websites are available to help teachers determine applications for these devices; many also delineate the research support for various curricula or technologies. These are presented in the top feature box on page 111.

Instructional hardware and software that facilitate RTI and differentiated instructional options are nearly endless, and many of these instructional options positively impact the opportunities for increased differentiation and Tier 2 interventions in middle and high school classes. At a minimum, schools should be establishing classrooms with the most basic technologies readily available, including the instructional tools, such as those listed in the bottom feature box on page 111.

Of course, educators must also realize that such technologies for each classroom can be expensive, and provision for all classrooms will probably take place over a period of time. Furthermore, schools must do more than merely purchase equipment and software (Manzo, 2010a). These technologies are most effective in improving academic achievement when teachers carefully weave them into the fabric of classroom instruction across the curriculum rather than manage them within a specialized computer lab or use them in only a handful of selected courses. Thus increased use of these as basic instructional tools should be every teacher's goal.

Web-Based Tools

Once the basic instructional hardware and software discussed previously are available, web-based tools for differentiated instruction become nearly endless. Various educators have presented instructional options based in these technologies (Bender & Waller, 2011; Busch, 2010; Cote, 2007; Elder-Hinshaw et al., 2006; Salend, 2009), and the following section discusses the types of differentiated instructional opportunities technology is now facilitating in middle and high school classes.

Websites on Technology Applications in Education

Center for Applied Research in Educational Technology

http://caret.iste.org

This website operates as an arm of ISTE and provides research analysis of questions on technologies and technology applications such as, "How can technology influence student academic performance?" or "How can technology improve student motivation, attitude, and interest in learning?" The organization cites research articles on these and other questions.

International Society for Technology in Education

www.iste.org

This is a member-supported nonprofit group dedicated to effective use of technology in preK–12 classrooms as well as in higher education. Various governmental lobbying activities, conferences, and public policy statements are available here, including the Top Ten in '10: ISTE's Education Technology Priorities for 2010.

One-to-One Institute

www.one-to-oneinstitute.org

The One-to-One Institute promotes student achievement through development of learner-centered programs to engage students via use of personal, portable technologies. This organization promotes one-to-one initiatives in which laptops and Internet capability are made available for every student. Professional development for instruction based on one-to-one initiatives is available from this source.

Technology Requirements for Differentiated Instruction in the Modern Classroom

Four to six computers per classroom (allowing a number of students simultaneous access)

Internet access for all computers

Presentation software for project and assignment preparation

Whiteboards (or smartboards) or other classwide projection and instructional systems

Classroom response systems

One-to-one laptop availability when possible

Webquests

Webquests are assignments generally given to individuals or small groups of students that require searching the Internet for information about a topic (Skylar et al., 2007). Webquests are not "scavenger hunts" on the Internet but, rather, represent a student or group of students seeking specific information on a particular topic in the context of a search guided by some input from the teacher (Okolo et al., 2007; Skylar et al., 2007). In a webquest, students follow links previously identified by the teacher to answer specific comprehension questions about the topic or to seek information for a project or report. Various sources provide different components that may be included in webquests (see www.internet4classrooms.com/using_quest.htm for more information). These typically include an orientation or introduction with background information, specifics on the required tasks for students to accomplish, the process students should undertake including recommended links to explore, an evaluation mechanism that clearly states expectations, and some method to summarize the experience.

A webquest is not an ill-defined search along the digital superhighway. Rather, students follow links identified by the teacher in order to answer specific comprehension questions about a particular topic.

Most webquests for the middle and upper grades provide a distinction between required links and optional links. Once students have viewed the required links and completed the assignments for those links, teachers may encourage them to explore the topic on their own by finding other Internet-based information.

To structure a webquest, teachers should create a guide that identifies specific links for students to explore and specific tasks to accomplish at each Internet location. Required and optional links within structured webquests provide an opportunity for differentiation within the assignment; teachers may require higher-functioning students to complete more of the activities or require students with different learning strengths to perform different aspects of the group's webquest task. Many websites can assist teachers in developing webquests; some of these are presented in the following feature box.

There are many advantages to using webquests in the classroom. First, students seem to be more motivated to research and study a topic when they are able to complete their assignment on the computer (Cote, 2007). Webquests also allow students to discover information for themselves instead of just hearing the information presented via discussion, lecture, or other traditional delivery. Webquests are likely to foster higher levels of student engagement with the learning content than pencil-and-paper tasks.

Useful Websites to Assist in Creating Webquests

Internet4Classrooms

www.internet4classrooms.com/using_quest.htm

This website describes five components of webquests: (1) introduction, (2) task description, (3) process for completion, (4) evaluation criteria and rubrics, and (5) conclusion. It provides additional links for development of webquests.

Knowledge Network Explorer

www.kn.pacbell.com/wired/fil/

This website offers free templates for creating webquests. Step-by-step instructions make it fairly simple for teacher use.

QuestGarden

http://questgarden.com/

This website was created by Bernie Dodge, the developer of webquests. This site requires membership, which costs twenty dollars for a two-year subscription. The site offers user-friendly templates for creating webquests and makes it easy to upload documents, images, and worksheets in the webquest. It also encourages users to share their work. Instead of creating a completely new webquest, teachers can use previously designed webquests and adapt them for their individual needs. A thirty-day free trial is available if teachers are interested in sampling the website before subscribing.

TeachersFirst

http://legacy.teachersfirst.com/summer/webquest/quest-a.shtml

This site provides a tutorial on creating webquests for the classroom, and while participating in that tutorial, teachers create a webquest they can subsequently use.

TeacherWeb

www.teacherweb.com/

TeacherWeb is another online tool that helps create webquests and web pages. The subscription costs twenty-seven dollars annually.

Zunal

www.zunal.com/

This website is another webquest maker that does not require a subscription.

As noted earlier, webquests can facilitate high levels of differentiation through individualization, allowing students to investigate a variety of topics within a given area as well as work at their own pace (Cote, 2007). For differentiation purposes, teachers might build many options into a single webquest assignment guide or merely design several versions of the same webquest, based on students' ability, learning style, interests, and reading levels. Students who need an extra challenge can be given additional links to higher-level reading material on the content, while students needing more assistance might have links to reading material specifically aimed at their reading level. In order to assist in this differentiation effort, various websites test the readability of other websites (for example, visit http://juicystudio.com/services /readability.php#readweb).

Webquest assignments are also highly versatile in that these activities can be completed in the classroom, in computer labs, in the media center at school, or even at home (Bender & Waller, 2011; Cote, 2007). Furthermore, webquests, like the frequent utilization of other modern technologies, help students learn about various technology applications, thus building skills they need for the 21st century (Cote, 2007). To illustrate this point, a sample webquest for a middle school science class is provided in the following feature box. Note that this webquest ties the content on the solar system to eventual development of a multimedia presentation on that topic.

Webquest: What Makes Up the Solar System?
(This webquest is recommended for students in grades 6 through 9.)

Webquest Question: What is the solar system and what types of objects exist in the solar system?

Assignment 1: Working in two- or three-person groups, complete the required assignments that follow.

Assignment 2: After most of the small groups complete assignment 1, the teacher will place you into three larger groups. The task for each of the larger groups will be to design a fifteen-minute multimedia presentation about the information you collect on the solar system.

I. Link 1: http://solarsystem.nasa.gov/planets/index.cfm

Required Questions and Activities:

1. List the planets in sequential order and write down one sentence about a primary characteristic of each.
2. What is the most modern definition of a planet? Write that down.

Optional Activities for This Link:

1. What is a plutoid? Write down the definition. How is that different from the modern definition of a planet?
2. List and describe the five major types of objects in the solar system.

II. Link 2: http://nineplanets.org/sol.html

Required Questions and Activities:

1. Why is this website named Nine Planets?

2. How large is the sun?

3. What is the sun made of?

4. How hot is the sun on the surface and in the interior?

Optional Activities for This Link:

1. What is solar wind? What is that made of?

2. Can one see solar wind on the Earth?

3. Go to link http://solarviews.com/eng/sun.htm and describe the interior and exterior of the sun.

III. Find Other Related Websites

Search the Internet (using Google, Google Maps, or other search tools) and provide a list of three additional websites that offer either photos or brief videos on this topic. Describe in three or four sentences the types of information found at each of these three additional websites. Once Assignment 2 begins, you will use these websites to obtain interesting and informative images related to the assignment.

IV. Reflection Questions

Use the following questions both for reflection and as a basis for some of the information included in your presentation.

1. What objects in the solar system produce energy?

2. What force holds the solar system objects in their constant relationship with each other?

3. How are objects in the solar system that are not on planetary orbits held within the solar system? Why are their orbits different?

This webquest offers various differentiation options. For example, as indicated in the rubric (table 5.1, page 116), advanced students would be required to complete all of the tasks, whereas students with more limited academic skills may complete only the first three activities. This webquest is initiated as a small-group or peer-buddy activity, which can greatly assist students with more limited skills. However, this particular webquest culminates as a larger-group multimedia development project, which will assist students who have an interpersonal learning strength. For spatial learners, the teacher might require a variety of questions related to the components of the sun or the map of the solar system, while limiting requirements to complete the other work. As this example indicates, teachers can use webquests as tools for differentiated instruction across the grade levels.

Educators recommend providing a rubric for evaluation of the final product of webquests (Larmer et al., 2009). Rubrics help students understand their task more concretely and allow them to focus their time and energy when they are involved in small-group projects on the Internet. Table 5.1 presents a sample rubric for the solar system webquest.

Table 5.1: A Rubric for Final Project Evaluation of the Webquest

	Indicators	Grade
Adequate	All six of the required activities were completed. Three additional websites were identified. A presentation was completed that involved at least three imported images relevant to the topic. At least two optional questions were answered.	C
Very Good	All six of the required activities were completed. Four or more additional websites were identified. A presentation was completed that involved at least six imported images relevant to the topic. At least four optional questions were answered. The presentation was interesting enough to involve the class members.	B
Excellent	All six of the required activities were completed. Six or more additional websites were identified. A presentation was completed that involved at least six imported images and two video segments that were relevant to the topic. All additional optional questions were answered. The quality of the presentation excited the other members of the class. Interactive options such as polling the class on certain questions or perspectives were used during the presentation. Answers to most of the reflection questions were provided.	A

In order to maximize motivation during webquests in middle and high school, teachers should create small-group or peer-buddy activities and specifically design them with fun in mind. They should show interesting sites including animation, sound, maps, videos, photos, and other visuals. Such sites will increase students' motivation and interest and make the webquest much more interesting overall.

YouTube, TeacherTube, and Podcasts

Teachers have long recognized that pictures and video images are highly effective as teaching tools. Not only do images capture actual events related to the content, but these tools also make academic content much more interesting, particularly for students raised in a digital, video-based environment. YouTube (www.youtube.com) is a collection of amateur videos that many teachers are using as instructional tools, after careful review, in middle and high school classes. Most YouTube videos are from one to three minutes long, though longer ones are available, and they cover many topics. A similar website, TeacherTube (www.teachertube.com), specifically identifies short videos teachers might use for instructional purposes.

For example, after only a quick search, I found a video that described the major events in the Civil War, in sequence, and presented a moving set of photos of various leaders and events, as well as President Lincoln's Gettysburg Address (www.teach ertube.com/viewVideo.php?video_id=434). This video could help launch a discussion of President Lincoln's thinking on the reasons for the war, as well as major events in the Civil War timeframe. Alternatively, this video could easily become an introduction to a unit of study on that topic or a component of a student-generated, multimedia production within such an instructional unit.

Podcasts are audio files that might be considered "episodes" addressing a particular content topic, and these digital files can be downloaded onto a computer or a personal audio device such as an MP3 player or an iPod.

Podcasts are another, similar tool that can enhance students' understanding of content in the subject areas (Salend, 2009). Podcasts are digital media files, usually created in audio form, that typically present information in a radio show type of format. These audio files are considered "episodes," with each episode addressing a particular content topic. Podcast files can be downloaded to a classroom computer or a personal audio device such as an MP3 player or an iPod. The options for use in the classroom are nearly endless, and the excitement generated by podcasts truly motivates students to work harder to understand the topic (Salend, 2009). The following feature box (page 118) presents websites that include podcasts for use in the classroom.

Student Production

Many middle and high school teachers use videos, still photography, and tools such as TeacherTube or YouTube to provide instructional presentations on various topics. Others create videos or podcasts for instructional purposes and then publish them on those websites or in other venues. Another option in the differentiated classroom involves having a group of students create the podcast or video content (Bender &

Waller, 2011; Salend, 2009). Many students enjoy activities that involve creation of content and that may result in publication of their work in various ways. In fact, even poorly motivated students respond to the opportunity to create a product on a topic of study, if that product—a video or podcast—will be published in some form. Even if teachers are reluctant to publish a student-produced video on TeacherTube or YouTube, publication of that student-generated product on a district, school, or class website can be highly motivational for many middle and high school students.

Websites That Feature Podcasts for Instruction
Audacity http://audacity.sourceforge.net/ Audacity provides free software for recording and editing sounds that can be of use in teacher- or student-created podcasts.
The Education Podcast Network http://epnweb.org/ The Education Podcast Network is a website with numerous podcasts for teachers broken down by subject area. There is also a catalog of podcasts created by students that will give teachers an idea of how podcasts can be used in their classrooms. As always, teachers should carefully listen to the entire podcast prior to using it in the classroom.
Grammar Girl http://grammar.quickanddirtytips.com/default.aspx Grammar Girl offers weekly podcasts for older students on tricky grammar rules, which can assist in a variety of reading and language arts areas. It is a fun way to get students thinking about their writing and their speech. Teachers can subscribe to the podcast through the website.
Learn Out Loud www.learnoutloud.com/Podcast-Directory/Education-and-Professional This site features a link to help teachers learn how to access podcasts, as well as a podcast directory to assist teachers in finding podcasts for educational use. Most podcasts are free, but some access options such as iTunes may require accounts for accessing podcasts.

Salend (2009) suggests that student creation of such media products might be used as an alternative form of assessment. As society moves further into the digital age, skills in these new communications technologies are becoming critical, and teachers should encourage students to produce projects for publication on these and similar media (Cote, 2007; Partnership for 21st Century Skills, 2007). As discussed previously, with the development of a wide range of Internet-capable mobile devices, publication of student work provides the opportunity for sharing that work more frequently with parents or the world at large.

Blogging

Various blogging websites allow students the opportunity to connect with teachers and other students worldwide for interactive discussions on almost any topic. A blog is akin to an online journal with postings about a particular topic, and all of the postings are generally categorized by topic and date (Bender & Waller, 2011). Those who read the blog are able to comment on the author's postings, making the blog similar to an interactive website on a particular subject.

The popularity of various social networking sites like Facebook certainly demonstrates that most adolescents enjoy high levels of connectivity, and middle and high school teachers should take advantage of that fact for instructional purposes (Bender & Waller, 2011; Cote, 2007; Salend, 2009). Of course, the security issues and misuses involved in these social networking sites have prohibited many educators from using them in the classroom. Newer websites, however, are much safer and reasonably convenient for teachers and students to use in the classroom. For example, Ning (www.ning.com) is a fee-based social networking site that allows teachers to set up a social network, including blogging options, specifically for their classrooms and their schools. Using the right website, blogging can be an important teaching tool, and it is currently being used in many middle and high school classes.

Davis (2010) reports that students used blogging to ask questions about algebra homework in one North Carolina high school. In that example, students were provided with smartphones (purchased by the school) and Internet capability. Manzo (2010a, 2010b) reports that the interactive nature of blogging can be quite motivational, even for middle and high school students who seem totally unmotivated by other learning tasks! In fact, many teachers have suggested to me that they found blogging to be a powerful incentive to read more in the content areas, and that seems to be particularly true for challenged readers. Blogs allow for connections between students in the same class, the same school, or even classrooms halfway around the world!

Should teachers wish to use blogging, they have the option of having students post comments to existing blogs or establish blogs themselves. In either situation, educators must protect students, since the Internet is by and large unregulated. Teachers should first elicit the support of the principal and the parents, and parents of the students should sign a permission form allowing students to participate. Many schools are already soliciting such permission from parents, and in those situations, the teacher should merely provide a paragraph description of what he or she intends to do with the blog to make sure student participation is covered under existing parental permission letters and current policies.

Teachers should use a secure blog that provides extra security for the students because it is password protected, and the teacher should monitor all comments and postings.

Unless the content demands that students participate in an open news blog (such as the blog managed by the Tea Party Movement of 2010 or one managed by MoveOn .org), teachers should consider using a secure blog. These are blogs established within the context of a single school or single class, and they provide an added degree of security for the students, since they are password protected and content is generally monitored and controlled by the teacher. The following feature box presents websites that provide secure blogs for use in public school classrooms. Of course, when teachers choose to use a particular blog site, they should fully investigate the security of the site, carefully noting any advertisements and links to which students may be exposed. Additional guidelines on student security in modern digital learning environments are discussed at the end of this chapter.

Websites for Creating Secure Classroom Blogs

21Classes

www.21classes.com/

21Classes is another blog option that offers several layers of protection for students, including password protection and additional teacher controls. Teachers can moderate the comments and edit specific posts as necessary prior to posting them on the blog. A free version is available, as is a fee-based version that offers higher levels of security.

Class Blogmeister

www.classblogmeister.com/

This is a free website that provides a template for teachers to create their own password-protected classroom blogs. Teachers in middle and high schools may wish to create a semester-long blog and then vary the postings and topics based on particular units of instruction.

Gaggle

www.gaggle.net

Gaggle provides free or fee-based email and blog tools for teachers and students. The site has numerous security options available that allow teachers to filter for inappropriate words and images, and teachers control who can post on the site.

Technology-Based Curricula and Progress Monitoring

Computers can facilitate RTI and foster increased differentiated instruction, particularly for students who may be struggling with the academic content across grade levels. In fact, it is extremely difficult to discuss either RTI or differentiated instruction without likewise discussing technology, since judicious application of various software programs frequently facilitates both.

As discussed in chapter 4, learning centers can foster high levels of differentiation, and having a computer learning center with appropriate content-oriented software in every classroom provides an excellent option for differentiating instruction. In a computerized lesson, students receive highly differentiated content targeted to their exact academic level. Of course, finding appropriate curricula for subject content instruction in middle and high schools can be challenging. In addition to the Study Island program discussed previously, the PLATO curriculum provides schools with a software-based instructional option, and several additional curricula are described in later chapters that cover a range of academic areas. For progress-monitoring purposes, the AIMSweb software program is one of the most frequently used programs in RTI.

The PLATO Curriculum

The PLATO curriculum represents nearly an entire middle and high school core curriculum available via computer. PLATO courses were developed by PLATO Learning (www .plato.com/Secondary-Solutions/Online-Learning/PLATO -Courses.aspx) as either make-up or replacement courses for middle and high school classes. Using the PLATO curriculum, students master course content online on their own schedules. These courses are designed to roughly parallel most state or provincial standard curricula in a variety of middle and high school subject areas. These self-paced, whole-semester courses include assessments that place students in the course content they most need. Thus students avoid spending time on content they have already mastered, which allows them to concentrate on their skill gaps and complete their course requirements quickly. Comprehensive reporting built into PLATO courses gives the teacher the information needed to ensure students have acquired knowledge and earned course credit.

> PLATO courses place students in the content they most need so they avoid spending time on content they have already mastered. This allows them to concentrate on their skill gaps and complete course requirements quickly.

Each course includes both online and offline activities, various Internet resources, built-in assessments throughout, and end-of-semester assessments that document course completion. Teachers can also use those final course assessments for grading student performance over the semester or the entire course. The instructional support materials are extensive, including a comprehensive teacher's guide for the course, a scope and sequence chart, a plan for instructional pacing, copies of all tests and grading keys for each assessment, and various grading rubrics. Courses are aligned with state or provincial standards and can be customized on a district-by-district or class-by-class basis. Course content is available for various grades, ranging from grades 7 through 12, in each of the core content areas:

- U.S. history
- World history
- Civics
- Geography
- U.S. government
- Biology
- Chemistry
- Life science
- Physical science

- English/language arts (all grades)
- Economics
- Algebra I and II
- Computer applications
- Geometry
- Consumer mathematics

While the PLATO curricula are widely used around the United States, the efficacy of this curriculum has not been demonstrated in rigorous clinical research. The company website presents a series of evaluation studies from around the United States, indicating that rigorous application and use of this curriculum would move students forward academically. A search of the What Works Clearinghouse website (http://ies.ed.gov/ncee/wwc) did not locate any studies documenting the efficacy of this curriculum. The research standards for the What Works Clearinghouse are extremely stringent, and it is not uncommon to find no research support at that location for other research-supported curricula that are widely utilized. Educators who wish to use PLATO or portions of it should investigate the evaluation studies available and should also carefully document the efficacy of this curriculum with the students in their classrooms to show its efficacy to both parents and administrators within their district, state, or province.

AIMSweb: A Tool for RTI Implementation

AIMSweb (www.aimsweb.com) is a benchmark and progress-monitoring system published by Pearson Education that focuses on performance assessment in reading and mathematics and several additional basic skill areas. Of course, computerized instructional curricula (such as Study Island) have built-in assessment options, meaning the teacher will not need additional progress-monitoring software. In the absence of such comprehensive intervention and assessment curricula, however, many middle and high schools are turning to the AIMSweb progress-monitoring and recordkeeping system.

AIMSweb uses various curriculum-based measures and is intended for use with students from grades 1 through 8, making it very applicable in middle school RTI implementation. According to the company website, many high schools are also using this system to monitor the progress of students struggling in their classes, as their academic progress tends to fall in the upper elementary and middle school grade levels.

Assessments available in AIMSweb include progress-monitoring measures in oral reading fluency (words read correctly per minute), reading comprehension, and various curriculum-based measures in mathematics, spelling, and writing, making this useful in a variety of mathematics and language arts areas in the upper grades. While the assessment system is web based, students actually take these curriculum-based progress-monitoring assessments via pencil-and-paper assessments printed out from the AIMSweb program. Because this progress-monitoring system is based on direct and frequent curriculum-based measurements, it can generate various reports for students, parents, teachers, and administrators via the web-based data management and reporting system, so the results are very useful in RTI procedures.

AIMSweb is not an intervention program; rather, this tool is purely a data-aggregating, performance-monitoring assessment, and recordkeeping program that monitors the effects of any RTI instructional intervention program at the Tier 1, 2, or 3 levels. The AIMSweb license subscription includes access to all necessary implementation guides and manuals for educators, and professional development is also available. Such professional development may involve onsite training, two-day open workshops, or online training. Subsequent chapters describe several of the AIMSweb measures in reading, writing, and mathematics, and many middle and high school teachers and administrators have reported their satisfaction with this tool as a component of their RTI implementation. One 2011 study of RTI implementation in forty-two middle schools indicated that this tool was used for progress monitoring in more than 50 percent of those schools (Allen et al.). Thus use of AIMSweb does seem to be increasing across the United States.

Digital Media Security and Media Literacy

The issue of students' security is a critical concern for every educator in the modern classroom, and as the learning experiences migrate increasingly toward Internet-based learning situations, issues of security become even more critical. Coupled with student and faculty security in the digital world is the issue of media and technological literacy (Gregory & Kuzmich, 2005). Schools must teach students how to seek, develop, evaluate, and interpret information found on the Internet, and because that environment is totally unregulated, educators in middle and high schools must address this issue in content-area classes (Partnership for 21st Century Skills, 2007, 2009).

Of course, when planning activities such as webquests, YouTube activities, and publication of student-developed podcasts, careful thought is in order. Very careful website selection is always necessary when teachers use the Internet for instructional purposes. Furthermore, either individual teachers or school faculty working as a group should develop policies on Internet usage; many middle and high schools already have such policies. These policies should stipulate what students should do if they find themselves in an inappropriate website. Certainly all teachers should regularly discuss with students what types of sites are and are not appropriate for use in schools.

No information about students should ever be posted on open blogs or open websites unless teachers have carefully screened that information. In general, student pictures, addresses, personal email addresses, phone numbers, or any other personal contact information should never be posted in the digital environment, though they may post teacher-reviewed pictures of students working in groups on class activities once they have obtained parental permission. Even those pictures, however, should not contain information identifying specific students by name. Of course, no student should have an online profile posted on the classroom blog or website unless the class uses secure classroom-only or school-only sites. In today's world, middle and high school teachers must discuss these security issues openly with students, including cautions of posting private information not only on school-related sites but also on social networking sites. While those sites are generally not related to school endeavors and should not be used for school activities, a discussion of the cautions is certainly appropriate.

Internet instruction provides a basis for teaching media-savvy interpretation and evaluation of information (Gregory & Kuzmich, 2005; Partnership for 21st Century Skills, 2009). Educators should repeatedly stress the difference between factual information and overt speculation or opinion that may be found throughout the web. Unlike school textbooks, which have been evaluated for accuracy and approved by various state/provincial or school district curriculum committees, information on the Internet is "raw" and may be quite misleading or inaccurate. Media-savvy students must learn to question authenticity of all information found using these unregulated information sources. Students should learn to search diligently for further information, seek out contradictory information, and determine the media orientation and general perspective of the author while making an evaluation as to the overall worth of any information found (Gregory & Kuzmich, 2005). In fact, evaluating digital information may be one of the most important skills students will need in the 21st century, and every class should address them.

Twenty-first century students will live their lives in an Internet world with ever-increasing connectivity, and some knowledge of how to evaluate information is absolutely critical to their success in using the information superhighway effectively. As content teachers increasingly implement this type of highly interactive instruction, every teacher will share a responsibility for teaching these media-literacy skills, and these technologies can increase the level of differentiation in every middle and high school class.

Conclusion

These technologies will facilitate both supplemental RTI interventions and progress monitoring for RTI. The various hardware, software, web-based tools, curricula, and progress-monitoring options discussed herein foster much higher levels of differentiation within most general education classes, and this chapter has only scratched the surface of how technology will affect instruction in the immediate future. These technology tools can make RTI and differentiated instruction realities in virtually every middle and high school class.

Many of these software-based curricula support RTI specifically because both completely individualized instruction and intensive progress monitoring are built in. Teachers should move toward increased implementation of these modern teaching tools, because that synthesis of targeted individualized instruction and repeated progress monitoring can save a great deal of instructional time. It seems clear that these technologies will characterize all classrooms in the 21st century school. One thing is certain: technology has and will continue to impact teaching, and middle and high school teachers must continue to explore these and additional technologies as they are developed, since these truly represent best instructional practices (Ash, 2010; Manzo, 2010b; Partnership for 21st Century Skills, 2007, 2009; Salend, 2009; Waller, 2011).

The combined impact of differentiated instruction, RTI implementation, and these technologies for teaching will result in middle and high school classrooms that look and function differently when compared to most current classrooms. There is every reason to believe that an instructional program rooted in differentiated instruction, supplemental RTI interventions, and technology applications will be more effective than any single instructional approach could have been previously.

An instructional program rooted in differentiated instruction, supplemental RTI interventions, and technology applications will be more effective than any single instructional approach could have been previously.

Many proponents of technology-based education (Cote, 2007; Partnership for 21st Century Skills, 2007, 2009; Waller, 2011) advocate that all educators and schools move in that direction. Not utilizing these technologies can drastically impair our overall instructional effectiveness for many students, and in that sense, we owe our students our best, most rigorous efforts in the application of these proven technologies and instructional techniques.

Part II will build on this basis and will explore specific instructional tactics for reading, writing, and mathematics instruction and interventions in middle and high school classes.

Part II

Chapter 6

RTI and Differentiation in Reading

Middle and high schools throughout North America are implementing RTI interventions in reading as a first priority, coupled with Tier 1 differentiated instruction in core, reading-dependent subjects (Canter et al., 2008; Gibbs, 2008; Pro & Thompson, 2010). While a limited number of RTI initiatives in certain areas have emphasized mathematics at the middle or high school level (Canter et al., 2008), most of the RTI efforts in those grades have taken place in the context of reading-dependent, content-area classes (Gibbs, 2008; Pro & Thompson, 2010). Thus upper-grade faculty need to understand how both RTI and differentiated instruction procedures fit within the general education reading activities for core curriculum classes in the upper grades.

This chapter initially describes reading problems that negatively impact academic performance in the upper grades. Next it presents an array of reading instructional strategies to facilitate differentiation during Tier 1 instruction in departmentalized content-area classes. Then it describes several supplemental reading curricula that are frequently used for Tier 2 and Tier 3 interventions in middle and high schools, along with several progress-monitoring examples for reading in the content areas. Finally, it presents a real-world example from Clark County, Nevada, that is specifically focused on reading skills (Pro & Thompson, 2010) and a case study RTI that emphasizes reading comprehension in a ninth-grade biology class.

Tier 1 Reading Challenges in Middle and High School

Teachers face a number of challenges when emphasizing reading instruction for students struggling with reading assignments in content-area subjects (Biancarosa & Snow, 2006; Faggella-Luby & Deshler, 2008). Educators have long recognized that reading in subject areas involves expository text and is, therefore, somewhat different from reading narrative texts such as the stories found in most core reading curricula in the elementary grades. While students primarily learn their reading skills using narrative stories, expository text—such as the descriptive, highly detailed text found in most content-area textbooks—requires a slightly different set of reading skills (Faggella-Luby & Deshler, 2008). For that reason, it comes as no surprise that students who struggle in narrative story reading struggle even more in upper-grade expository reading (Faggella-Luby & Deshler, 2008).

The very focus of reading instruction changes from the lower grades to the upper grades. Whereas basal reading instruction in the elementary grades fosters reading success exclusively, the reading of expository texts in content-area classes increases understanding of content.

The structure of reading content changes as students progress through the grade levels. Specifically, the overall structure of a story problem or story plot rarely supports the information as it does in most elementary-grade reading selections. Thus elementary reading techniques focused on story structure that students may have mastered during the lower elementary grades are not necessarily as helpful in the content-area reading assignments in the higher grades. Most veteran elementary teachers from grades 3 and up have experienced many students who demonstrated some overall reading ability yet display great difficulty in reading and comprehending textbooks in science, health, history, or other core subjects. For this reason, discussions of adolescent literacy have received much more attention, particularly regarding national educational goals (Biancarosa & Snow, 2006).

Reading expository texts requires different reading skills and necessitates somewhat different instructional strategies than those necessary for reading narrative texts.

Another complication for reading instruction in middle and high school involves teacher preparation for content-area instruction. In some sense, elementary teachers are trained to be both child specialists and reading specialists, in that certification as an elementary teacher typically requires numerous courses on educational psychology, cognitive development in childhood, and reading instruction. In contrast, some teachers in the middle and high school grades may be certified in one or more specific content areas (history education, science, or health) without any particular emphasis on instruction for reading skills. Some states and provinces require no specific reading instructional courses at all for middle and high school teachers. Overall, upper-grade teachers in general have less preparation for reading instruction for struggling readers than do their elementary counterparts.

Both the curriculum and current instructional practices in middle schools and high schools emphasize coverage of extensive content rather than reading skills. Many upper-elementary and middle-grade teachers may feel pressure to cover all of the subject-area content in a science or English literature class, and consequently, they may devote less time to reading instruction itself. If a student's reading problems are compounded by other factors, as for EL students or students with learning disabilities, subject-area teachers may become overwhelmed.

One additional complication can manifest, particularly during the middle and upper elementary grades: a lack of motivation to read (Biancarosa & Snow, 2006; Morgan & Fuchs, 2007; Roberts, Torgesen, Boardman, & Scammacca, 2008). If students have struggled in reading for two, four, or six years in the earlier grades, or if they have been embarrassed by repeated expectations to display their oral reading skills in the classroom and those skills were somewhat limited, by middle school those students may be quite reluctant to read any material at all (Biancarosa & Snow, 2006). They may seek to avoid reading their textbook assignments altogether, or they may pass their eyes over the words in text without any serious cognitive investment with the content. Alternatively, they may simply refuse to participate in reading activities at all. For that reason, the *Reading Next* report on middle and high school literacy (Biancarosa & Snow, 2006) identified motivation as one of fifteen critical elements in reading instruction for middle and high school students. Other research has also consistently shown a lack of motivation to read among some middle and high school students (Morgan & Fuchs, 2007; Roberts et al., 2008).

Such a lack of motivation to read for some struggling readers becomes increasingly obvious and detrimental with each passing grade level (Biancarosa & Snow, 2006; Morgan & Fuchs, 2007). In fact, Morgan and Fuchs (2007) demonstrate a direct relationship between poor reading skills and the lack of motivation to read, which frequently becomes more apparent in the upper grade levels. Poor reading skills lead to less mastery of vocabulary terms, less understanding of the content, and less ability overall to succeed in reading expository texts (Morgan & Fuchs, 2007). As reading skills decline, so does motivation to read, which, to continue the vicious causal cycle, leads to even poorer reading skills. For this reason, teachers at all grade levels must focus some attention on a student's motivation to read; that need becomes increasingly important with each successive grade.

Given this array of concerns in reading instruction, teachers in middle and high school classes will need preparation in a variety of differentiated instructional strategies to facilitate effective Tier 1 instruction in reading-dependent content areas. Such strategies are available and have become more widespread. These instructional tactics will enhance both students' reading skills overall and students' understanding of the content area under study.

> **There is a direct relationship between poor reading skills and a lack of motivation to read that becomes more apparent in the upper grade levels.**

Cognitive Strategies for Differentiated Content-Area Reading

Explicit instruction in cognitive strategies involves providing guidelines and directions for specific activities students complete when reading content from a subject-area textbook, the Internet, or any other source (Biancarosa & Snow, 2006; Faggella-Luby & Deshler, 2008). Cognitive strategies tend to focus a student's efforts while reading and give some intentional structure to his or her activities during the reading process. A cognitive strategy approach emphasizes not only literal comprehension but also higher-order comprehension skills and will help students master not only vocabulary in subject-area classes but also conceptual issues. Many cognitive strategies have been shown to be effective in increasing comprehension for a variety of different types of reading texts, and some of these strategies have improved students' motivation to read as well (Biancarosa & Snow, 2006; Faggella-Luby & Deshler, 2008; Gajria, Jitendra, Sood, & Sacks, 2007; Wolgemuth, Cobb, & Alwell, 2008).

For these reasons, cognitive strategy instruction is one research-proven strategy for differentiated instruction that virtually every middle and high school classroom should employ. In fact, many subject-area textbooks include various cognitive strategies as suggested activities in the instructors' manual to increase comprehension of the subject material (Faggella-Luby & Deshler, 2008; Gajria et al., 2007; Wolgemuth et al., 2008), similar to the various descriptions that follow.

Text Structure

Text structure involves teaching students the basic components of various types of text (Faggella-Luby & Deshler, 2008; Gajria et al., 2007; Gately, 2008). Terms such as *story grammar* or *story components* represent this concept in stories during the elementary grades. In fact, the basic components of story structure in most basal reading stories (plot, story problem, characters, story setting, climax of the story, and so forth) are commonly taught in the lower grade levels. However, as noted, the text found in middle and high school textbooks is almost never structured as a narrative, so various other types of structure must be taught (Espin, Cevasco, van den Broek, Baker, & Gersten, 2007; Williams et al., 2007). Many struggling readers may not even be aware of that fact and may struggle to find a "plot" in a ninth-grade science chapter on invertebrates!

When considering text structure, the structures identified in basal reading stories may sometimes fit the reading assignment in content areas. For example, imagine a tenth-grade student struggling with a chapter on the history of the British Empire in the 1600s to the 1800s. That history is largely related to setting, one of the story components taught in the elementary years. Specifically, England is an island nation that developed a powerful navy during that timeframe, which, in turn, eventually led to a worldwide empire. Thus the setting element (England as an island) is an important component to emphasize in reading instruction involving expository texts on the British Empire at any grade level.

However, the same struggling reader may read that chapter while seeking other story elements, such as plot, and that could lead to frustration. While understanding setting could support the student's comprehension of that reading material, a story plot would not support his or her comprehension in that context.

With that stated, one reading method many middle and high school teachers use is to teach the expository content under consideration as if it were a narrative or a story (Espin et al., 2007). For example, stories that emphasize sea power highly define the history of the British Empire. When faced with the threat of the Spanish armada, the British sent their smaller but swifter and more agile fleet into the English Channel to do battle. A teacher can use the story of the defeat of the Spanish armada as a story plot in some sense to illustrate those historical events, even when using expository text on that content. In many cases, various cause and effect relationships in expository text lend themselves to creation of a "story" (Espin et al., 2007). Some teachers take this idea further and actually obtain various videos that present history as stories. For the previous example, consider a more modern series of movies on the life of Queen Elizabeth that focus on the defeat of the Spanish armada.

In addition to finding ways to relate expository text to a story line, teachers should directly teach alternative text structures to middle and high school students (Espin et al., 2007; Williams et al., 2007). Various text structures to emphasize include causal events described in text, descriptive text, critical sequences of events, persuasive or opinion-based text, and so on. Students will learn to look for such relationships in the content and will highlight them or make notes as they find them in text.

To emphasize text structure and to differentiate the reading assignments for expository texts, the teacher may develop a study guide in several different forms and present those various forms to different students. In this example, he or she might give partially completed story guides with explicit and clear text structure components to students struggling with comprehension, whereas more successful readers would receive broader, less exact study guides.

Middle and high school students should specifically learn to understand the difference between a narrative story and expository text. Rather than reading to find the main characters, the setting, or the plot, they should be asking other questions based on the general structures found in expository text, and the study guide can emphasize those structures (see the following feature box on page 134).

Cognitive Mapping for Differentiating Instruction

Cognitive mapping is an excellent way to emphasize the elements presented in many expository texts. Using this strategy in middle and high school classes, some advanced readers might generate their own cognitive maps entirely from scratch; in contrast, struggling readers might receive a teacher-made diagram or outline for a cognitive map related to reading content and then fill it in with accurate vocabulary terms and definitions. (Gately, 2008; Lenz, Adams, Bulgren, Pouliot, & Laraux, 2007).

Cognitive maps can enhance comprehension for expository texts, help students learn new vocabulary, and increase overall cognitive involvement with the reading material.

Educators have used many terms for this instructional idea over the years, including *semantic mapping*, *graphic organizer*, and *participatory organizer*; still, the idea is the same. Use of cognitive maps can enhance comprehension for expository texts, help students learn new vocabulary, and increase the overall cognitive involvement with the reading material (Lenz et al., 2007).

Self-Questioning for Expository Texts

1. What is the main event, relationship, or topic described here?

   _____

   _____

2. Is there a particular thesis or point of view in this text? If so, describe it in a few words.

   _____

   _____

3. How is this text structured? Is there a breakdown of heading subsections or subtopics that appear to be critically important?

   _____

   _____

4. Is there a sequence of events, and are they related to each other? In what way?

   _____

5. Does this text explain the cause of something? Which event causes other events?

   _____

6. What is the overall purpose of this author in writing this text? Is this author trying to influence my opinion or merely providing information?

   _____

   _____

7. Can I determine the audience for whom this text was intended?

   _____

   _____

8. Are there facts in this text that seem unbelievable or outrageous? Has the author presented believable facts and evidence to support his or her thesis?

   _____

   _____

As a general guideline for all middle and high school subjects, whenever students must read content in a subject-area class, they should also complete a cognitive map (or some other type of participatory organizer) during that reading assignment. The cognitive map should present all or most of the critical elements within that reading content and may also present suggested questions, reflections, definitions, or fundamental factual statements. The activities required for different cognitive maps vary. As students read the text material, they might be responsible for completing a definition related to each of the major concepts, drawing and labeling lines between the main concepts, or explaining those relationships in written notes on the cognitive map. In most cases, the cognitive map can easily emphasize the critical vocabulary terms within the reading assignment (Faggella-Luby & Deshler, 2008; Gajria et al., 2007; Gately, 2008; Lenz et al., 2007). As students complete various cognitive maps during an instructional unit, they should also use them as study guides. In order to maximize the efficacy of cognitive maps, teachers should refer to them as the instructional unit progresses to emphasize their importance. A sample cognitive map for a middle school ecology lesson is presented in figure 6.1.

Food Chain	Definition	Examples
Carnivores		
Herbivores		
Primary Food Sources		

Examples may include: squirrels, corn, deer, snakes, wolves, grass, moose, humans, fungi, bears, nuts, cows, antelope, or other appropriate species.

Reflection Questions:

1. Do some animals fit in more than one category?

2. How are herbivores different than carnivores? Which of these should be considered predators?

Figure 6.1: Cognitive map for the food chain.

Many teachers report that use of cognitive maps during reading-based homework assignments increases the likelihood that students will complete those assignments, because students must complete the cognitive map during the reading assignment (that is, students must produce a product as they read the chapter). Some teachers choose to grade students' work on these cognitive maps, but it is also possible to merely have students exchange, discuss, and grade these cognitive maps in class as a part of the instruction. Alternatively, teachers may choose to merely check the content and not assign grades for the cognitive map at all. Prior to encouraging students to use their cognitive maps as study guides, however, teachers should make certain that the content of the map is accurate.

Study Guides for Prediction of Text Content

Research has shown that prediction of what one might find in expository texts can enhance reading comprehension (Faggella–Luby & Deshler, 2008; Gajria et al., 2007; Gately, 2008). As students are initially exposed to the chapter content in a new instructional unit, it is often beneficial for them to scan the chapter subheadings, look at photographs included in the text, and then predict the content the chapter is likely to contain. Teachers can easily construct worksheets to facilitate such prediction by merely listing chapter subheadings and requiring students to scan the chapter and write a one-sentence prediction about what is in that section.

Prediction is an important component of student comprehension. For example, if a class of ninth graders is studying a chapter on invertebrates in science, the successful readers in the class are quite likely to be able to predict what the next section or even the next chapter might be (in this case, probably vertebrates). Less successful readers, however, are not as likely to make even these simple predictions accurately, so they miss the understandings that might arise from seeing how sections within chapters or sequential chapters fit together.

A Prediction Exercise: Picture Walk Through the Chapter

For struggling readers, one prediction-based assignment idea involves a "picture walk" (Gately, 2008). This activity requires students to look at pictures within a chapter and predict what the chapter might include prior to reading. In many texts, the pictures can be quite interesting and will prove to be useful teaching tools. Teachers can make time during class to call students' attention to the important pictures, graphs, and charts in the text and then discuss them. In a picture walk, prior to making a chapter reading assignment, students should read the captions while considering the content of each picture in the chapter.

Furthermore, these picture-walk activities lend themselves to high levels of differentiation. Students with strengths in bodily/kinesthetic learning may enjoy the opportunity to act out their reflections on the chapter pictures, whereas learners with a strength in linguistic learning may complete an outline based on the picture walk or other cognitive map activity, emphasizing the relationship between their predictions and final summarizations.

Summarization and Self-Checking

Many educators recommend coupling summarization activities with most Tier 1 reading assignments to enhance comprehension of expository content in general education classes (Biancarosa & Snow, 2006; Faggella-Luby & Deshler, 2008; Gajria et al., 2007; Gately, 2008). In fact, many study guides or cognitive maps might involve both prediction of the reading content as a prereading activity and summarization as a postreading activity. These activities, coupled together, will enhance reading comprehension in middle and high school classes (Biancarosa & Snow, 2006; Faggella-Luby & Deshler, 2008; Gajria et al., 2007).

The impact of prediction and summarization can best be understood in terms of the self-checking/self-monitoring required within these activities. Research has shown that monitoring one's own understanding of reading content results in higher levels of comprehension (Biancarosa & Snow, 2006; Faggella-Luby & Deshler, 2008; Roberts et al., 2008), and prediction/summarization activities foster that type of self-monitoring. In most reading assignments in core classes, students should complete these activities during each reading assignment (Faggella-Luby & Deshler, 2008; Gajria et al., 2007; Roberts et al., 2008).

Paraphrasing and Retelling Reading Content

Paraphrasing or retelling the content of a section of text from a chapter can be another postreading activity that is highly effective for building comprehension (Faggella-Luby & Deshler, 2008; Gajria et al., 2007). Like summarization, this technique requires the student to identify the important points and restate them in relationship to each other. Subskills of this task include identification of the main idea of a text as well as critical supporting details. Particularly for expository text, researchers strongly recommend requiring students to paraphrase the text.

As one differentiated instructional alternative, having teams of two or three students complete these restatements together increases on-task participation and decreases the possibility of embarrassment for students who may not understand the content. They can complete paraphrase restatements either verbally or in writing. The teacher should devise a worksheet to help struggling students retell the critical content in written form. Like a cognitive map, a completed paraphrasing worksheet, once checked by the teacher, can then serve as a study guide for the student for the rest of that unit.

Paraphrasing requires students to state complex concepts from the reading and, thus, emphasizes higher-order comprehension skills.

Research has shown that this text-retelling or paraphrasing technique enhances both comprehension and retention (Faggella-Luby & Deshler, 2008; Gajria et al., 2007).

Brain-Friendly Instruction for Reading Activities

As discussed in chapter 3, brain-friendly instructional tactics provide the very basis of differentiated instruction, and these techniques can certainly enhance a student's understanding of reading content. Teachers should use the SHEMR tactics frequently in conjunction with every reading assignment to make the reading more engaging and to foster increased recall of the material. For example, the teacher can use various movements to illustrate portions of the content from the assigned read-ing, because movement does enhance students' learning overall as well as their desire to participate in reading-based activities (Sousa, 2010). Walkthroughs, such as the example with the blood flow in the heart, will also help illustrate the reading content and will assist students in concept mastery. Finally, when teachers or students cre-ate songs and chants, the class should sing them each day as long as they are rich in essential content. Again, these SHEMR activities will aid students' memory for that content when both the unit assessment and the end-of-year assessments roll around.

Differentiation Through Repeated Reading

Repeatedly reading the same content will increase comprehension of that content and lead to improved reading overall (Therrien, Wickstrom, & Jones, 2006; Welsch, 2007). This technique involves having middle and high school students repeatedly read the same passage three to five times. It was originally intended to increase a student's reading fluency, and it works well in that regard, but research has demon-strated that repeatedly reading the same passage is a highly effective strategy for improving reading comprehension as well (Morgan & Sideridis, 2006; Therrien et al., 2006; Vandenberg, Boon, Fore, & Bender, 2008; Welsch, 2007).

Repeated reading involves having a student read the same passage three to five times to achieve fluency, learn content vocabulary, and increase comprehension.

In the repeated reading technique, the student reads along simultaneously with a fluent reader, which may be a teacher reading the same passage, a peer buddy, or a voice presented by computer software. Through repeated practice, the strug-gling reader will pick up use of the correct phrasing, punc-tuation, and word timing during reading, resulting in more fluent reading, increased understanding of vocabulary, and increased comprehension. Of course, any student's fluency for and comprehension of a single passage is likely to increase with each exposure to that passage as long as it is approximately on that student's reading level. Research has also shown that as students' fluency improves through practice in repeated reading, their fluency and comprehension on reading passages to which they have not been exposed will also increase over time (Morgan & Sideridis, 2006; Therrien et al., 2006; Vandenburg et al., 2008; Welsch, 2007).

Generally, in a repeated reading intervention, a student would repeatedly read the same passage until he or she reaches a criterion of 95 to 100 percent correct on the words in the passage. Teachers can present instruction for new vocabulary prior to reading the passage as well as between readings, and discussion of the content will also assist in improving comprehension. Research presents guidelines for using a repeated reading strategy with reading material from textbooks and other sources (Conderman & Strobel, 2006; Mastropieri, Leinart, & Scruggs, 1999). It has also demonstrated that individual teachers can develop a repeated reading instructional procedure using materials from content passages in various subject areas, such as those materials that are typically available in the classroom (Vandenberg et al., 2008).

A set of systematic guidelines for implementing a repeated reading procedure as a partner reading activity is presented in the following feature box.

Guidelines for Repeated Reading as a Partner Activity

1. The teacher should identify a series of appropriate reading passages that range in reading level to meet the needs of all students in the class. While a number of reading curricula are available, middle and high school teachers will need to be creative in finding content material that covers various topics, carefully seeking out selections that are written on lower grade levels as well. Each passage should include a minimum of several hundred words and should be accompanied by five to ten comprehension questions.

2. If the teacher finds appropriate reading material that does not have comprehension questions available, the teacher or other students in the class can develop them. For example, teachers may have a group of advanced students identify, select, and develop ten comprehension content-area questions for a passage. The teacher can then use that passage and those questions for repeated reading activities.

3. The teacher should explain to the class how repeatedly reading a passage builds both reading fluency and comprehension of the material. He or she should point out that repeated readings will help students on the coming unit test. Most middle and high school students with reading problems can be motivated to use this tactic if the activities are presented in that fashion.

4. The teacher should partner students with approximately the same reading level. For part of the period, one student will serve as the tutor and the other as the target student, and then they will reverse roles. In some cases, teachers may wish to partner advanced students with some of the struggling students on a case-by-case basis. However, the overall goal is to partner students who are at approximately the same level.

5. The teacher and each student should select an appropriate reading rate goal and write down that goal in terms of words read correctly per minute and/or comprehension questions answered successfully for each passage. Here is an example: "I will be able to read sixty words per minute correctly and answer 80 percent of the comprehension questions correctly on each reading passage."

Continued→

6. Particularly in the higher grades, students of approximately the same reading level can do this as a partner activity. After selecting a reading passage for each student, the peer buddy serving as a tutor should listen to the target student read the passage and time the student's initial reading while noting reading errors. The tutor will mark a copy of the passage, indicating each error the target student makes during the reading. Then the tutor and the target student should calculate the words per minute read correctly for that passage by dividing the number of words read correctly by the number of minutes and seconds it takes to read the section.

7. The students change roles and the student who had initially been serving as the tutor reads his or her targeted passage as the other student counts errors and words read correctly per minute.

8. Once both students have done an initial timed reading and calculated their reading fluency score (the number of words read correctly per minute), each should take the comprehension test associated with the passage and score that using a scoring key the teacher provides. Teachers should check carefully to ensure that all students are correctly scoring their reading fluency and comprehension.

9. At that point, each student should chart his or her reading fluency score and comprehension score.

10. Each student should silently read his or her target passage three times while carefully decoding unknown words and rehearsing new vocabulary. Students should jot down unfamiliar vocabulary terms and, between reading sessions, review those words with the tutor or teacher.

11. When each student has completed reading the passage three times, the pair should again work together to complete another timed reading and comprehension test for the passage and chart those scores.

12. Encourage the student to compare that performance with the reading rate goal set earlier and also with previous performance. In almost every case, the correct words per minute will improve from the first reading of a story to the last, so praise students for that improvement. When the chart begins to show those data, point out that positive result to the student as another indicator of improved reading.

13. Depending on students' reading skills, they may complete these activities for a single reading passage in one or two instructional periods. The class might spend one or two days per week in repeated reading partner activities, with students reading selections on the content under study for that unit.

In using repeated reading instruction in a differentiated classroom, the differentiation could take several different forms. First, for this to be an effective comprehension strategy, students should tackle reading passages at their own instructional levels (Welsch, 2007). Next, teachers should consider students' learning styles and interests when selecting the content and instructional procedures. Students are more likely to read something that interests them, and teachers in content-area classes frequently have access to supplemental textbooks or software on topics that might be more interesting to students than the material in the text.

Then teachers can require various activities along with the repeated reading. For example, students who learn best using bodily/kinesthetic approaches could role-play a segment of the text after they read it several times. In this fashion, a repeated reading strategy in middle and high school classes can function as a highly differentiated reading instructional approach.

After the student repeatedly reads the same passage, he or she should complete a comprehension assessment on that content. Providing the student access to the comprehension questions during the repeated reading activity will also enhance overall comprehension.

Supplemental Reading Curricula for Tiers 2 and 3

While most reading difficulties in elementary schools become evident within reading classes, reading problems in middle and high schools most often crop up in the context of subject-area classes. Increasingly, middle and high school teachers are having to prepare for teaching reading within the context of their subject areas. Reading difficulties, however, are often related to broader language arts difficulties, and all of these problems affect a wide range of academic areas, including writing papers, listening, taking notes, and so forth. This is one reason many Tier 2 and 3 RTI procedures in middle and high schools to date have involved language arts teachers implementing a supplemental, research-proven curriculum in reading and literacy skills.

There will certainly be occasions in which students' reading difficulties may be too extensive to address in the context of a content-area class, and middle and high school language arts faculty will need access to specific instructional curricula to assist with those difficulties. Many middle and high schools are implementing various supplementary curricula as Tier 2 or Tier 3 interventions (Gibbs, 2008; Protheroe, 2010). While some of these broadly address various reading- and language arts-related skills, others exclusively target improving reading comprehension. This section presents several specialized curricula that middle and high school faculties may wish to consider as options for Tier 2 or Tier 3 interventions in their school.

The Voyager Passport Reading Journeys

The Voyager Passport Reading Journeys program is a multilevel comprehensive language arts program structured into three levels: Voyager Passport Reading Journeys, Journeys II, and Journeys III. This interesting curriculum teaches reading and language arts skills in the context of subject-area studies on various topics in social studies, science, and fine arts. All of the lessons include both reading and writing skills, making this a particularly effective program for learners who are struggling in both reading and writing assignments.

The program provides thirty weeks of intervention lessons for each of the three levels, and each daily lesson requires approximately fifty minutes to complete. The third level of the program (Journeys III) is aimed directly at high school students who are at least two years below grade level (www.voyagerlearning.com/prj; Gibbs, 2008). High school students who are struggling in particular subject areas may receive this curriculum to develop reading and language arts skills while working, at least in part, in the content of a particular class.

The program is motivational, and each level features a variety of "expeditions"; these are structured lesson activities involving nonfiction reading in two-week lesson units related to different high-interest topics. Journeys III, for example, includes fourteen such expeditions for students to work through. Each expedition opens with a high-interest video intended to engage interest and provide background knowledge for that unit of instruction. Other supports for this program include the Passport Reading Journeys Library—a collection of novels and short stories for use in either independent or partner reading—and an online VocabJourney to provide a vocabulary component to the lessons. The curriculum includes weekly assessment, making it a good fit within the RTI model for middle and high schools.

Research evidence on this program is still in development, but several studies have shown its efficacy (Slavin, Cheung, Groff, & Lake, 2008; also see the research evaluation at www.bestevidence.org/reading/mhs/limited.htm). The focus specifically on struggling students in the higher grade levels in Journeys III, coupled with the various video and assessment supports, makes this program highly motivational.

The Learning Strategies Curriculum

The learning strategies curriculum is one component of a broader content literacy continuum instructional model Don Deshler and his associates at the University of Kansas have developed (Bulgren, Deshler, & Lenz, 2007; Deshler et al., 2001; Lenz, 2006; Lenz et al., 2007). Some experts now recommend it as one option for RTI initiatives in the upper grade levels (Bender, 2009a; Gibbs, 2008). It is based on the types of academic tasks students must undertake in content-area classes, and the specific strategies are designed to be applicable in a wide variety of curriculum areas.

Learning strategies instruction is not specifically directed at reading. Rather, this curriculum provides students with the cognitive steps needed to complete various types of academic tasks in the middle and high school grades, and some of the strategies are aimed at reading and language arts tasks. The literature has used various terms to represent this instructional approach, including *metacognitive instruction*, *learning strategies instruction*, and *cognitive instruction*, and research on cognitive strategy instruction has shown the efficacy of this instructional approach in the middle and higher grade levels (Deshler et al., 2001; Lenz, 2006).

In considering the types of skills struggling students need to have in order to succeed, Deshler and his associates have identified a variety that are relatively independent of the subject-area content itself (Deshler et al., 2001). These skills include the following:

- Comprehending subject matter
- Checking written paragraphs for errors
- Writing research papers/themes
- Self-questioning during a reading selection
- Word attack skills for vocabulary terms
- Test-taking skills
- Searching for answers in text material
- Interpreting pictures in text
- Using visual imagery for comprehension

As this list indicates, these skills are not related to any particular subject area, but they are essential for success. Mastery of strategies that assist with these tasks, therefore, can help middle and high school students in a wide variety of subject areas (Deshler et al., 2001; Lenz, 2006). Since 1990, Deshler and his colleagues have devised a set of cognitive strategies, most of which are represented by acronyms, that facilitate a student's work in these and other tasks. For example:

COPS: *Strategy for editing/checking written work*

Capitalization (check each sentence)

Overall appearance of written paragraph

Punctuation (check each sentence)

Spelling

This type of strategy comprises the core of the learning strategies curriculum (Bulgren et al., 2007; Deshler et al., 2001; Lenz, 2006; Lenz et al., 2007). By learning these strategies, a student can enhance his or her performance in many academic classes, including future ones. For example, once a student learns the COPS strategy for checking and editing a paragraph in a written theme, he or she can use that strategy throughout his or her academic life. The universal application of the strategies makes this curriculum very appropriate for implementation within an RTI process, and this should be one option all middle and high school faculties consider as they move into development of RTI procedures (Gibbs, 2008).

The creators of the learning strategies curriculum developed an instructional procedure involving multiple instructional steps, ranging from pretest and initial student buy-in through a maintenance and generalization step (Bulgren et al., 2007; Deshler et al., 2001; Lenz, 2006; Lenz et al., 2007). Teaching a strategy thoroughly requires daily work over an extended period of time ranging from twenty-five to fifty days or more (see Bender, 2008, pp. 94–105, for an extended description of these steps), and generally students learn only one strategy at any given time. In addition to memorizing the steps in the COPS strategy, the student would receive a daily reading selection to use it with. This curriculum also involves frequent progress-monitoring assessment on application of the strategy (Gibbs, 2008).

The learning strategies curriculum results in very frequent assessment that could serve as a daily progress-monitoring measure during an RTI procedure.

The learning strategies curriculum, coupled with other learning strategies, can certainly serve as a basis for the RTI process for middle and high school students struggling with reading assignments in the general education classroom. In fact, I had the opportunity to work with a middle school in Southeast Arkansas that adopted this curriculum in the context of its RTI efforts, specifically as a Tier 2 intervention option. The faculty felt that some students struggling in various academic classes were having difficulty because of poor reading and language arts skills dealing specifically with expository texts. The students did not have access to cognitive strategies that facilitate successful reading and conceptual understanding. The faculty had already implemented a high-quality supplemental reading program, so supplementing that reading program with this curriculum seemed to provide the students with more instructional options. The faculty viewed this curriculum as a major thrust within the overall RTI initiative and were pleased with the results, believing this to be an option that every middle and high school should consider in the RTI context.

Researchers recommend this learning strategies curriculum as one possible Tier 1 instruction or Tier 2 intervention option for both middle and high schools (Gibbs, 2008). Research has shown it to be effective in general education classes, and this will result in increased student success in subject content areas (Bulgren et al., 2007; Deshler et al., 2001; Lenz, 2006; Lenz et al., 2007).

Like every curriculum, the learning strategies curriculum is most effective when implemented with fidelity, and teachers will require training on its appropriate application. Such training is available through the learning strategies institute associated with the University of Kansas (Bulgren et al., 2007; Deshler et al., 2001; Lenz, 2006; Lenz et al., 2007).

LANGUAGE!

The LANGUAGE! curriculum (Greene, 1996) was developed to assist struggling students in reading, including language-delayed students and English learners across the grade levels (Denton, Wexler, Vaughn, & Bryan, 2007). This supplemental curriculum has received research support for use with struggling readers (see the website: www.sopriswest.com/language). It is particularly effective for EL students since it teaches about the English language as well as teaching specific reading and language skills. The program features activities including phonemics and phonics through listening, reading, and comprehending more complex reading material on grade level, and it is useful from elementary grades through grade 12.

Because difficulties in English only compound learning difficulties in the content areas in the upper grades, this curriculum is a great option for Tier 2 or Tier 3 interventions for older students struggling in reading. It is formatted into three levels, comprising a total of fifty-four instructional units. Each unit includes sixteen instructional lesson plans, but not all students receive all lessons. Rather, built-in assessments determine the level at which individual students should begin. There are also various performance-monitoring assessments built in, including an online assessment option. The extensive range of lesson plans and the suggestion for delivery of such lessons to small groups of students make this curriculum very appropriate for small-group instruction.

Schools with large populations of EL students should consider the LANGUAGE! program as one option within their RTI initiatives.

This integrated, comprehensive curriculum includes reading, spelling, and writing, and it teaches these as a complex whole using explicit, highly focused instruction (see www.fcrr.org/FCRRreports/PDF/Language.pdf; Greene, 1996). It is intended for implementation in two daily sessions of ninety minutes each, though some schools have implemented it successfully in less intensive formats. It is a research-supported curriculum, and while research is limited, the company website does present a variety of anecdotal studies and one controlled study that demonstrate the program's efficacy. Most of the research has shown the efficacy of this program with middle and high school students rather than younger students, making this program particularly appropriate in the upper grade levels (Denton et al., 2007; Greene, 1996).

Fast ForWord

Fast ForWord is a computer-based reading intervention curriculum founded on brain-functioning research (Doidge, 2007). Michael Merzenich, Bill Jenkins, Paula Tallal, and Steve Miller collaboratively developed it through the company Scientific Learning (Doidge, 2007; www.scientificlearning.com). Fast ForWord focuses on phonemic-based instruction for students with reading difficulties and is useful across the grade levels. A series of comprehensive computer-driven, intensive lesson activities covers phonemic, prereading, and reading skills ranging from preschool through the high school grades. Sample tasks involve the blending of sounds to recognize correct pronunciation, word segmentation, oral reading fluency, and passage comprehension.

Students enter the curriculum based on their specific needs, and the program tracks individual progress and generates individualized progress reports for each student. Different lessons present different skills in a variety of engaging formats, most of which involve game-like activities the student completes on the computer. The Fast ForWord program also includes a series of reading instructional packages, and the last of these packages, described here, are very appropriate for the struggling readers in middle school and high school:

- **Language to Reading**—This package helps struggling readers in middle school grades make the connection between oral and written language, including decoding, vocabulary, grammar, and word recognition.

- **Reading**—This package concentrates on word recognition and fluency, advanced decoding, spelling, vocabulary, and passage comprehension. It is intended for middle and high school students and emphasizes sustained focus of attention, reading skills, listening comprehension, sequencing, and organization.

> The Fast ForWord reading program represents perhaps the best merger of brain-compatible instructional research, reading research, literacy and language development research, and technology applications for reading instruction.

The early research results on applications of this program among students with learning difficulties are quite impressive, and the company website supplies a bibliography of journal articles from this research. Temple and colleagues (2003), for example, demonstrated changes in brain processing after using Fast ForWord in a study with students with dyslexia. In the anecdotal research examples presented on the company website, many students demonstrated one- to three-year gains in reading and language in just a one- or two-month intervention using this program. Among struggling readers in high school, one anecdotal report indicated that students' reading skills advanced by a grade equivalency of slightly more than a year in only a thirty-day intervention period (Kolonay & Kelly-Garris, 2009).

The Fast ForWord reading program, perhaps more than any other program, represents the merger of brain-compatible instructional research, reading research, literacy and language development research, and technology applications for targeted reading instruction. Because various educators concerned with the time constraints of RTI implementation have recommended judicious application of effective intervention software (Bender, 2009a; Bender & Shores, 2007), reading programs such as this may well represent the primary approach to supplemental reading instruction for many struggling middle and high school students.

Read Naturally

The Read Naturally curriculum employs a repeated reading approach as well as a "read with a fluent model" tactic (described earlier) to enhance fluency and improve comprehension (Hasbrouck, Ihnot, & Rogers, 1999). This curriculum features brief stories, typically 100 to 200 words each, written at a variety of grade levels up through grade 8 (Ihnot, Mastoff, Gavin, & Hendrickson, 2001; Wahl, 2006). The program can also serve struggling readers beyond that grade level. This program is receiving attention from educators and researchers across the United States since emphasis on reading fluency is increasing and educators are seeking scientifically validated reading curricula for RTI procedures in that specific area. Several studies have indicated the efficacy of this curriculum (Denton et al., 2006; Hasbrouck et al., 1999; Wahl, 2006), and a Spanish version of this intervention curriculum is now available, making this an excellent curricular choice for English learners who may require RTI interventions.

The program is designed to enhance both reading fluency and reading comprehension by presenting a safe, structured, and highly motivating opportunity for struggling readers to engage with brief reading stories on a variety of interesting topics. The program includes research-based strategies for improving fluency, such as teacher modeling (having the student read along with a fluent reader), goal setting, vocabulary practice and development, repeated readings, and daily or weekly progress monitoring. The program provides twenty-four high-interest reading selections in each of three levels within the curriculum, and a placement assessment helps place students at their individual instructional level within the curriculum.

Implementation of Read Naturally involves the student selecting a story at his or her reading level and making a prediction about the content of the story. The student then reads the same story several times. Initially, a teacher will listen to a student read the story while marking oral reading errors, as well as noting the time the student began and ended the passage. The teacher then calculates the number of words read correctly per minute for that initial read-through. This initial reading is referred to as the "cold timing." Based on this correct-per-minute reading score, the teacher and the student should jointly set a goal for how quickly the student should read the passage by the end of the instructional period.

Next, the student rereads the same passage several times, which may involve the teacher or another student chorally reading the passage or having the target student read alone or with an audio version of the story presented on the computer. Once the student feels he or she has reached proficiency, the student and teacher would again go through the story with the student reading and the teacher noting errors and reading time. This is referred to as the "hot timing." In almost every case, the student's hot timing will represent an improvement on the cold timing for reading fluency, and teachers can then reinforce students for their improvement. Teachers monitor comprehension via a comprehension quiz and a story retelling activity the student completes.

Read Naturally has received research support as an effective instructional reading fluency and reading comprehension curriculum. Furthermore, it is quite useful in RTI Tier 2 and Tier 3 interventions, given the emphasis on daily progress monitoring of oral reading fluency. It will help struggling readers across the grade levels develop better reading fluency and comprehension (Wahl, 2006).

Accelerated Reader and STAR Reading

The Accelerated Reader program by Renaissance Learning has been available for a number of years and is perhaps the most widely used reading practice software available in elementary schools. Since so many students and elementary teachers are familiar with this program, it is likely that teachers will have heard of it, making adoption of this curriculum in middle and high schools somewhat easier. While the program activities do vary by grade level, elementary teachers who are familiar with this curriculum can provide some degree of in-house professional development for middle and high school teachers who may wish to adopt it in the higher grade levels.

As explained on the company website (www.renlearn.com/ar/RTI.aspx), students are assigned specific Accelerated Reader hard-copy books at their reading levels, which they then read at their own pace. When they complete a story or reading selection, they take a comprehension quiz on that reading content. The curriculum provides reading material for students through the high school grades, and a fairly large body of research has shown that this program is effective in helping students progress in virtually every reading skill from decoding to comprehension (Husman, Brem, & Duggan, 2005; Nunnery & Ross, 2007; Nunnery, Ross, & McDonald, 2006).

In conjunction with implementation of the Accelerated Reader program, many schools are also adopting STAR Reading, a computer-based progress-monitoring system Renaissance Learning developed (www.renlearn.com/ar/RTI.aspx). STAR Reading provides norm-referenced reading scores on a variety of reading skills for students in grades 1 through 12, as well as criterion-referenced measures of students' instructional reading levels. The criterion-referenced measures provide an excellent progress-monitoring tool for Tier 2 or Tier 3 RTI interventions (Gibbs, 2008). STAR Reading uses computer technology to tailor each student's instructional lessons based on assessments of previous performance, making this program highly responsive to each individual's intervention needs. STAR Reading enhances reliability and minimizes testing time by administering test items that are closely matched to student achievement levels, such that it can assess students' reading levels in as little as ten minutes.

Like most computerized programs, the software can generate a variety of progress-monitoring reports for one child or a group of students. For individual progress monitoring, the charts depict student growth compared to a target line depicting growth necessary to reach the individual student's RTI goals.

Progress Monitoring for RTI Efforts

Mellard, McKnight, and Woods (2009) document that most RTI initiatives in their study used either commercially available progress-monitoring tools (such as AIMSweb) or progress-monitoring assessments that came with specific intervention curricula such as Voyager Passport.

However, Rebora (2010) raises questions concerning the necessity of commercially available progress-monitoring tools in the RTI process. Specifically, has conventional usage reduced RTI to merely a universal screening and progress-monitoring business? Certainly that would not be an optimal outcome of the nationwide emphasis on RTI.

By way of explanation, Rebora (2010) states what many proponents of RTI have perceived: RTI has now become a *multibillion-dollar business* across North America. In an era of extremely tight budgets, RTI initiatives seem to be one place school districts are spending their limited funds, and much of those funds go to progress-monitoring tools rather than instructional intervention programs. Virtually every curriculum and assessment company has generated progress-monitoring tools schools and districts can purchase for use in the RTI process (Rebora, 2010), several of which this text has described. Many of them are excellent assessments, but most do involve the expenditure of funds, and in today's tough budget battles, that is a serious concern. While progress monitoring is certainly essential in the RTI framework, perhaps schools should purchase research-proven interventions with assessments built into them rather than progress-monitoring tools themselves. This seems to be the most effective way to stretch the RTI dollar.

> Has conventional usage reduced RTI to merely a universal screening and progress-monitoring business?

Teachers with no funds at all can devise excellent, research-supported progress-monitoring procedures within the context of their own curricula (Gibbs, 2008; Rebora, 2010), and while such assessments would not include schoolwide data-collection options for administrators, these self-developed, curriculum-based assessments can provide an excellent basis for monitoring a student's intervention progress. The next section provides a few guidelines on how teachers might accomplish this in subject-area classes.

Progress Monitoring Without Commercial Assessments

Given tight budget dollars in schools, middle and high school faculty can certainly consider independently developing curriculum-based reading assessments for use in Tier 2 or Tier 3 interventions (Gibbs, 2008; Rebora, 2010). As indicated previously, reading involves a variety of skills, and different reading skills receive emphasis at different grade levels. For example, while kindergarten and primary grades tend to emphasize phonemic instruction and phonics (sounds associated with particular letters), decoding, and reading fluency, reading instruction in higher grades tends to emphasize reading fluency, vocabulary instruction in content areas, and reading comprehension (Bender & Waller, 2011; Espin, Wallace, Lembke, Campbell, & Long, 2010; Gibbs, 2008). Gibbs (2008) indicates that measures of reading fluency may not be appropriate for progress monitoring during RTI procedures in high schools, and she emphasizes measures associated with vocabulary development in content areas and reading comprehension. In contrast, Espin and colleagues (2010) document that reading fluency measures were highly related to reading skills as measured by standardized assessments. Based on this research, secondary teachers conducting Tier 2 interventions might have to assess reading skills in their subjects in all three of these ways. Of course, in many cases, certain measures will be more appropriate for certain students. For example, some students may have few problems with fluent reading but may lack comprehension of the material, and in that case, the measures associated with comprehension are more appropriate for progress-monitoring purposes. Each of these measures is described as follows.

Monitoring of Reading Fluency

This chapter has already covered measurement of a student's reading fluency in the section on repeated readings and in the section on the Read Naturally curriculum (Hasbrouck et al., 1999). In essence, subject-content teachers can periodically assess a student's reading fluency by having the student read a passage for one minute while the teacher follows along with another copy of the passage and marks words read incorrectly or words skipped. To get a measure of words read correctly per minute, the teacher would count the total words in the passage that the student completed in one minute and subtract the number of errors (Espin et al., 2010). This is an excellent measure of reading fluency for content-area subject matter that can serve as a progress-monitoring measure in Tier 2 and Tier 3 interventions.

Progress Monitoring of Subject-Area Vocabulary

Vocabulary is critically important in most content-area subjects in middle and high schools, and teachers can easily create assessments of vocabulary for progress monitoring. For example, a student's ability to match vocabulary terms to their definitions highly correlates with that student's understanding of the content (Gibbs, 2008; Espin & Foegen, 1996; Espin, Shin, & Busch, 2005), and general education teachers can easily construct progress-monitoring tools for that type of matching task simply by using a matching procedure similar to various matching assessments many teachers use during unit tests. In fact, most teachers have, at one time or another, used a vocabulary-matching worksheet in an instruction unit, and vocabulary-matching assessments for performance monitoring in RTI are very similar. The following feature box presents guidelines for such a vocabulary-based progress-monitoring assessment.

Creating a Progress-Monitoring Assessment for Subject-Area Vocabulary

To create this type of an assessment worksheet for a single instructional unit, teachers typically list critical vocabulary terms on one side of the worksheet and definitions on the other. They then require students to match those items. This procedure is somewhat different from unit-long assessments, however; for RTI purposes, the vocabulary-matching list of terms shows students' progress over a series of instructional units rather than on one instructional unit (Gibbs, 2008). Since Tier 2 and Tier 3 interventions typically take longer than a two- or three-week instructional unit, the teacher must modify the progress-monitoring assessment to assess student growth over a longer timeframe as well (Gibbs, 2008). To make this vocabulary-matching procedure work in an RTI context, teachers should think in terms of progress monitoring across at least a nine-week grading period or perhaps a semester-long grading period of eighteen weeks. In that context, teachers should follow these guidelines:

1. Select critical vocabulary from each of the instructional units to be covered in that timeframe.

2. Use that vocabulary list as the basis for vocabulary-matching assessments for RTI purposes.

3. Identify anywhere from 75 to 150 vocabulary terms that will be covered in those instructional units.

4. From that list, construct five progress-monitoring assessments that present twenty-five randomly selected terms/definitions.

5. Use a different list of randomly selected works every two weeks for progress monitoring.

6. Score those using a raw score and a percentage correct score. The raw score (twenty-three of twenty-five definitions correctly matched to terms) provides a sensitive measure on comprehension of those units, whereas the percentage correct on each assessment is more similar to a student's typical grades and, thus, may be more understandable.

7. Chart the raw score on an x/y-axis chart over time to show a student's progress on those vocabulary terms.

Of course, one would not expect even highly successful students to achieve high levels of mastery on the first several of those assessments, since some of those terms would come from instructional units that they have not seen up to that point, and teachers should make certain that the students understand that. By administering that type of assessment every one or two weeks for a semester, however, teachers can generate a data chart of a student's performance overall. In most cases, that chart will show some academic growth as the class completes more of the instructional units and covers more of the vocabulary terms. Thus teachers will get a highly accurate picture of overall academic growth relative to the student's understanding of the subject-area vocabulary (Gibbs, 2008).

Progress Monitoring of Comprehension in Subject-Area Reading

It may also be necessary in Tier 1, 2, or 3 interventions to monitor students' progress in reading comprehension in specific subject areas rather than merely monitor their understanding of vocabulary. Fortunately, there is a relatively easy-to-use procedure for this purpose: the maze-comprehension monitoring procedure (Gibbs, 2008). The maze procedure requires students to select a term that will correctly complete a sentence from the reading material. Because research strongly supports this procedure (Espin & Foegen, 1996; Espin et al., 2005), many commercially available assessment systems (such as AIMSweb) use it to assess reading comprehension.

The maze procedure is very similar to fill-in-the-blank worksheets subject-area teachers in many high school classes frequently use. A maze-comprehension monitoring worksheet consists of a passage selected from a textbook with every seventh word deleted and replaced by a blank. Rather than require students to provide the word, the sheet presents three choices under or immediately after each blank, including the deleted word and two other words that are the same part of speech as the deleted word but do not correctly complete the sentence. The following feature box presents a sample maze for a literature selection.

A Maze-Comprehension Monitoring Selection for a Middle School or Secondary Literature Course

The attack came at dawn from a brace of light _____ (sticks, cannon, tables) Colonel Williamson had mounted on the hills to the east above the Tugaloo Council _____ (House, Apartment, Lake). The British column had moved into position much _____ (cleaner, softer, faster) than anyone had anticipated, and even with the rumors of a British _____ (dress, wagon, army) on the move, the Cherokee of the lower towns were still dispersed and totally unprepared. The first cannon _____ (impression, salvo, whisper) rudely awoke the four hundred Cherokee in Tugaloo _____ (lake, Towers, Town) on the morning of June 12, 1761, and those first several shots _____ (destroyed, replaced, painted) for all time the Tugaloo Council House, and the sacred_____ (fire, supports, stars) within. That building was the _____ (smallest, ugliest, largest) in the town and was thus the logical _____ (monster, enemy, aim-point) for Williamson's artillery officer.

Source: Waters, 2008, p. 212.

As this example shows, it is relatively easy to construct a maze reading passage from various literature selections, and it is also fairly easy to develop a maze from a textbook passage. In using mazes to monitor progress for secondary reading comprehension, experts generally recommend constructing maze passages so that students can read them for at least three minutes (Espin et al., 2005). In general terms, secondary students who are performing at grade level can correctly complete between twenty-five and twenty-eight correct answers in this type of passage during a three-minute timeframe, and that performance level should increase by six to eight answers during the year (Gibbs, 2008; also see the information on the maze reading procedure at the Florida Center for Reading Research website, www.fcrr.org). The National Center on Student Progress Monitoring (www.studentprogress.org) describes a number of commercially available progress-monitoring tools for high schools that employ a maze procedure, and various sources have provided more specific guidelines for creating maze reading passages (Espin et al., 2005; Gibbs, 2008).

Real-World RTI Example: Clark County, Nevada

High schools in Clark County, Nevada, have implemented a model RTI program in reading (Pro & Thompson, 2010). While various other models of RTI procedures were described in chapter 2, I'm presenting this particular implementation model because this faculty focused specifically on reading in high school content-area classes. As faculty began the RTI process, they reviewed earlier RTI initiatives in various schools and determined that using RTI procedures from elementary grades was similar to "trying to put a square peg in a round hole" (Pro & Thompson, 2010). In short, they decided that elementary RTI models will not work well in departmentalized schools, as discussed in chapter 2 (Bender, 2009a; Gibbs, 2008; Protheroe, 2010). The following feature box presents a synopsis of their model. Note the interesting choices concerning how to subdivide Tier 2 interventions in the context of these Clark County high schools (Pro & Thompson, 2010).

High School RTI Model From Clark County, Nevada

Resources Restructuring: As noted in chapter 2, schools may have to restructure available resources to facilitate RTI implementation (Gibbs, 2008). While the initial report on this secondary RTI implementation project in Clark County, Nevada, did not specifically address the issue of resources or resource allocation, readers can identify some suggestions of the necessary resources from the report itself (Pro & Thompson, 2010). Clark County implemented a variety of reading programs in the RTI secondary school effort, but it was not clear from the initial report whether the district had purchased programs specifically for RTI purposes (Pro & Thompson, 2010) or if they were previously in use in the schools.

Continued➜

This report stressed the importance of building a team of secondary professionals committed to RTI within the school and indicated that educators should expect RTI implementation at the secondary level to involve at least a five-year process. Specific concerns involved teacher buy-in, scheduling changes, and administration concerns such as meeting and exceeding AYP (Pro & Thompson, 2010).

Universal Screening and Progress Monitoring: In this example, various types of data were used as progress-monitoring data sources during Tier 1 instruction, including benchmarking data, statewide assessment scores, and classroom-based performance measures such as grades, progress reports, and teacher-made assessments (Pro & Thompson, 2010). Examples included individual student performance data from the state testing program as well as from commercial norm-referenced assessments. The data charts shared by Pro and Thompson (2010), which were generated during Tier 1 instruction, used either a bar graph or an *x/y*-axis format to depict a specific student's reading and/or mathematics score in relation to criteria labeled "meeting state standards" or "exceeding state standards" (Pro & Thompson, 2010).

The Tier 1 Instruction: As in all RTI procedures, general education teachers in this example were responsible for Tier 1 instruction. However, the document was not clear on who collected progress-monitoring data in Tier 1. Do these general education teachers collect all of the data used, including benchmarking data, or were other educators responsible for collecting those assessment data? While Tier 1 evaluation involved both class grades and teachers' assessments, it was not clear whether a biology teacher, for example, collected data on the number of words read correctly per minute (one such example was shown in this document as a Tier 1 benchmarking chart; Pro & Thompson, 2010) or whether such data were collected by the language arts teachers.

The Tier 2 Intervention: Tier 2 intervention is described in this example as differentiated instruction at the students' instructional levels (Pro & Thompson, 2010). This is an interesting recommendation, since differentiated instruction in the models presented previously in this text is specifically identified as something that general education teachers should be doing at the Tier 1 level.

This school district also chose to subdivide the Tier 2 intervention phase into two separate phases, which they labeled Stage 1 and Stage 2 monitoring within Tier 2 (Pro & Thompson, 2010). Both AIMSweb (measuring reading comprehension using the maze-comprehension measure) and Voyager Passport (using the words read correctly per minute measure) generated sample data charts that exemplify the Stage 1 performance monitoring in Tier 2. Students showing little progress in Stage 1 of Tier 2 moved on to Stage 2 of Tier 2, which again involved increased progress monitoring. In Stage 2 of Tier 2, the examples show that teachers monitored students' progress every other week. Unfortunately, the printed document provided no indication of actual interventions that might take place during Tier 2 (Pro & Thompson, 2010).

However, the subdivision of the Tier 2 intervention phase makes this implementation model somewhat unique.

The Tier 3 Intervention: Students showing no improvement in Tier 2 moved into Tier 3, and again the document discussed progress-monitoring procedures but not actual supplemental interventions for the students (Pro & Thompson, 2010). The writers described progress monitoring at this intervention phase as more frequent, and the examples suggested that progress monitoring was completed every other day in Tier 3. This again raises the question of who is doing both the progress monitoring and the interventions at Tier 3; the document itself provides no insight into that question.

Results: The available document provides no results of this RTI implementation, though clearly such results would be available from the data collected for the students.

Of particular interest, the Clark County RTI implementation model involved conducting an inventory of school resources—an attempt to consider resources and opportunities they could use for RTI at each tier level. Researchers recommend a survey of school resources that may facilitate RTI, and one such form is presented in figure 6.2 (Bender, 2009a). As shown in this inventory, faculty should seek a wide array of resources that can support RTI efforts, including curricula that might already be available or that they might use in elementary or middle schools within the district, specialized training that faculty might have, and other resources that can support RTI. Visit **go.solution-tree.com/rti** for a reproducible version of this figure.

Hard-Copy Supplemental Curricula Interventions
List all supplemental curricula that are "hard copy" (that is, not primarily computerized curricula, for example, various "curricula in a box"). Note the grade range and the areas or subjects for each. Include curricula used by every teacher within the school, including curricula used by particular teachers within specialized programs. Note who is using these and for what group. Also remember to consider any curricula that may be unused in the media center or storage areas in the building.
Computerized Supplemental Curricula Interventions
List all supplemental curricula software (for example, Read Naturally, Academy of READING). Note the grade range and the areas or subjects for each. Include curricula used by every teacher within the school, including curricula used by particular teachers within specialized programs. Note who is using these and for which students.

Figure 6.2: A schoolwide RTI inventory.   Continued➔

Hard-Copy Assessments for Universal Screening
List all individual assessments that are appropriate for universal screening or repeated assessment for performance monitoring (for example, Dynamic Indicators of Basic Early Literacy Skills). Note the grade range and the areas or subjects for each. Include curricula used by every teacher within the school, including curricula used by particular teachers within specialized programs. Note who is using these and for which students.
Curricula Recommended for Specific Tiers
Are there reasons for recommending particular curricula for specific tiers? For example, a limited site license for a certain computerized curriculum may suggest use of that curriculum only as a Tier 3 intervention. Explain.
Specialized Training
Have teachers received specialized training for particular supplemental curricula (for example, learning strategies training for the learning strategies curriculum or training in Fast ForWord)? Can or will these teachers be responsible for certain tiers of interventions or prepare other teachers for such intervention? Can other teachers receive such training, as necessary?

Source: Bender, 2009a.

A Case Study: RTI in Content-Area Reading

In this scenario, Mr. Duggan, the academic counselor and one of the biology teachers at Rabun County High School, noted that Tony Tramati had always struggled in reading-based content subjects in middle school. Tony's reading scores at the end of the eighth-grade year suggested that he was reading at approximately a fifth-grade reading level, and his eighth-grade academic report indicated that he had not passed his science class, while he managed only marginally passing grades in his other subjects. In short, Mr. Duggan was concerned with Tony's prognosis for the biology class prior to the year beginning, and in his role as academic counselor, he suggested that Tony receive some instructional assistance. A description of Tony's RTI is presented in figure 6.3.

For the purposes of this example, we'll describe a high school RTI model similar to the model of the Long Beach schools in California described in chapter 2 (page 48). That RTI model for middle and high schools includes the option of doubling the period in order to provide Tier 2 interventions, as well as specific instructional practice on reading skills that affect academic performance in the subject areas.

Student: Tony Tramati	Age: 16	Date: 12/08/2012
Initiating Teacher: Mr. Duggan	School: Rabun County High	Grade: 9

1. Student Difficulty and Summary of Tier 1 Instruction:

    Tony is having difficulty in reading, and his scores indicate he is reading at approximately a fifth-grade level. This difficulty resulted in his failure in science in grade 8 and difficulty in most other subjects. I called and had a conversation with Tony's science teacher from last year, as well as with the guidance counselor at the middle school, and both recommended that Tony receive additional support for science in grade 9. These problems suggest that Tony can benefit from academic support, particularly in science.

    Mr. Chas Duggan, 12/08/12

2. Tier 2 Intervention Plan:

    As a Tier 2 intervention, I recommend placing Tony in a double period of biology that I will teach. We anticipate that twelve students will require that double biology period this fall, and while Tony's first biology class will include twenty-eight or twenty-nine students, the second biology period will include only twelve students. On that basis, Tony will receive support in the subject that gave him the most trouble last year, as well as additional time and support in reading.

    In the double biology period, I use a number of supports for the second biology group, including a computer-based program, Study Island (www.studyisland.com). In the first portion of the second period, I review the concepts covered in the first-period biology class. During the second half of the second biology period, all of the students use Study Island to review scientific concepts. Thus Tony will work on that curriculum every other day for approximately twenty minutes.

    We plan on keeping Tony in the double period for the first semester (eighteen weeks) and then reviewing his progress. I will also develop a vocabulary-matching assessment for progress-monitoring purposes that includes vocabulary for every instructional unit we will cover in the next eighteen weeks. Each week, Tony will complete a twenty-item vocabulary-matching assessment, and that will serve as a progress-monitoring tool for Tony's Tier 2 intervention.

    I discussed this Tier 2 intervention plan with Mr. Engles, the chairperson of our student support team. He indicated that this intervention seemed appropriate and that I would be expected to present results of this intervention and

Figure 6.3: RTI documentation form for Tony in content-area reading. Continued➜

a chart of data from this intervention to the student support team in eighteen weeks—or sooner if this intervention doesn't seem to be working for Tony.

Mr. Duggan, 12/08/12

3. Tier 2 Intervention Summary and Recommendations:

On 08/12/12, Mr. Duggan presented Tony Tramati's educational progress to a subcommittee of the student support committee for Rabun County High School. The members of the subcommittee included Mr. John Engles, chair of the student support team; Ms. Alice Grubber, assistant principal; Ms. Janice Webber, department chair in science; Mr. Al McLaughlin, high school reading coach and special education inclusion teacher; and Mr. Frederick West, Tony's world history teacher.

The vocabulary-matching assessment data over the eighteen weeks indicated that Tony has made some progress on the Tier 2 intervention over the last semester. On the accompanying graphic [fig. 6.4, page 160], each indicator at the bottom of the chart represents an assessment conducted every two weeks over the eighteen-week semester, and the scale on the left represents the percentage of terms matched to the correct definition. These data indicate that he improved over the eighteen weeks, but by the end of the time period, he should have been at 80 to 100 percent on these vocabulary terms, and he did not reach nearly that level. As indicated, his progress was very slow and, in the opinion of this committee, this level of growth will not allow him to catch up with his classmates by the end of the year in his overall reading comprehension skills.

In addition, while Tony is currently passing biology, Mr. West has indicated that Tony is not succeeding in history, and that seems to be related to Tony's reading deficits. While Tony did complete most of his work on the Study Island curriculum, that work was focused exclusively on biology and not in history. The subcommittee also noted that Tony failed his health class during the last grading period and only barely passed his consumer economics class.

These data suggest that Tony will need more intensive intervention in order to develop reading skills that will allow him to succeed in ninth-grade subjects. The committee recommends placing Tony in a Tier 3 intervention with Mr. McLaughlin, the reading coach, while at the same time continuing the double period in biology. Mr. McLaughlin will submit a Tier 3 intervention plan, including those components, for Mr. Engles to review.

Mr. Engles, chair of Rabun County High School student support team, 12/09/12

4. Tier 3 Intervention Plan:

Tony will continue during the remainder of this year (one more semester) in the double biology period taught by Mr. Duggan, and Mr. Duggan will continue to monitor Tony's vocabulary development performance in biology. However, since he has completed driver's education, he has an open scheduling slot we will fill with a Tier 3 intervention in reading during fifth-period reading lab. In that lab, I typically have up to twenty students, but they each work individually on computerized reading. We will use the Voyager Passport Journeys II or Journeys III series for improving reading skills among adolescent learners. That curriculum will expose Tony to various reading journeys in a variety of subject areas, but with help in biology from Mr. Duggan, we will emphasize other subjects in the reading lab for Tony. Thus Tony's Tier 3 intervention will take place daily for an entire period for the remainder of the school year. The subcommittee believes that the work in Mr. Duggan's class, coupled with specific work in this Tier 3 intervention, should help Tony move toward success in reading overall.

Mr. Albert McLaughlin, reading coach, 12/11/12

Figure 6.3: RTI documentation form for Tony in content-area reading.

Academic Content Stressed in RTI Interventions

As indicated previously, most RTI initiatives described in the literature present Tier 2 and Tier 3 interventions focused on reading and mathematics rather than on biology, history, health, science, or other core-subject content. While there are exceptions, most examples of actual RTI models currently used in middle and high schools are building Tier 2 and Tier 3 interventions within the context of separate periods of instruction, centered primarily around reading and mathematics content and taught by language arts/English teachers or mathematics teachers, respectively.

As RTI procedures for middle and high school continue to develop, however, educators should anticipate Tier 2 combination options within content areas that pair a subject-content emphasis with an emphasis on reading (Bender, 2009a). The description of the Berkeley Springs High School RTI model in chapter 2 presented an example in which a general education teacher in history used technology to provide a Tier 2 intervention that stressed reading skill and history content. This case study is likewise designed to demonstrate what such an intervention might look like.

In this case, Tony received a double period of biology—because science was his weakest subject—in conjunction with an emphasis on reading in the content areas during both the Tier 2 and Tier 3 interventions. Of course, the emphasis on reading skill in that double period should assist Tony in other subject areas as well. While researchers encourage doubling English/language arts classes, algebra I classes, or general math classes, perhaps middle and high school faculty should also consider providing doubled classes in the other core courses in secondary schools,

While researchers encourage doubling English/language arts, algebra I, or general math classes, high school faculty may also consider doubling other core courses as well, particularly at the freshman and sophomore years.

particularly at the freshman and sophomore years. In most cases, such double classes must be scheduled at the beginning of the academic day (as period 1 and 2 classes) to avoid scheduling around lunch periods or vocational education classes. This way, students such as Tony will receive help not only with the basic skills of reading or mathematics but also with particularly difficult reading-based content-area classes.

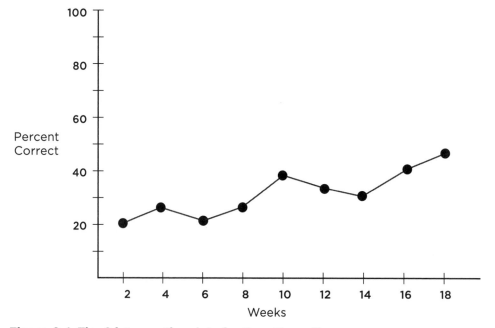

Figure 6.4: Tier 2 intervention data for Tony Tramati.

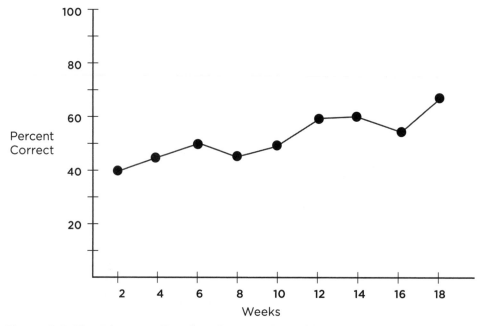

Figure 6.5: Tier 3 intervention data for Tony Tramati.

With that suggestion noted, schools probably will not find it necessary to offer double sections of all core classes. In the higher years of high school, the courses tend to be somewhat more homogeneously based, and if extensive interventions are provided for ninth and tenth graders, there should be fewer struggling students in the upper grades. In fact, the Long Beach model described previously reported exactly that finding; the entire district has many fewer students receiving special education assistance than the national average (Buffum et al., 2009).

Intervention Overlap/Replacement in the Upper Grades

One issue Tony's RTI plan exemplifies involves intervention overlap and intervention replacement. In most elementary school RTI models, students progress through the RTI tiers in numeric order, as determined by their individual instructional needs, and Tier 2 and Tier 3 do not generally overlap. While all RTI implementation models involve continuation of Tier 1 instruction throughout the process, the committee typically terminates Tier 2 interventions if it determines that a Tier 3 intervention is necessary for a particular student. While this has been the general intervention pattern in almost all elementary models, there are exceptions in middle and high schools. Specifically, Allen and his colleagues (2011) documented that in half of the middle schools they studied, Tier 1 and Tier 2 instruction overlapped, but for students with very serious deficits, Tier 3 instruction actually replaced Tier 1 instruction.

In the example here, the team determined that both the Tier 2 double period intervention and a more intensive Tier 3 reading lab intervention would support Tony at the same time. Thus the Tier 2 and Tier 3 interventions overlapped for the second semester of Tony's ninth-grade year. This forces the question: should interventions at the Tier 2 and Tier 3 levels overlap? To date, that is an unanswered question. This example emphasizes maximum flexibility in RTI procedures. Middle and high schools should maintain the option of overlapping Tier 2 and Tier 3 interventions or replacing Tier 1 instruction with Tier 3 intervention as dictated by the needs of individual students. While intervention overlap will not be critical for most students, for some, such support will be necessary.

In order to maximize flexibility, middle and high school faculty should consider the option of overlapping Tier 2 and Tier 3 interventions.

In fact, this might be another way in which RTI functions differently in middle and high schools as compared to elementary schools. As students become more exposed to schooling over the years, larger and larger deficits between their grade level and their reading achievement may develop. Specifically, a grade 3 student can only be a maximum of four years behind in reading achievement, whereas a grade 10 student can be eleven years behind! Furthermore, educators in high school will have significantly fewer years to help a student with massive skill deficits catch up with his or her peers. For those reasons, flexibility in intervention options, including the option of overlapping Tier 2 and Tier 3 interventions, seems necessary in the upper grade levels, and middle and high school faculty should consider implementing RTI procedures with this option available.

Learning Disability Eligibility

In this example, the team noted that Tony was making some progress in reading (specifically in vocabulary development) but that the rate of progress would not allow him to eliminate his deficits in one year. The team then considered the option of referral to the special education eligibility committee. Such a referral was not recommended in this example—as indeed it is not recommended in most RTI procedures, since well over 50 percent of students in Tiers 2 and 3 of an RTI process demonstrate significant progress (Bender, 2009a).

On occasion, a student's progress may suggest a different decision, and middle and high school educators need to understand how the RTI process fits within the context of eligibility decisions for special education placement. Educators make comparatively few referrals to special education eligibility teams in the upper grades compared to the elementary grades (Bender, 2009a). Three of every four students placed in special education for learning disability services are placed by grade 5, with most referrals for special education services coming in grades 3 and 4 (Bender, 2009a). Thus teachers are likely to identify students with significant learning disabilities prior to the middle and high school years.

In this case, however, the committee may have decided that some consideration was warranted for Tony. In that case, the student support team would have forwarded Tony's RTI file to the chair of the school eligibility team at the high school, complete with the data charts for the Tier 2 and Tier 3 interventions, along with the recommendation that the school eligibility committee consider Tony for possible special education placement (Bender, 2009a; Buffum et al., 2009).

It is important to note that a student's failure to respond to a Tier 2 or Tier 3 intervention does not prove the existence of a learning disability (Bender, 2009a). Rather, a child study eligibility team, as mandated in federal statute, will consider the RTI interventions and the resulting data charts in combination with other factors that may include possible medical factors that could negatively affect Tony's academic performance, language-based factors, motivation, learning processing, or other factors (Bender, 2009a; Kame'enui, 2007). In short, failure to respond to Tier 2 and Tier 3 interventions is a necessary but not sufficient condition to make a determination that a child has a learning disability (Bender, 2009a).

With that noted, general education teachers in middle and high schools will be much more involved in eligibility determinations for special education than they have been previously (Bender, 2009a; Bender & Shores, 2007). In fact, the data the general education teachers generated in this example—specifically by Mr. Duggan (fig. 6.4, page 160) and Mr. McLaughlin (fig. 6.5, page 160)—could provide a critical basis for a determination of learning disability status had those data been reviewed by the eligibility team. In particular, the data Mr. Duggan generated showed very sluggish academic progress.

Conclusion

Reading is an essential skill for middle school, high school, and lifelong success. However, many students in the upper grades struggle in reading, and this negatively affects their performance in many subject-area classes (Bender & Waller, 2011; Gibbs, 2008). For this reason, implementation of rigorous RTI procedures in middle and high schools in reading is not only timely but also long overdue. The techniques and approaches described in this chapter will assist struggling students not only to master academic content in their subject-area classes but also to develop improved reading skills over time. Both RTIs and differentiated instruction will assist many students in that regard, and middle and high schools are gearing up to implement these important curricular modifications in all reading-based content-area classes. The techniques and ideas described in this chapter should help teachers in that regard.

Another task that fosters success in many high school classes involves writing skills. In fact, almost every upper-grade subject involves writing skills to one degree or another, and for that reason, the next chapter provides information on RTI along with a variety of differentiated instructional tactics for writing that cut across the subject areas.

Like skills in reading, writing skills impact students' success in life. Many states and provinces now assess writing skills in their assessment programs, and districts encourage middle and high school teachers to emphasize these skills more in virtually every subject area. The next chapter should help in that regard.

Chapter 7

RTI and Differentiation in Writing

Writing is, arguably, one of the most important skills students must develop since they will use it for communication throughout life (MacArthur & Philippakos, 2010). Given the importance of writing, it is somewhat surprising that most middle and high schools do not directly teach it, nor do early middle and high school RTI implementation models emphasize it (Spectrum K–12 School Solutions/CASE, 2008). Of course, this doesn't mean the students are not writing in their subject-area classes or even in personal communication. In fact, as surprising as it may seem, one favorite pastime of many adolescents involves writing—specifically writing in the form of texting their best friends. Schools do not directly teach or evaluate texting as a form of writing. However, one could arguably build an interesting dictionary of specialized acronyms used in that form of written communication (lol, u, bff, rofl; if u don't recognize these acronyms, u are clearly not txting!).

In addition to that very modern and very informal form of written communication, school curricula emphasize many other forms of writing, including expository, creative, letter, and technical writing. All of these forms may be required in one's occupation, and in the 21st century, writing is essential in the job market; very few professions require no writing skills. For example, very few attorneys could function without highly developed writing skills.

> Writing is one of the most important skills students can develop, but middle and high schools do not directly teach it.

Given this important and lifelong emphasis on writing, it is interesting that there is no writing course in most upper grades. Like reading, writing is a skill the lower grades teach, and traditionally, faculty assume students master it by the time they reach the upper grades. Also like reading, writing involves many different skill sets, and students may be quite adept at some of these skills (such as forming sentences or paragraphs) and quite weak in others (such as creating a cohesive five-paragraph theme on a topic or developing a research paper).

Perhaps for this reason, only a small percentage of schools have undertaken RTI efforts in writing skills. One 2008 American survey of educators indicated that only 17 percent of the districts that completed the form reported using RTI procedures in writing (Spectrum K–12 School Solutions/CASE), though veteran teachers recognize that many middle and high school students have not mastered them.

For that reason, it is fair to say that nearly all subject-area classes in the upper grades teach writing skills, though perhaps indirectly, to some degree. In fact, schools now see writing skills as a critical component of reading instruction in the middle and upper grades, since writing instruction does positively impact a student's reading (Biancarosa & Snow, 2006).

This chapter begins by describing different types of writing. Next it presents various strategies teachers may use for differentiation of writing assignments in middle and high school classes. It then discusses several cognitive strategies as well as curricula options. Finally, it presents an RTI for writing skills in a ninth-grade biology class.

Different Types of Writing

Which skills should teachers include in writing instruction in the upper grade levels? What skills, exactly, do most middle and high school writing assignments involve? To answer that critical question, one might consider a typical assignment in almost any secondary class—writing a five- to ten-paragraph theme on an assigned topic. In order to write such a theme, students would need to:

- Research a topic, determining what information relates to the assignment and what does not

- Collect that information from various sources (texts, Internet, newspapers, and so on)

- Organize that information

- Determine a format for the written assignment based on what type of writing they wish to present (expository, compare-contrast, narrative, or writing involved in a multimedia presentation)

- Develop an outline structure for the written product

- Draft the written assignment by writing the sections of the outline (skills here involve developing sentences and presenting theses or the main idea along with appropriate details)

- Determine what information might be necessary that is not presented in the initial draft and research further to acquire that information

- Develop paragraphs that tie together to present the body of the theme rather than merely individual, stand-alone paragraphs

- Develop beginning and ending paragraphs and put them together with the other paragraphs in the body of the theme

- Revise and edit the theme several times

- Write the final paper for evaluation prior to turning in the assignment

Given this relatively extensive and complex set of skills, it is not surprising that middle and high school curricula emphasize writing skills more than previously. In fact, writing is one of the basic skills assessed in many state/provincial assessment programs across the grade levels, and at least fifteen states require students to demonstrate writing skills prior to high school graduation (Jacobson & Reid, 2010). These facts, taken together, suggest the overall importance of written expression, and thus almost every middle and high school teacher needs strategies for teaching these skills.

Not all writing assignments, however, involve writing a cohesive theme on a topic. For example, some assignments involve specific types of writing or different purposes for the written work. Persuasive writing, writing that argues for a stated position (Jacobson & Reid, 2010), is somewhat different from expository or creative writing, such as writing a story or poem. Other writing assignments differ based on the intended use of the written work. For example, some assignments may involve merely developing bullet points for a presentation on a topic or notetaking during a lesson, while others involve creating a longer cohesive piece. These differences in perspective, purpose, or type of writing force the question of how teachers can enhance writing skills in all those areas while continuing to teach their individual subject areas.

> Writing is one of the main skills assessed in many state/provincial assessment programs, and at least fifteen states require students to demonstrate writing skills prior to high school graduation.

While we can categorize writing in various ways, for purposes of this text, we shall use a relatively simple six-category system.

1. **Narrative writing**—This type of writing includes stories in a basal reading text in the elementary grades, stories in magazines, or paragraphs a student may write to illustrate the events in a story. Students have experience in this type of writing from the earliest grades.

2. **Expository writing**—This writing presents information, such as the writing in a middle or high school history or science text. The early school grades often introduce expository writing.

3. **Persuasive writing**—This type of writing intends to convince others to change their attitudes or beliefs or to state one's own beliefs forcefully. Students learn persuasive writing a bit later in school, typically during the mid-elementary years, and it receives increasing emphasis as the years progress.

4. **Creative writing**—This type of writing is associated with creative works such as poems or song lyrics. Some might suggest that the first category

is really a subcategory of creative writing, but creative writing is often graded in terms of "creativity" whereas writing a narrative about a story or a description of events typically is not; thus these forms of writing are separated here. Students do creative writing most frequently from the mid-elementary years onward.

5. **Writing for social networking**—Of course, this type of writing is the most recently developed, and it has developed independently of school assignments. This writing type often involves limitations from various social networking sites (such as limits of 140 characters in a "tweet" on Twitter, or limitations on entry length on Facebook). Most students begin this type of written communication during their middle school years, and to date, schools have not directly taught it.

6. **Technical writing**—Some writing does more than merely describe an object or process and is, instead, intended to demonstrate the functioning of the object or process. Technical writing is often coupled with technical diagrams that illustrate how a machine works. If students study technical writing at all, it tends to be somewhat later in the school years, and it is limited to various technical or vocationally oriented courses (such as drafting, mechanics, and the like).

While there is clearly some overlap in these categories, this sequence of writing skills suggests a hierarchy in writing that most school curricula reflect. Students study narrative writing and expository writing first and then progress to the more demanding forms, including creative and persuasive writing. While most school curricula teach the first four types of writing, they generally do not teach writing in the context of social networking. Instruction in technical writing is considerably less frequent than the other writing formats and tends to be limited to upper grades.

Of course, one can subdivide each of these types of writing. For example, one can separate expository writing into the structure associated with the text, as such texts may be based on cause and effect, compare/contrast, the sequence of events, or a problem-solution structure. In general, once students understand these basic types of writing, they will have a firm grasp on the various writing styles.

Most curricula emphasize these categories of expository writing in one form or another. Over the years, teachers have developed many "typical" writing assignments (book reports, notes, research papers, and the like), and they can now devise many newer types of writing assignments based on newer technologies and the media-rich environment in which today's adolescents live. The following feature box provides suggestions concerning how teachers may vary their subject-area writing assignments to emphasize these basic categories of writing while, in many cases, using technology. Note how some assignments represent particular types of writing from the list (for example, letters to the editor often represent persuasive writing).

Differentiated Instruction Via Alternative Types of Writing Assignments

Tweets (Twitter). If students are using Twitter, have them write a tweet to someone else and explain to the class the process (for example, How does one get "followers"? What limitations are imposed on length of a tweet?). Inviting students who have not used that written communication form to do so can be highly motivating and exciting.

Texting or Emailing. One free writing tool used by many students involves computer or smartphone technology for texting or emailing. These technologies offer nearly unlimited options for teaching writing. For texting or emailing, teachers can partner their class with another teacher's class and have students set up the modern equivalent of pen pals. Of course, students' personal security is an issue schools must address carefully, and most school districts have policies on use of these tools as instructional approaches.

Facebook. Facebook is one of the commonly used social networking sites, and as teachers realize that students enjoy this communication format, some have begun to use it for educational purposes. Some teachers now use Facebook pages (typically Facebook pages dedicated exclusively to a particular class) in high school classes. This can facilitate written communication with students. For example, teachers might use such a page to allow students to ask the teacher specific content questions on the night before the unit test. In that case, the communication would not emphasize writing skills directly, but writing would be part of the communication mechanism, and certainly it could be taught in that format. Furthermore, many students who are not motivated to write in any other format seem motivated to write in this context. Ning and Moodle, described previously, are two other sites that teachers can use instead of Facebook for this type of written communication within the classroom.

Songs and Chants. Students enjoy developing songs, chants, and jingles for helping memorize the content, and teachers should use that strategy. Present students with eight to ten main conceptual points and have them develop a song or chant to teach those concepts. All students should learn the chant and practice it daily during a two- or three-week unit; they will then learn those abbreviated versions of the main concepts in that unit.

YouTube. YouTube allows anyone to post brief videos online, and students are often quite motivated to develop such videos. While some school districts prohibit postings on YouTube, others allow it as one mechanism for students to publish their work. Of course, that gives teachers the option of having students write out their presentation beforehand, as that develops many writing skills such as topic selection, research, organization, initial drafting, adding presentation elements such as pictures or charts, and editing. Prior to initiating a YouTube assignment, teachers should check school policies and secure parental permission.

Continued➔

Cartoons. Humor is an excellent teaching tool; students are more likely to remember material they found funny. Students may work individually or as a small group and create a cartoon or comic strip based on information in the instructional unit, and the finished cartoon can be an instructional tool for all class members.

Magazine or Newspaper Articles. Writing an article for a newspaper or magazine is highly motivating. Students should select a specific newspaper or magazine based on its editorial perspective and then write on a topic of interest covered in that instructional unit. If possible, have the students submit the articles for publication by those publications. Some local newspapers will occasionally accept such an article, though publication should not be required. Students often enjoy that creative experience.

Letters to the Editor. Writing a letter to the editor in a local newspaper is somewhat different from writing an article. Articles tend to be expository in nature, presenting news items and some factual information about a topic, whereas letters to the editor tend to be persuasive in nature, expressing a clear point of view and urging a change in attitude or behavior.

Cognitive Strategies for Teaching Writing Skills

As described in previous chapters, schools have successfully used the cognitive strategies or learning strategies instructional approach across the grade levels on a variety of different school tasks, and it should come as no surprise that researchers have developed various cognitive strategies for teaching writing for middle and high school classes (Chalk, Hagan-Burke, & Burke, 2005; MacArthur & Philippakos, 2010; Mason & Graham, 2008; Troia, Graham, & Harris, 1999). We'll take a look at strategies for mechanics, strategies for higher-order thinking, and some tips on strategy implementation.

Mechanics

The learning strategies curriculum, developed by Deshler and his associates at the University of Kansas (Bulgren et al., 2007; Deshler et al., 2001; Lenz, 2006) and discussed in chapter 6, includes strategies for teaching mechanical writing skills.

> Researchers have developed various cognitive strategies for teaching writing for middle and high school classes.

Other researchers have developed a number of additional cognitive strategies (Jacobson & Reid, 2010; Korinek & Bulls, 1996; Therrien, Hughes, Kapelski, & Mokhtari, 2009; Troia et al., 1999). Troia and colleagues (1999) used a cognitive strategy to assist several fifth-grade students to develop a written story. They taught the students to actively plan their writing assignment using three major steps: (1) setting goals, (2) brainstorming ideas, and (3) sequencing their ideas. Students practiced those steps on a variety of written assignments during the instructional phase of the study. Afterward, the multiple-baseline design demonstrated that once the students had learned these planning strategies, their written stories got longer and the overall structure of the stories improved.

Similarly, Korinek and Bulls (1996) developed a writing strategy called SCORE A that can assist students in developing a research paper:

Select a subject.

Create categories or areas to be researched.

Obtain sources on each topic or category (and revise categories as needed).

Read and take notes on each topic from each source.

Evenly organize the information into subheadings.

Apply the writing process steps.

   a. Planning and prewriting
   b. Drafting each section
   c. Rewriting and revising each draft

These authors taught the SCORE A strategy to five students in grade 8 who were struggling with writing skills, and after instruction, four of the five students completed their writing assignment with a grade of "C" or higher. Of course, teachers should implement this type of strategy across a number of writing assignments, until the student has mastered application of the strategy. When taught and practiced extensively, this strategy will assist students in the various steps of extended research writing assignments, and as students use this strategy more frequently, they will internalize this process.

Harris and Graham (1996) developed a cognitive strategy called DARE for helping students write short essays that emphasizes self-regulated strategy development (Harris & Graham, 1996; Jacobson & Reid, 2010):

Develop a topic sentence.

Add supporting ideas (at least three ideas).

Reject at least one argument for the other side, and support your own opinion.

End with a strong conclusion.

In this strategy, students learn to consistently self-check against a set of organizational components. This strategy has proven effective in increasing the overall quality of students' written work in several research projects, as reviewed by Jacobson and Reid (2010).

Finally, helping students develop the skills of self-checking can assist in overall development of writing skill. Figure 7.1 (page 172) presents a self-checking form that might be used in middle or high school for checking a theme-based writing assignment or as students complete an argumentative or persuasive writing assignment.

1. Is my position or argument clearly stated as a defensible thesis early in the paper?

_____

2. Have I presented one or more points that support my thesis?

_____

3. For each point supporting my thesis, do I provide evidence of some type? Do I present a good case that the evidence supporting my thesis is strong?

_____

4. Have I presented counterarguments and shown why they should be discounted?

_____

5. After developing the body of the paper, including the components mentioned, have I developed a good introductory paragraph that leads to and explicitly states my thesis?

_____

6. Have I developed a good summary paragraph that restates my thesis and indicates, in short form, the various points supporting it?

_____

Figure 7.1: A self-checking sheet for writing a persuasive paper.

Higher-Order Thinking

In addition to strategies that address the mechanics of writing and editing, various authors emphasize higher-order thinking skills in written assignments, using several newer learning strategies (Bulgren et al., 2007; De La Paz, Morales, & Winston, 2007; Mason & Graham, 2008). For example, De La Paz and her coworkers devised a cognitive strategy to help students develop critical thinking for both reading and writing assignments in a secondary history course. While there is no acronym for the strategy, they did develop a breakdown of steps students could use to evaluate the information they collect during the research phase of writing a paper. The following feature box presents an adaptation of that strategy.

As these various steps indicate, strategy training of this nature can emphasize more than merely a specific task such as editing a paragraph (as in the COPS strategy) or planning a written theme (as in DARE). This instance stresses higher-order thinking skills such as evaluation of author's intent, purposes, and possible biases. With these steps in mind, content-area teachers can easily apply these broader concepts to various other subject areas, such as comparing and contrasting scientific theories or developing alternative interpretations of sociological perspectives.

Historical Thinking and Evaluation Strategy

I. Sourcing the information: Who said or wrote this (primary or secondary source)?

    A. What was the author's purpose?

    B. Do the reasons make sense?

    C. Is there evidence of bias?

II. Comparing details via alternate sources

    A. Are there conflicting views?

    B. Are there inconsistencies between sources?

    C. Is a person or event described differently?

    D. What is missing from one or more authors' arguments?

    E. What can you infer from reading across the sources?

III. Believability: What can you believe from each source?

    A. Make notes on consistencies and inconsistencies between sources.

    B. Consider each author's purpose and any possible biases.

Adapted from De La Paz et al., 2007.

For differentiation purposes, many students may already be completing this type of evaluative thinking, and use of such a strategy would not be likely to assist them a great deal. For students who struggle to write even the simplest theme, however, having strategies such as these can be of great benefit. Teachers across the content areas should identify students who struggle more with their written assignments and present a strategy such as this to assist with their thinking and planning for longer written assignments.

Strategy Implementation

Using these types of learning strategies will enhance students' writing over time (Bulgren et al., 2007; Deshler et al., 2001; Lenz, 2006; Therrien et al., 2009), and for that reason, researchers recommend using learning strategies to enhance writing in middle and high school grades. Implementation of these strategies is reasonably straightforward, and teachers can conduct it in any core content area without taking much time away from the content instruction itself, a critical concern for subject-area teachers in middle and high schools.

First, the teacher should select one learning strategy and teach it directly using explicit instruction techniques such as description, discussion, modeling, and repeated practice while emphasizing the context of the class content. As mentioned

Using these types of learning strategies will enhance students' writing over time.

earlier, these learning strategies are effective when practiced extensively over a period of eight to twenty-five days, so she should select the strategy that most closely aligns with the writing demands in a given class. Whereas teachers can typically teach one writing strategy in a content-area class, teaching more than one would be problematic time-wise.

Once the teacher has selected a strategy, she should make a poster of the steps in that strategy for class display. She should then discuss the steps in the strategy at length with the class while modeling use of the strategy. A think-aloud procedure, in which the teacher writes while using the strategy and thinking aloud along with the class, works well here. After initial instruction, she should require students to write every day, using the strategy, for a period of days. Typically teachers should arrange to use the strategy daily for eight to ten days, and in classes where this schedule does not work, try using the strategy two or three times per week for six to ten weeks. Of course, those writing assignments should address topics from the content area the class is studying so teaching these writing strategies does not deduct instructional time from the class content.

Next, the teacher must grade each daily text the students write based on both the overall writing quality and the specific steps in the selected learning strategy. The teacher should collate and chart those grades by student to show their improvement in writing over time. In that sense, using any of these learning strategies can provide teachers with charted data on writing performance across a period of days, which would be very appropriate as a Tier 2 intervention on writing skill. The following feature box summarizes these steps in writing strategy instruction.

Cognitive Strategy Instruction Guidelines for Writing Instruction

1. Select one specific learning strategy that best addresses the demands of the type of written work required in a particular class.

2. Develop a poster of the strategy steps for long-term display in the room.

3. Teach that strategy directly and repeatedly using explicit instruction techniques, including a description of the strategy, specifics on when to use it, and a discussion of how to apply the strategy.

4. Model the strategy while using a think-aloud procedure to discuss strategy application. Emphasize the strategy for specific types of assignments that are common in the class.

5. Have students practice the strategy once or twice in partnership with each other, using each other to respond to their strategy application on a writing assignment.

6. Provide extensive practice requiring the students to apply the strategy and offering immediate feedback. Typically, teachers should arrange to use the strategy daily for eight to ten days, and in classes where that schedule does not work, try using the strategy two or three times per week for six to ten weeks.

7. Evaluate each written assignment during that practice period based on both the overall writing quality and the specific steps of the selected learning strategy. Chart those grades for each student to demonstrate progress.

It is not an overstatement to say that nearly all instructional research on writing for the upper grades over the last decade has focused on use of cognitive strategies and learning strategies. As our schools increasingly emphasize literacy, all teachers will take some responsibility for teaching writing skills, so teachers in middle and high school classes should build many writing assignments into their course outlines, as well as directly and explicitly teaching students using one or more of the cognitive strategies for writing described here. Differentiation and enhanced learning will occur for many struggling students because students who need the supports of these writing strategies will continue to use them as they see the benefits of strategy application.

Notetaking and Storyboarding for Written or Presentation Assignments

One writing skill that has been essential in the upper grades for many years is the ability to take notes when a teacher is speaking. This skill involves listing points while developing a general outline, and in that way, notetaking is similar to the more modern skill of storyboarding a presentation. Notetaking, however, differs from other types of writing assignments and, at a minimum, involves the following tasks: writing down brief expository facts or statements, organizing those into outline form (often while writing them down initially), and editing them to make the notes cohesive and comprehensive.

To date, very little research on notetaking skills among struggling students in middle and high school students is available. One may assume that because of the difficulties in reading and cognitive organization many struggling students experience in the upper grade levels, notetaking is a difficult task for them.

Notetaking is similar to the more modern skill of storyboarding a presentation.

The research that has been done on notetaking among struggling students has indicated that the more cognitively involved students are with the notetaking task, the higher the recall (Igo, Bruning, McCrudden, & Kauffman, 2003). In a 2006 study on notetaking among students with learning disabilities, Igo, Riccomini, Bruning, and Pope investigated use of computer technologies to assist in notetaking. Computer-based notetaking, coupled with web-based texts, offers the possibility of cutting and pasting content to formulate one's notes as opposed to mentally constructing notes in non-web-based learning, such as lectures and class discussions. Using seventh- and eighth-grade students, including some students with learning disabilities, Igo and his colleagues (2006) questioned the efficacy of cut-and-paste notetaking versus writing notes out and paraphrasing text. These researchers anticipated that writing notes out would result in increased comprehension, but their results were somewhat mixed. Writing out notes enhanced recall for written answers on texts, whereas, contrary to expectation, cut-and-paste notetaking enhanced recall on multiple-choice tests (which tend to be merely factual/literal recall). More research will be done on notetaking skills among struggling students, but these results do indicate the efficacy of electronic, cut-and-paste notetaking in enhancing some types of comprehension.

Regardless of how that research turns out, notetaking is a skill that schools can and must emphasize in most core classes in the upper grades. Teachers should help students understand the advantages of developing outlined notes and then check those notes for accuracy and completeness. Furthermore, students should learn to make notes on a computer, if possible, since that is probably a skill they will need in the working world throughout their lives. Finally, emphasizing the similarities between notetaking and more comprehensive presentation development can entice students to improve their notetaking skills as well as prepare them for the world of tomorrow.

Supplemental Writing Curricula

Curricula for writing instruction in middle and high school classes are somewhat limited compared to curricula for reading or mathematics instruction. This section looks at one writing curriculum for content-area classes at the secondary level: Step Up to Writing by Maureen Auman (www.sopriswest.com). It then explores several web-based tools, and discusses how such technologies affect writing instruction.

Step Up to Writing

Step Up to Writing presents three separate instructional programs that cover the public school age range. The secondary-level kit from this curriculum focuses on writing skills from grades 6 through 12. It includes research-based writing instructional strategies such as explicit instruction, modeling, and repetitive practice.

In Step Up to Writing, students study various writing genres and develop understanding of the types and purposes of writing. They study writing as a tool for content learning and specifically connect reading and writing as tools for learning subject-area content. In particular, the secondary Step Up to Writing kit teaches the traits of strong expository and narrative writing. It emphasizes improving writing by adding details and varying word choice, sentence types, and structure. It also emphasizes revision and editing skills, and students learn to think critically about their written work prior to submitting the assignment.

The company website (www.sopriswest.com) presents several anecdotal research reports that attest to the efficacy of this program. After it was implemented in a school district in Washington State, a higher percentage of the students passed the writing assessment on the statewide test. Given that states increasingly include writing skills on statewide assessments, applying this curriculum in middle and high schools can assist efforts to enhance learning and improve statewide writing assessment scores overall.

Web-Based Tools

Every teacher is aware of the types of support for writing available through modern technology such as grammar and spell checkers, but students have to complete their writing assignment on a computer in order to access these tools. One term frequently used for these and more sophisticated technology-based instructional options is *TELE*, which stands for *technology-enhanced learning environments* (Wang & Hannafin, 2005), since the computer becomes the learning environment for the student when he or she completes a given writing assignment. These and many other such technologies clearly enhance writing instruction, so schools should utilize them to provide the basis for writing in the real world.

Texting increased drastically between 2008 and 2010 among adolescents, many students use email frequently, and use of social networking technologies has increased writing among youth even more.

Even a cursory knowledge of how adolescents spend their time indicates that students love to write, at least in certain venues! As mentioned previously, texting increased drastically between 2008 and 2010 among adolescents, many students use email frequently, and use of social networking technologies such as Facebook and Twitter has increased writing among youth even more (Dretzin, 2010). Given that students are highly motivated to write using these technology venues, teachers should consider using technology as instructional tools in various subject areas (Castellani & Jeffs, 2001; Salend, 2009; Shapiro, 2010).

Wikipedia

Shapiro (2010) discusses an interesting, highly motivational writing assignment concept that can be either an individual or a small-group assignment using Wikipedia, an online encyclopedia in which the entries are written by the general public. While some educators may consider this reference source problematic (some teachers may even prevent students from using Wikipedia, since it is not written by experts), Shapiro (2010) suggests that teachers use Wikipedia both as a source for information and as a teaching tool. Specifically, one must check entries from Wikipedia for accuracy since anyone can write or modify them. This provides an excellent opportunity for students to consider the reliability of sources they use in their research as well as to evaluate an author's perspective. Furthermore, the students themselves can edit and improve the accuracy of the entry on a particular topic, and they are often highly motivated to complete this type of assignment, since they realize their work will be published on Wikipedia for all the world to see!

There are other benefits for this writing assignment, too. Shapiro (2010) points out that such an editing process is exactly the same editing process students must master in order to improve their own writing skills. Thus this Wikipedia assignment improves skills in written expression in many other assignments. Given the extensive range of topics on Wikipedia, virtually every middle school and high school teacher could use this assignment in almost any subject area.

Science.net

Salend (2009) describes another TELE, a web-based writing assignment available at Science.net (www.epistemicgames.org/eg/?cat=10). At that website, a gaming format encourages students to adopt the roles of journalists. They then gather factual material and write stories about various science and technology issues for online magazines (Shaffer, 2007). Again, students are quite motivated to accurately research and develop their articles, as well as edit them for clarity, because they realize their work will ultimately be published.

WriteToLearn

The WriteToLearn website (http://writetolearn.net/) is another TELE Pearson Learning setup. It is devoted to instruction and assessment in writing. The activities focus on reading and writing together, emphasizing both summary writing, which is writing of brief expository texts, as well as essay writing. The site then scores the written product on six traits of writing: ideas, organization, conventions, sentence fluency, word choice, and voice or writer's perspective. It provides instruction on each of those six aspects of writing, and having these writing assignments scored on the site itself can save teachers a great deal of time.

Castellani and Jeffs (2001) identified a number of other technology tools for writing instruction across the grade levels. For example, visual concept organization software provides graphic templates that help students organize and outline their thoughts and concepts prior to writing. Graphic-based writing software provides storyboarding frameworks for developing a written product and incorporates sound, music, voice recording, and other elements to make the written product an effective presentation (Castellani & Jeffs, 2001).

Is Traditional Writing Instruction Enough?

This type of software begs the following questions: Is teaching writing in a traditional, pencil-and-paper fashion enough? Is development of traditional hard-copy writing skills during the school-age years truly preparing our students for the 21st century? Alternatively, will students need writing skills they can automatically and seamlessly couple with presentation, computer production, or web design skills to meet the communication demands the new century will place on them? In the 21st century world, it would seem that writing instruction might be coupled not only with extensive use of word processing packages and the tools available therein but also with presentation software instruction, since writing a report and preparing a class presentation on a topic do represent, in many ways, the same set of skills. These would include selecting and defining a topic, researching, preparing outlines, developing the outline, putting it together, editing, revising, and so forth.

While most curricula in 2011 reflect traditional writing skills instruction, some proponents of technology suggest that schools should teach writing in the context of developing effective, technology-based communication skills for the next century (Partnership for 21st Century Skills, 2007), such as presentation planning and presentation software. It seems clear that all middle and high school teachers should be developing skills in teaching writing using some of the modern technologies described herein.

Readers should note that this book presents only a few options for technology-based writing instruction and that hundreds of other technology-based options are also available. In writing instruction, as in reading and mathematics, it seems a different world is soon coming as technology increasingly impacts the way people communicate through written expression.

A Case Study: RTI in Writing

In the United States, only 17 percent of school districts indicate that they provide RTI interventions in writing (Spectrum K–12 School Solutions/CASE, 2008). Some districts are providing RTI writing support, however. In most cases, writing RTI, like reading RTI procedures discussed previously, will probably be undertaken in a separate language arts or literacy support class, but on occasion it may be possible for some RTI work in writing to be completed in various general education classes. This case study presents an RTI example in writing that involves a Tier 2 writing support intervention in a general education class and a Tier 3 intervention in a literacy support class. The documentation form for this RTI procedure is presented in figure 7.2.

Student Name: Emma	Age: 16	Grade: 9
Initiating Teacher: Mr. Jessup	School: Baton Rouge High School	Date: 9/15/2013

1. Student Difficulty and Summary of Tier 1 Instruction:

    Emma and several other students are having difficulty expressing themselves in written form. In particular, Emma cannot formulate a coherent

Figure 7.2: RTI documentation form for Emma in content-area writing.   Continued→

paragraph or check her work prior to handing it in. Her grades from the eighth-grade writing assessment likewise indicated substantial difficulties in writing. I have instituted a journal writing assignment and have tried informally coaching Emma on her writing in that assignment. Still, those journal entries suggest difficulties in writing.

Mr. Jessup, 9/15/13

2. Tier 2 Intervention Plan:

    As a Tier 2 intervention, I recommended to Ms. Megan Thurston, the literacy coach at our school, that Emma be placed in a Tier 2 writing intervention that I plan to undertake in my biology class. She will receive this intervention along with four other students who are likewise having difficulties in writing. I will teach these students the COPS self-checking strategy for written work and will require them to complete that strategy every Monday, Wednesday, and Friday when they do their journal entries. While all students will be taught the COPS strategy, for the students in the Tier 2 intervention, I will count the errors they make in their writing as a progress-monitoring score on those three days each week.

    Ms. Thurston agreed that this seemed to be an appropriate Tier 2 intervention for Emma and further agreed to review the data from this intervention in five weeks.

Mr. Jessup, 9/16/13

3. Tier 2 Intervention Summary and Recommendations:

    On 10/26/13, Mr. Jessup presented Emma's progress-monitoring data to Ms. Megan Thurston, the literacy coach, along with two other members of the student support team at Baton Rouge High School, Ms. Renee Lovorn, the assistant principal, and Ms. Norma Schnider, the reading coach. [Those data are presented in figure 7.3.] That subcommittee of the student support team agreed that a more intensive Tier 3 intervention would be necessary for Emma.

Ms. Renee Lovorn, assistant principal, 10/26/13

4. Tier 3 Intervention Plan:

    Emma will be assigned to work with me in the literacy class, beginning at the start of the next grading period (10/31/13). All of Emma's work will focus on writing, with an emphasis on paragraph structure and organization, as well as self-checking to eliminate errors. Emma will write a paragraph daily, which will be graded as a progress-monitoring score on her Tier 3 intervention for writing skills.

Further, Mr. Jessup has agreed to continue his work, using the COPS strategy with Emma three times each week in conjunction with her biology assignments.

Ms. Megan Thurston, literacy coach, 10/27/13

5. Tier 3 Intervention Summary and Recommendations:

[Data on Emma's daily written paragraphs from Ms. Thurston's class are presented in figure 7.4, page 182.] As these data show, Emma's writing skills improved with this combination of intensive writing support in the literacy class, as well as her ongoing work in writing paragraphs in Mr. Jessup's biology class. She seems to have grasped the concept of paragraph structure as well as the importance of self-checking her writing prior to handing it in. Emma even noted that she had used the COPS strategy in another class during the Tier 3 intervention, indicating some generalization of that strategy to other written work. Based on these data, there is no need to continue with Emma's placement in the literacy class after the current grading period.

Ms. Megan Thurston, literacy coach, 12/5/13

Figure 7.2: RTI documentation form for Emma in content-area writing.

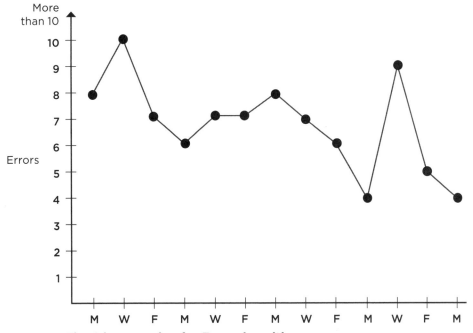

Figure 7.3: Tier 2 intervention for Emma in writing.

A Tier 3 Intervention in Writing

After the student support team examined the data chart and looked over a couple of Emma's initial journal entry drafts, the team determined that a more intensive tier of instruction, specifically focused on writing skill, would be necessary for her. The team encouraged Mr. Jessup to continue his work on paragraphs by continuing the journal-based instruction three times each week. In addition, they decided to place Emma in a literacy intervention class, focused jointly on reading and writing skills, as a Tier 3 intervention in writing. That class was scheduled to begin within two weeks at the beginning of the next grading period.

A literacy coach at the school, Ms. Thurston, was leading instruction in that literacy class. She indicated she would be able to focus all of Emma's work on her writing, specifically eliminating errors and improving overall paragraph structure. On paragraph structure, Ms. Thurston planned to emphasize creation of a clear, concise topic sentence and identification of supporting details on that topic sentence. Thus Emma would receive daily writing instruction with Ms. Thurston, and Ms. Thurston would grade one paragraph she wrote each day. She would use those daily grades to monitor Emma's performance during the Tier 3 intervention. As Emma participated in the literacy intervention class, Ms. Thurston collected her daily scores on her written paragraphs and graphed those data for the next five weeks. Those compiled data are presented in figure 7.4.

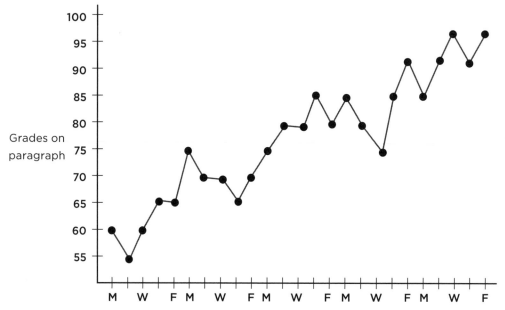

Figure 7.4: Tier 3 intervention for Emma in writing.

Intervention Summary

As the data indicate, this combination of interventions—the COPS editing strategy in Mr. Jessup's class coupled with the daily intensive instruction in paragraph structure with Ms. Thurston—worked to improve Emma's writing skills. At the end of that grading period, Ms. Thurston recommended that Emma not be required to continue in the literacy intervention class, since it had dealt with her problems. The student support team accepted that recommendation but did suggest that Mr. Jessup continue his work on helping Emma in paragraph writing.

In this instance, the advantage of a scheduled intervention period in a departmentalized school is clear. When teachers cannot alleviate problems with additional intensive Tier 2 interventions, which they often present in the general education class, they can supplement with a Tier 3 intervention such as the literacy intervention period described here.

Conclusion

Though a small percentage of districts have developed RTI procedures to assist in written expression (Spectrum K–12 School Solutions/CASE, 2008), there is clearly an immediate need for writing interventions. Differentiated strategies such as the strategies and interventions described in this chapter should assist in that regard, and all teachers in middle and high schools should make every effort to assist students in developing the critically important skill of written expression.

While RTI procedures in writing may become a concern for many middle and high school teachers in the future, clearly there is an immediate need for writing interventions.

Many students likewise struggle in mathematics during middle and high school. Like reading and writing, mathematics involves a set of skills that affects success in life and can impact success in other upper-grade subjects such as science, economics, or geography. The next chapter will present an array of effective suggestions for RTI procedures and differentiated instruction at the Tier 1 level to address students' needs in mathematics.

Chapter 8

RTI and Differentiation in Mathematics

While most RTI programs in middle and high schools have dealt with reading, some, like the Tigard High School RTI model described in chapter 2, provide RTI interventions for students struggling in mathematics. It will come as no surprise that students entering high school are often not prepared for algebra, and many are ill prepared for even lower-grade mathematics (Cole & Wasburn-Moses, 2010). It seems clear that upper-grade teachers of mathematics, like teachers in the reading-dependent core content areas discussed previously, will need to implement various RTI interventions as well as a wider array of differentiated instructional tactics and strategies in Tier 1 to deal with this widening gap between top- and bottom-level achievers in mathematics. In short, both RTI and differentiated instruction have become increasingly essential to meet students' needs in mathematics.

One subtlety within these reports involves the number of students who require intensive interventions to succeed in mathematics. In fact, the data cited suggest that the need for RTI procedures and differentiated instructional supports in mathematics may be considerably greater than the need for supports in reading in the upper grade levels. As discussed in chapter 1, the traditional RTI model suggests that traditional whole-class instruction in reading, coupled with differentiated instruction, meets the needs of 80 percent of students. In contrast, these statistics suggest that by the end of eighth grade, traditional instruction in mathematics meets the needs of only 32 percent of all students (Lee, Grigg, & Dion, 2007; National Mathematics Advisory Panel [NMAP], 2008). It is quite possible that many more students need Tier 2 interventions in mathematics, as well as more intensive instruction at the Tier 1 level, to succeed. Indeed, the available data suggest that as many as 66 percent of all students in grade 8 and above may require some type of supportive Tier 2 intervention in mathematics. Middle and high school faculty may need to create many more mathematics than reading or writing intervention options for their students (Bender & Crane, 2011).

With this point in mind, chapter 8 will initially present an array of innovative, differentiated instructional strategies for Tier 1 instruction in mathematics. These strategies have received research support but have not yet been widely applied in mathematics in middle and high schools. All mathematics teachers from grade 7 and higher would do well to begin applying one or more of these innovative strategies in their classes.

Specific mathematics interventions at the Tier 2 and Tier 3 levels will, of necessity, become a concern as RTI is implemented in upper-grade mathematics, and this chapter describes a number of technology- and non-technology-based curricula for faculty to consider. Then it presents progress-monitoring options. In addition, an RTI case study in mathematics appears at the end of the chapter to show the issues involved in RTIs in mathematics in middle and high schools.

Cooperative-Learning Strategies

Some studies indicate positive results on motivation among students struggling in mathematics when students participate in math activities with a partner or a group, as this can seem less threatening than doing them alone (Kroeger & Kouche, 2006; Stevens & Slavin, 1995). This section presents peer tutoring options as well as problem-based learning.

Peer Tutoring for Differentiation in Mathematics

One of the instructional examples in chapter 6, repeated reading with partners, emphasized using peers as tutors within the general education class. Since 1990, a large body of research has demonstrated the efficacy of peer tutoring in various grade levels, including the middle and high school grades, in a variety of subject areas such as history, science, and mathematics (Fuchs et al., 2008; Harper & Maheady, 2007; McDuffie, Mastropieri, & Scruggs, 2009; Wood et al., 2007). Specifically, research has shown the efficacy of various peer tutoring programs in mathematics up to and including algebra (Allsopp, 1997; Foegen, 2008; Fuchs et al., 2008; Kroeger & Kouche, 2006). A variety of these authors and researchers have recommended peer tutoring as a Tier 1 instructional tactic within the context of an RTI procedure (Harper & Maheady, 2007; Kroeger & Kouche, 2006).

Doing math activities with a partner or tutor can seem somewhat less threatening than doing them alone.

Students are also more likely to remain cognitively involved in the mathematics lesson during a peer tutoring exercise (Foegen, 2008; Fuchs et al., 2008; Kroeger & Kouche, 2006; Stevens & Slavin, 1995), and that increased engagement is likely to result in increased achievement. In this sense, peer tutoring provides one method for delivering highly differentiated instruction in mathematics within general education classrooms. Reciprocal peer tutoring involves a tutoring partnership similar to peer buddies in which each student serves as both tutor and tutee. In reciprocal peer tutoring activities, students are provided highly detailed instructional guidance and immediate feedback based directly on their misunderstandings in learning situations, and research has shown that both students will benefit from this instructional practice (Foegen, 2008; Fuchs et al., 2008; Kroeger & Kouche, 2006; Stevens & Slavin, 1995).

For these reasons, middle and high school mathematics teachers should investigate reciprocal peer tutoring instructional options as one component of their differentiated instructional efforts. In fact, with the growing evidence on the efficacy of peer tutoring programs, teachers of mathematics who are not using some type of peer tutoring are missing an excellent opportunity for increasing the mathematics achievement of their students, not to mention the enjoyment of mathematics as students work together on their practice activities.

In short, peer tutoring approaches generate increased on-task time and enjoyment, since working together on mathematics activities is more engaging than completing a practice worksheet. Peer tutoring should be one component of effective, highly differentiated mathematics classes, and teachers might consider replacing most individual worksheet practice assignments with some version of reciprocal peer tutoring in

> Some version of reciprocal peer tutoring can replace most individual worksheet practice assignments in every middle and high school mathematics class.

every middle and high school mathematics class. The next section describes several peer tutoring systems for middle and high school mathematics teachers to consider.

The Peer-Assisted Learning Strategy

The peer-assisted learning strategy (PALS) is an instructional tactic built on a reciprocal relationship between peers working through mathematics problems (Fuchs et al., 2001; Fuchs et al., 2008; Kroeger & Kouche, 2006). PALS moves beyond the one-way tutoring relationship in which high-achieving students tutor lower-achieving students and instead allows students in general education classes to tutor each other. This reciprocal tutoring approach fosters higher engagement among all students in the mathematics lessons since all students are vested in the process and all recognize that their work supports other students' learning (Kroeger & Kouche, 2006). According to the research on PALS, collaborative reciprocal learning activities also enhance students' enthusiasm for learning and their determination to achieve academic success, resulting in increased achievement for students of all abilities (Kroeger & Kouche, 2006; Stevens & Slavin, 1995).

The PALS program combines explicit instruction, clear models, an array of examples, think-aloud tactics, use of physical and visual representations of number concepts for problem solving, and extensive practice (Fuchs et al., 2001; Kroeger & Kouche, 2006). PALS engages students supporting each other in reciprocal roles of coaches (tutors) and players. In the course of practice activities, all students serve in both roles. The PALS program provides explicit scripts including step-by-step directions for problem solving, complementing these activities with gaming activities that increase student engagement.

In PALS, the coach reads the scripted lesson while the player solves the mathematics problem. The coach reads instructions on how to complete a problem and stands ready to provide additional coaching as needed. When the player makes a mistake, the coach draws a circle around the mistake, calling the player's attention to it, and then helps the player rethink that work. In this reciprocal relationship, both students develop a deeper conceptual understanding of the mathematics learning in combination with improved computational skills. Classroom interactions like those provided in the PALS program enhance learning with understanding (Kroeger & Kouche, 2006), and research has supported this approach to mathematics instruction in general education classes across the grade levels (Fuchs et al., 2001; Greenwood, Delquadri, & Carta, 1997).

Kroeger and Kouche (2006) described the use of PALS in several co-taught mathematics classes in the seventh grade; these classes included 150 students. While the PALS curriculum has been designed for elementary and secondary grade levels (Kroeger & Kouche, 2006), Kroeger and Kouche used it but devised their own instructional lesson scripts to meet the specific needs of their middle school classes. In each class, the teachers assigned students to pairs by splitting the class into two lists, one of higher-achieving students and another of lower-achieving students. They formed the pairs by partnering the highest-achieving student on the first list with the highest-achieving student on the second, and so forth down each list.

The PALS instructional approach requires specific training in peer tutoring for five days during which students learn the roles of coach and player and practice with various mathematics lessons in each role. They receive points for correct coaching, including things such as reading the script word for word while coaching, helping the player accurately figure out where the mistake was, and staying on task.

Classroom interactions like those provided in the PALS program enhance learning with understanding, and research has supported this cooperative learning approach to mathematics instruction in general education classes.

In using PALS, the lead teacher should teach the target skill (for example, dividing fractions with unlike denominators) in the same fashion as always. Rather than practicing individually, students use the PALS procedure and the script to coach each other on that task. One student would serve as coach for about ten to fifteen minutes, and then, with a signal from the teacher, the students would change roles. During that time, the teachers would visit various pairs of students and offer assistance with coaching as necessary. In that fashion, PALS served as a supplementary support for practice on various problems in the general education class. Typically, students do this type of reciprocal peer tutoring three days per week (Kroeger & Kouche, 2006). The results documented the efficacy of this instructional approach in terms not only of increased mathematics achievement but also of increased engagement in and dramatically improved attitudes toward mathematics (Kroeger & Kouche, 2006).

Classwide Student Tutoring Teams

The classwide student tutoring teams (CSTT) approach depends on a classwide peer tutoring approach initially developed by Greenwood and his associates (Greenwood et al., 1997; Harper & Maheady, 2007), but in CSTT, instructional teams replace pairs of students. Because of this "group project" basis, the CSTT approach is somewhat more appropriate for students in the higher grades (Harper & Maheady, 2007). Like many peer tutoring approaches, CSTT relies on the concept of reciprocal tutoring, in which all students on the team tutor all others on the team. A videotape and manual for implementing CSTT are available (Harper, Maheady, Mallett, & Sacca, 1992), and teachers can easily implement this approach in virtually any subject area in high school or middle school.

In this system, as in most peer tutoring approaches, the classroom teacher initially introduces and initially teaches new content. Students then have the chance to interact with each other in two or more thirty-minute reciprocal tutoring sessions per week, with those interactive tutoring sessions taking the place of independent practice seatwork activities (Harper & Maheady, 2007). Initially, the class will be comprised of teams of three or four students, with the overall goal of forming heterogeneous learning teams. Each team should include one high-performing student, one average student, and one low-performing student; this division makes teams roughly comparable, making the competition between the teams relatively fair (Harper & Maheady, 2007). Teachers can encourage students to name their teams, decorate their work folders, and generally take pride in their teams. These CSTT teams should remain constant at least through a four- to six-week grading period unless significant disparities develop between the teams (Harper & Maheady, 2007).

Teams have the responsibility to make certain that each team member learns the content each week. Teachers using CSTT develop weekly study guides to accompany the new content for that week, and each study guide should include ten to thirty questions and answers (Harper & Maheady, 2007; Harper et al., 1992). After a teacher has delivered the initial instruction on a new concept or mathematics problem, the teams work together using those study guides. When it is time for CSTT, the teacher hands each team a folder that includes a study guide and a deck of cards numbered 1 to N, with N corresponding to the number of questions on the study guide. The teacher then sets an audible timer for thirty minutes, and the teams begin the CSTT work as described in the following feature box (page 190).

> In CSTT, students complete two or more thirty-minute reciprocal tutoring sessions per week, with those interactive tutoring sessions taking the place of independent practice seatwork activities.

Like the PALS tutoring approach, CSTT provides teachers in high school mathematics, as well as in many other subjects, the opportunity to replace worksheet practice activities with a team activity that results in increased engagement and higher levels of learning among the students (Harper & Maheady, 2007). It also provides an excellent differentiation opportunity in that students receive immediate assistance for their misunderstandings in a highly engaging manner.

CSTT Peer Tutoring Activity Directions
1. To begin the CSTT team activity, one student selects the first card from the deck, and the number on that card indicates the question number on the study guide they will address.
2. The student seated to the left of the card selector is the "tutor" for that question, and that tutor reads the designated question to his or her teammates.
3. Each of the teammates then writes down an answer to that question and shows it to the tutor, who checks them against the answers on the study guide.
4. If the answer is correct, the tutor awards the students five points. If an answer is incorrect, the tutor shares the correct answer with the teammate who answered incorrectly and requires that student to write the correct answer to the question two or three times.
5. That student then receives two points from the tutor. Students who refuse to cooperate with the tutor or do not correct their mistakes get no points.
6. After each teammate has earned points for that question, the next teammate on the left becomes the new tutor, and the person on the new tutor's left draws a card.
7. Students continue through the study guide and through the deck as many times as possible, repeating questions if they finish the entire deck. This allows them to earn more points. Teachers should review Harper and Maheady (2007) for additional information on implementation of CSTT.

Problem-Based Learning

Problem-based learning (PBL) is an instructional technique that more and more middle and high schools are applying in a variety of subject areas, including mathematics (Fleischner & Manheimer, 1997; Knowlton, 2003; Marzano, 2007). In problem-based learning, students address a relatively complex problem and, working together, generate solutions or address smaller problems within the larger overall problem. The literature has used various terms for this concept, including *project-based learning* and *inquiry-based learning*, but the concept of students seeking a solution to a real-world-based problem and then working to implement that solution remains constant across these terms (Cole & Wasburn-Moses, 2010; Fleischner & Manheimer, 1997; Knowlton, 2003; Marzano, 2007).

In the context of mathematics, problem-based instructional units can reach far beyond merely the one-paragraph story problems currently used in mathematics, and some problems may take days or weeks to solve completely (Bender & Crane, 2011; Fleischner & Manheimer, 1997; Knowlton, 2003). Problems typically appear as longer-term endeavors, since they are intended, to the degree possible, to closely resemble tasks adults might confront in the real world (Fleischner & Manheimer, 1997; Knowlton, 2003). The following feature box presents an example of a problem a teacher might use over a period of weeks in a problem-based learning instructional unit.

Problem-Based Learning Project: Purchasing a New Home and the Doodle Family Budget

Project Assignment: The Doodle family is growing. Mom and Dad now have two children, ages five and nine. The parents feel they need a bigger house, and they have found a three-bedroom house they wish to purchase. Can they do so given their current salary and expenditures?

In this project, teams of five students will work together to answer a question about a family budget: should the Doodle family purchase a new home? The budget folder, which will remain in the front of the class, includes information on this family's finances, presented in typical form for this type of data.

Available Information in the Budget Folder:

- Salary information (salary and deductions) for both Mom and Dad

- Copies of the last three checking account statements for the joint checking account

- Copies of the stock fund savings plan for the family for the last three months

- Price information and escrowed mortgage payment on the new house

- Information on yearly bills (bills paid not every month but every six months or every year, such as life insurance)

Required Tasks to Complete: In order to complete this project, the team must finish a variety of tasks. Note that these activities are not listed in any particular order.

- Calculate the amount of savings (monthly and yearly) that this family places in the stock fund using a dollar cost averaging investment arrangement. What percentage of their take-home pay are they currently saving? By how much will they have to reduce those monthly savings after they purchase the new house?

- Using the checkbook, construct a current monthly budget for this family, including all expenditures as shown in the checkbook. Then determine the total fixed costs (the total monthly bills the family cannot change, like car payments, life insurance for Dad and Mom, and so forth). What percentage of their take-home salary is spent on fixed costs each month?

Continued➔

> - Using the current budget, determine the nonfixed monthly expenditures for the family (utility bills, cable TV, cell phone bills, grocery bills, entertainment). What percentage of their salary is spent on nonfixed costs? What savings might be possible by reducing these costs?
>
> - What funds must they save each month in the family checking account to pay nonmonthly bills? What percentage of the family budget do such bills require?
>
> - What interest, on average, does the money held in the checking account generate? Can this money be applied to the potential house payment?

As indicated in the example, problems used for problem-based learning involve real-world considerations, and this factor alone typically increases student interest in the mathematics work they may face. In addition, problem-based learning results in deeper, richer instruction in mathematics, which, in turn, leads to more complete examples of mathematical thinking and stronger connections between mathematics and other content areas. By way of example, compare the example problem with the typical math problem most educators may remember from their own mathematics instruction:

> A train traveling from Chicago is heading to Los Angeles at 75 miles per hour, and another train left Los Angeles on the same track, heading to Chicago. The second train is traveling 8 miles per hour slower than the first train. What percentage of the 1,872-mile journey will the first train complete before it meets the second train?

Which type of problem is more engaging for students? Which type of problem is likely to represent something the students eventually have to confront in the real world? Furthermore, the problem-based learning project presented here could easily be expanded into more complex areas. For example, imagine adding the following to the list of required activities in this assignment.

> Students must determine whether purchasing the house results in more or less savings for the Doodle family based on savings associated with deductions for interest they will pay on the new home. Given a tax rate of 34 percent for this family and an escrowed monthly mortgage that includes $597 in interest payments each month, students must calculate the yearly tax deduction resulting from those interest payments, since that represents a form of "savings" that current tax law allows for home owners. If the stock savings fund for the family generates an average of 7.3 percent per year, how does the tax deduction for the new house compare to the overall reduction in savings in the stock fund on a yearly basis?

With that item added as a required task, the overall PBL becomes much more complex, since students would have to calculate yearly tax deductions and compare that value to earned income from a stock market investment. As this example shows,

PBL experiences can be as complicated as any real-world decisions that most society members have to make every day, and all of these depend, to some degree, on mathematical understanding.

Finally, in all of the calculations, students will learn some of the subtle points of family budgeting. This type of real-world experience can help make mathematics more interesting and typically results in a higher level of student interest in mathematics activities.

How Does PBL Fit Into the Classroom?

When middle and high school teachers consider moving to problem-based learning, one immediate question is, when can the class undertake these projects? Specifically, in the example provided in the previous feature box (page 191), students must complete a wide variety of mathematics activities, including operations with decimals, calculations using percentages, fractions, comparative discussions of budgeting priorities (such as what nonfixed funds can the Doodles save monthly?), and researching various budgeting terms (such as *dollar cost averaging*, *life insurance*, *home interest deduction*, *tax rate*, and so on). Should the teacher assign this problem in an instructional unit on percentages or one on decimal operations?

> **Problem-based learning results in deeper, richer instruction in mathematics, which, in turn, leads to more complete examples of mathematical thinking and stronger connections between mathematics and other content areas.**

When most teachers move into problem-based learning using longer-term problems such as this, they do so on the basis of split periods: on certain days each week, the teachers split their instructional time between traditional teaching and the problem-based learning task. For example, teachers may introduce this sample problem in a unit on decimals, percentages, or fractions, and during that unit, the teacher would continue to teach on Tuesday and Thursday for the entire period as he or she typically does on the content unit. Likewise on Monday, Wednesday, and Friday, the teacher would teach the content in a traditional fashion for the first twenty-five minutes of the period. However, during the last twenty-five minutes of the period on those three days, students could move to sit with their teams and work on the various required tasks in the problem. The teacher might also offer rewards for teams that complete certain required tasks first.

What Are the Advantages of PBL?

There are a number of advantages to using PBL as a differentiated instructional approach in middle and high school mathematics classes. First, PBL provides richer content coverage. In the problem presented on page 191, students must use a variety of mathematical concepts that are inseparable from the task presented to students. Students must also explore and identify financial costs of activities and extend those to an annual projected budget in order to address the primary question on the purchase of the house. Of course, working with percentages and decimals can be quite problematic for many students, and showing the relationships between fractions, decimals, and percentages is often very beneficial.

PBL also fosters higher rates of active engagement with the mathematics content. When work on fractions, decimals, and percentages appears in the context of long-term PBL that is completed through team efforts, students often get quite interested and excited about the project. Teachers, at times, experience the relatively unusual circumstance of students asking to learn more about these mathematical concepts and showing other signs of excitement about learning based on PBL assignments (Partnership for 21st Century Skills, 2007).

Teachers may experience the unusual circumstance of students asking to learn more about these mathematics concepts as a result of PBL.

As indicated in the example, PBL activities relate directly to real-world learning experiences and allow students to experience work-like situations. These activities develop problem-solving skills that reach far beyond the skills they can develop through more traditional story-problem instructional methods. It should come as no surprise that PBL overall will increase mathematics achievement (Fleischner & Manheimer, 1997; Knowlton, 2003; Partnership for 21st Century Skills, 2007). One research summary indicated that students may improve as much as 30 percent in their understanding of concepts as a result of problem-based learning (Gijbels, Dochy, Van den Bossche, & Segers, 2005).

PBL also provides an array of differentiated instructional opportunities (Bender & Crane, 2011). For example, groups of students with similar learning styles may work as teammates, with the required assignments modified accordingly. The teacher may assign either heterogeneous or homogeneous groups to PBL tasks or vary those groups once the class completes a PBL project.

With these advantages noted, the initial planning of project-based learning experiences can be somewhat labor intensive (Bender & Crane, 2011; Fleischner & Manheimer, 1997). Nevertheless, high-quality learning experiences often result when students meet the challenge of solving problems that arise in real life as opposed to the more predictable patterns of traditional story problems (Fleischner & Manheimer, 1997). For that reason, PBL is increasing in a variety of subject areas including mathematics, and research has generally been supportive of this trend (Fleischner & Manheimer, 1997; Partnership for 21st Century Skills, 2007; Strobel & van Barneveld, 2009). General education teachers in middle and high school mathematics should consider incorporating this instructional activity into their Tier 1 instruction as well as develop Tier 2 interventions that are specifically tied with the types of required tasks presented within the PBL.

Cognitive Strategies for Mathematics

Many cognitive learning strategies apply directly to reading- and language arts-based activities in middle and high school classes. However, while Deshler and his colleagues have focused on reading and language arts types of tasks (Bulgren et al.,

2007; Chamberlain, 2006; Lenz, 2006), other researchers have developed a number of learning strategies that focus on mathematics activities. In particular, several learning strategies provide assistance for students learning to solve story problems, and research has generally shown these cognitive strategies to be effective (Bender, 2009b; Foegen, 2008; Maccini & Hughes, 2000; Sousa, 2008; Witzel, Mercer, & Miller, 2003).

From a conceptual point of view, learning strategies that focus on problem solving make sense. While most students can master rote performance of mathematics operations, transferring those operations skills into problem-solving contexts can be difficult for students with a variety of learning challenges (Bender & Crane, 2011), and at that point, many students seem to require additional assistance—perhaps even a Tier 2 intervention specifically focused on problem solving. Unlike solving calculation problems, solving complex story problems requires students to generate a solution plan that might require them to perform a series of operations correctly and in sequence to generate a correct solution. Of course, many high school students have great difficulty with the organization and planning tasks story problems require. Other students merely seem to get lost in the steps.

> Some students have great difficulty with the organization and planning tasks story problems require, while others seem to merely get lost in the steps.

STAR

The STAR strategy facilitates problem solving among students in middle and high school mathematics classes (Maccini & Gagnon, 2006; Maccini & Hughes, 2000; Maccini & Ruhl, 2000). This strategy guides the translation of story problems into mathematical equations and encourages the student to monitor his or her own performances while solving the problem. In that fashion, STAR provides scaffolded support for the student in the solution planning and calculations stages. Following are the steps of the STAR tactic (Maccini & Gagnon, 2006; Maccini & Hughes, 2000; Maccini & Ruhl, 2000):

Search the problem.

- Read the problem carefully.
- Ask, "What do I know and what do I need to know?"
- Write down the facts in the problem.

Translate the words into an equation in picture form.

- Choose a variable to solve for.
- Identify the operations necessary (using cue words and other hints).
- If possible, represent the problem with counters, sticks, or manipulatives.
- Draw a picture of the equation, including known facts and operations.

Answer the problem.

- Perform the necessary operations, solving for the unknown variable(s).

- Check that the equation is balanced in each operation.

Review the solution.

- Reread the problem.
- Ask, "Does the answer make sense? Why or why not? Does it answer the question?"

Check the answer.

The S in the STAR tactic represents the first step: search the problem (Maccini & Gagnon, 2006; Maccini & Hughes, 2000). Students should make certain they understand the problem by reading it carefully and identifying what they know and what they need to know. They then write down the available facts before moving forward. While the need to carefully read the problem may seem overly simplistic to many upper-grade teachers, struggling students often do not correctly read the story problem because of reading difficulties (Bender & Crane, 2011). They may search the problem for cue words or phrases that tell them what to do and may not carefully read and consider the entire problem. This often leads to mistakes.

The STAR tactic provides struggling students with scaffolded support for real-world problem solving.

Reading the story problem correctly is critical, and one quick suggestion is to have students write down cue words. Or perhaps teachers should require students to put a circle (in pencil) around each word in the story problem that suggests a particular mathematical operation. They can then compare those circled words with a list of cue words on a poster in the classroom. The important point here is that among struggling learners, teachers must encourage a strategy that involves carefully reading the problem.

The T in STAR represents translation of the word problem into an equation in picture form (Maccini & Gagnon, 2006; Maccini & Hughes, 2000). Students must use the facts from the first step and create an equation of the problem. In this step, students choose a variable to solve for, using cue words and other information in the problem to identify the operations necessary as well as any sequencing of steps they may need. Students may use counters and pictures to represent the equation if that assists them. Finally, they draw a picture representing the problem and then compare that picture with the various facts and cue words they previously identified (Maccini & Gagnon, 2006; Maccini & Hughes, 2000).

This translation process involves a student's imagination of the story problem and will activate various areas of the brain involved with conceptual understanding and perhaps spatial reasoning (Bender & Crane, 2011; Sousa, 2008). This also allows students to focus their own learning strengths on the problem. For example, if a student is gifted visually, this step might result in a "movie in their mind" that represents the problem solution. Musically creative students might create short lyrics describing the steps they need to undertake. The important aspect is that students mentally process the problem and translate that information into a reasonable problem solution.

The *A* step in STAR instructs the student to answer the problem by performing the operations in the equation (Maccini & Gagnon, 2006; Maccini & Hughes, 2000). Students should double-check their operations and computations at each step.

Finally, the *R* step indicates that students should review their solution in a structured, predictable fashion. This includes such activities as rereading the problem, asking questions about the answer, and checking the answer.

Research on STAR has shown this to be an effective problem-solving strategy (Maccini & Gagnon, 2006; Maccini & Hughes, 2000; Maccini & Ruhl, 2000). This strategy increases students' engagement with the mathematics problem, since various steps in STAR specifically target things like careful reading and checking one's work. Teachers in middle and high school mathematics classes should have some version of this strategy on display via a poster in their classes, and they should emphasize these problem-solving steps in their curricula.

Diagrams

Another research-supported instructional strategy for middle and high school mathematics classes is the use of diagrams that students develop to plan their story problem solution (Goldman, 1989; Jitendra, 2002; van Garderen, 2007). Drawing a picture of the problem was a significant component in the STAR strategy described previously, but the diagramming strategy focuses directly on picturing the story problem elements. This strategy is particularly useful for students with strength in spatial learning.

In teaching this instructional strategy, consider various types of diagram tools that will assist in solving the word problem (Goldman, 1989; Jitendra, 2002). For example, some story problems involve changes in quantity based on either addition or subtraction, and presenting those problems in a linear fashion can frequently assist students. Other story problems may make more sense as grouping problems, part/whole diagrams, or comparison diagrams, and some problems involve combinations of these types. In fact, one can represent many, though certainly not all, story problems with only a few common diagrams such as those in figure 8.1 (page 198). Teaching these diagrams to students can help them plan the steps toward problem solution.

In seeking to provide highly differentiated instruction in middle and high school mathematics classes, teachers should consider which students might need a structured learning strategy to succeed at problem solving. For example, many students in the upper grades can review a written problem, generate a plan for solving it and/or an equation representing it, and perhaps even draw a diagram representing that equation. Other students, however, do not spontaneously generate these keys for problem solving. Some students need a different set of instructional tactics that provides them with instruction on how problem solving might progress, and this problem diagramming strategy would work well for those students.

Change Problems include a change in quantity over time within the problem.

Tammy had eight text messages on her iPhone, but she read and deleted five of those prior to class. How many texts will she have to read through after class?

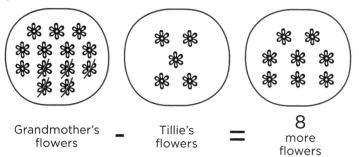

8 messages — 5 messages = 3

Comparison Problems are characterized by more than/less than types of questions.

Tillie's grandmother had a flower bed with thirteen flowers in it. Tillie loved the flowers and began a flower bed of her own when her grandmother bought five new roses for her on her birthday. How many more flowers did Tillie's grandmother have to tend than Tillie?

Grandmother's flowers — Tillie's flowers = 8 more flowers

Multischema Problems involve combinations of these major diagrams, and in most cases, such multioperation problems involve performing the various types of problems in sequence.

On Monday, Ricky came to school with a lunch that included ten small pieces of candy. He knew that his friend Jason usually brought some candy to share, and on that particular day, Jason had nineteen pieces of candy to share. In third period, Alphonse gave Ricky four additional pieces of candy to share during their lunch. How much more candy did Jason share than Ricky at lunch?

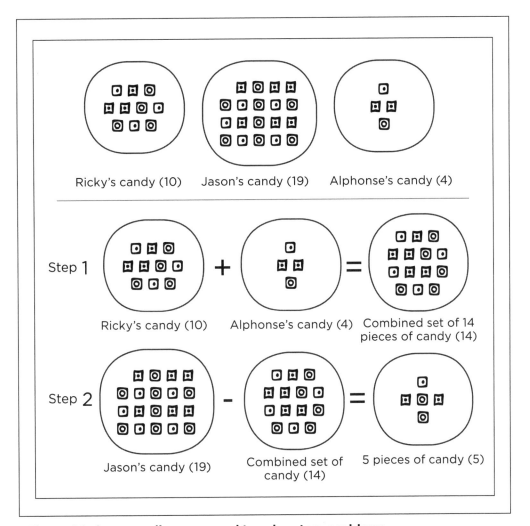

Figure 8.1: Common diagrams used to solve story problems.

Supplemental Mathematics Curricula

In RTI procedures in mathematics and in differentiating the math classes at all grade levels, teachers may wish to implement a computerized supplemental mathematics curricula or a hard-copy supplemental curricula. Here are several curricula in mathematics that are currently being used in middle and high schools.

SuccessMaker Math

SuccessMaker Math is one of the most widely used computer-driven mathematics curricula (www.pearsonschool.com/index.cfm?locator=PSZk99). This curriculum has been designed and updated to meet U.S. state and national content standards across the grade levels from kindergarten through grade 8. At the beginning of the program, students complete an initial placement module that determines their correct beginning starting levels. As they complete the daily assignments on the computer, the program adapts automatically and presents more complex work or revisits skills that students need extra practice with.

The lesson activities are highly engaging and visually stimulating. Full audio support and online manipulatives in many of the lessons aid students. The course includes real-world examples of problem solving at various grade levels. Students set their own pace, and teachers can target specific learning objectives. With more than 3,300 hours of instruction available at different levels, this software program can serve a wide range of learners, including students struggling in mathematics, which makes this program very appropriate for use in RTI procedures in mathematics in the elementary years.

Like most modern software programs, SuccessMaker Math provides individualized computer-driven instruction that allows every child to proceed at his or her own pace. The individualized interactive lessons are highly adaptable, and each student can reinforce weak skill areas or work to understand basic concepts. For students struggling in mathematics, the programmed instruction includes instructional scaffolding, multimedia presentations, and work on basic mathematics foundations.

SuccessMaker Math is also one of the most widely researched computerized mathematics learning curricula available, and evaluation studies using SuccessMaker courseware have consistently shown improved student achievement in the elementary grades (www.gattieval.com/SM_Math_Pilot_Report.pdf; see also www.swest .k12.in.us/documents/SuccessMakerEvidence.pdf). Based on this research, experts recommend this program for students in the elementary years as well as for students who are consistently behind in mathematics across the grade levels (Bender & Crane, 2011).

TransMath

TransMath is a higher-level supplementary mathematics curriculum developed by John Woodward and Mary Stroh that focuses on moving students from elementary mathematics skill levels up to algebra readiness (2004; www.sopriswest .com/transmath/transmath_home.aspx). This curriculum is intended for students functioning at or below the fortieth percentile in grades 5 through 9, but the content covers a wider range of skills, reaching from number sense to algebraic expression. Consistent with the recommendations of the National Mathematics Advisory Panel (2008), this curriculum covers fewer overall topics than most core mathematics curricula but covers those topics in much more conceptual depth. This program progresses in three levels that focus on specific mathematics areas.

- *Level 1: Developing Number Sense* focuses on number sense involving whole numbers and number theory. It includes operations, measurement, interpreting graphs, and early geometry.

- *Level 2: Making Sense of Rational Numbers* focuses on working with formulas, fractions, decimals, line graphs, percentages, and two-dimensional geometry.

- *Level 3: Understanding Algebraic Expressions* focuses on understanding algebraic expressions, negative numbers, exponents, properties, simple algebraic equations, probability, ratios, and proportions.

Three placement assessments (one for each of the levels mentioned) come with the curriculum, and each instructional unit within each level also includes two performance assessments. Together, these assessments allow for frequent progress monitoring, making this a useful curriculum in the RTI context. Several research studies have demonstrated the efficacy of this mathematics curriculum, as reported by the publisher and authors (Woodward & Stroh, 2004).

Given the focus on various skills explicitly identified as high-priority skills by the National Mathematics Advisory Panel (2008)—skills such as fractions, ratios, percentages, and the like—this curriculum will certainly be implemented by many elementary, middle, and high schools in their RTI efforts. In addition, the transitional nature of this curriculum is relatively unique in the mathematics area, another reason for using it in the RTI context for students in middle and higher grades.

Accelerated Math for Intervention

Accelerated Math for Intervention and the related curriculum, Accelerated Math, are research-based curricula and assessment tools published by Renaissance Learning (www.renlearn.com/am/). Accelerated Math has been available for some time, and the complimentary component Accelerated Math for Intervention became available in 2010. The Accelerated Math for Intervention curriculum presents mathematics practice activities for students struggling in mathematics from grades 3 through 12 and is specifically intended as either an RTI Tier 2 or 3 intervention program.

This program is self-paced and completely individualized. Students see multiple forms of practice problems on the tasks they have difficulty with. The program fosters mastery on mathematics content at each level, so students receive the level of intensity they need on each mathematics objective. An extensive system of ongoing professional development focused on RTI concerns supports this program, including using this program for universal screening, progress monitoring, and providing evidence-based documentation for intervention decisions. This curriculum can generate a wide variety of reports; some focus on a single student's performance, while others focus on school- or districtwide data. Student data reports are highly detailed and identify specific skills on which the student has worked (for example, multiplying money expressions involving whole numbers or estimating products and rounding). The program presents a variety of scores. Research has supported the use of the Accelerated Math curriculum (Yeh, 2007).

> The Accelerated Math for Intervention curriculum presents mathematics practice activities for students struggling in mathematics from grades 3 through 12.

Progress Monitoring in Mathematics

In middle and high school mathematics, as in reading-based upper-grade tasks, many students are struggling, and RTI procedures will probably be necessary. While most RTI efforts are currently based on progress-monitoring assessments that are built into various supplemental curricula (Mellard et al., 2009), middle and high school math teachers may, on occasion, need assessments that independently measure a student's performance. Teachers may also need a deeper understanding of a student's mathematical abilities, and various assessment procedures allow teachers to investigate them more directly (Allsopp, Kyger, & Lovin, 2007; Bender & Crane, 2011). For that reason, the next sections cover the mathematics components of AIMSweb and a comprehensive informal assessment procedure referred to as mathematics dynamic assessment (Allsopp et al., 2007).

AIMSweb in Mathematics

The AIMSweb comprehensive assessment system was described in chapter 5, but AIMSweb also includes a variety of assessments intended to help RTI efforts in mathematics (www.aimsweb.com). This assessment includes a curriculum-based assessment in mathematics that is appropriate up through grade 8 and for students having mathematics difficulties in the higher grades. Using a curriculum-based measurement (CBM) procedure, this assessment provides math probes that assess skills on narrow-band tests with items in each grade range or on each type of mathematics computation problem. The CBM measures should be relatively easy to administer and score, making them time efficient in the RTI process.

This company has also released the M-CAP, the mathematics concepts and applications assessment device, which can be quite useful in RTI. This assessment, in combination with the curriculum-based measures in mathematics from AIMSweb, measures students' abilities to apply mathematical reasoning, analytical skills, calculation, and computational skills. The assessment for grades 7 and 8 takes only ten minutes, and items are based on the mathematics standards developed by the National Council of Teachers of Mathematics (NCTM, 2006). Items address operations, patterns and relationships, measurement, probability, statistics, algebra, and geometry. The discussion of these assessments on the company website provides various research articles that document the efficacy of the measures incorporated into these assessments but provides no documentation of the reliability and validity of these specific assessments. Regardless, schools across the United States have embraced these assessments in many academic areas, including mathematics, and this trend toward increased use is likely to continue.

Mathematics Dynamic Assessment

As middle and high school teachers gear up to undertake RTI in mathematics, they should give some consideration to using mathematics dynamic assessment (MDA) as one foundation of RTI (Allsopp et al., 2007; Allsopp et al., 2008). Dynamic assessment provides teachers with in-depth insight into a student's mathematics understandings, and the process is useful from grades 1 through 12.

The developers of this assessment process suggest undertaking mathematics dynamic assessment two or three times per year and tying those administrations of MDA to the curricular focal points recommended by the National Council of Teachers of Mathematics (2006). This number of yearly administrations makes this procedure consistent with the universal screening procedures typically recommended for RTI and suggests the usefulness of MDA in RTI procedures for struggling learners (Allsopp et al., 2007; Allsopp et al., 2008).

Allsopp and his co-authors (2007, 2008) do not recommend the MDA procedure as a progress-monitoring tool for Tier 2 or 3 interventions; rather, Allsopp et al. suggest that curriculum-based measurements are more appropriate for progress monitoring on a repeated basis. Thus in that context, MDA might serve as a universal screening type of individualized assessment two or three times a year (Allsopp et al., 2007; Allsopp et al., 2008). Again, the purpose of MDA is to help the teacher develop a complete understanding of a student's mathematics capability rather than to be a repeated assessment tool during a specific intervention. This procedure integrates several research-supported assessment practices, including assessment of students' interests, assessment of their level of comprehension (using the concrete-representational-abstract metric), analysis of the students' errors, and interviews with students on their mathematics work (Allsopp et al., 2008).

Assessment of a Student's Interests

Students will work much harder on work that interests them, so teachers should consider students' interest in planning mathematics assignments. The MDA process begins with several informal ideas for soliciting information on the students' interests. Teachers may ask students questions about the types of worthwhile authentic learning experiences they have had previously, or teachers may require students to write letters about what they like. Teachers can use one of the student interest inventories others have developed (Allsopp et al., 2008) such as the interest inventory presented in figure 8.2 (page 204).

This aspect of mathematics assessment and instruction is vitally important. While educators have long used interest inventories, some mathematics teachers in the upper grades may be reluctant to spend precious time conducting this type of survey, but they will not be wasting their time. As indicated in chapter 3, some secondary students fear mathematics more than other subjects (Kortering, deBettencourt, & Braziel, 2005), and these fears can impede brain function. In short, mathematics teachers have a unique responsibility to make students emotionally comfortable with mathematics in order to maximize both brain functioning and student motivation to complete the assignments. Using interest inventories and planning authentic mathematics problems around students' interest areas can help.

Name: _____School: _____ Date: _____

I'd like to know a bit about you so I can plan mathematics activities that can help you personally. Please complete these questions to give me some information about you. I'll select some assignments based on this information.

1. Circle the topics that interest you!

iPhones	NASCAR	Football	Texting	Baseball
National news	Dating	Music	Video games	Fast cars
Movies	Friendships	Twitter	Science	Basketball

Other interests: _____

2. List two or three things you often do after school.

_____

3. What are your hobbies?

_____

4. What do you want to learn about?

_____

5. Are there particular types of mathematics or science activities you can recall that you really enjoyed?

_____

6. Do you like to do work in groups of students, in student pairs, or alone?

_____

7. Can you tell me anything else about you that might help me in planning interesting learning experiences for you?

_____

Figure 8.2: A student interest inventory for MDA.

Concrete-Representational-Abstract Assessment

The literature on mathematics instruction has often described concrete-representational-abstract assessment (CRA) as an important and effective instructional and assessment technique, and while elementary mathematics teachers have long used this approach, experts now recommend CRA in high school mathematics as well (Allsopp et al., 2008; Bender, 2009b; Foegen, 2008; Witzel, Riccomini, & Schneider, 2008). For example, while using stick counters as representations of numeric problems can be cumbersome, students can do this form of CRA procedure in complex multidigit math problems as well as in more simple problems (Bender, 2009b). Diagrams can provide representations of algebra problems that facilitate student learning (Bender, 2009a, 2009b; Foegen, 2008). A representative example of a simple algebraic equation is presented in figure 8.3.

When solving for y in the equation $3y + 4y + 3 = 24$, try representing the problem with a diagram. Substitute a point or fulcrum for the equal sign to suggest the equality of the terms in the number sentence.

$$OOOy + OOOOy + \because \underset{\triangle}{=} 24$$

Isolate the variable y in order to solve the problem. Whatever is done to one side of the equation must be done to the other side. First, subtracting 3 from each side eliminates that numeral from consideration, and the equation remains balanced.

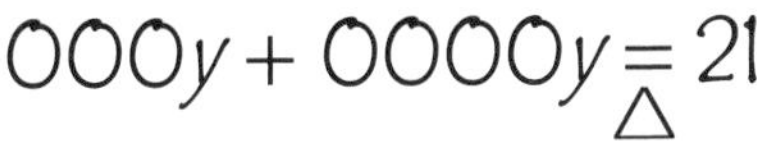

$$OOOy + OOOOy \underset{\triangle}{=} 21$$

Next, adding $3y$ and $4y$ together yields $7y$, and since the other side is already added together, nothing is to be done on the right of the equal sign.

$$OOOOOOOy \underset{\triangle}{=} 21$$

Next, dividing each side of the equation by 7 produces the answer.

$$y = 3$$

Figure 8.3: A representation of an algebraic equation.

When using representations for MDA, teachers should present an equation or problem and have the student attempt to develop a representation of it as the teacher closely observes. By asking judicious questions, teachers can gain deep understanding of the student's exact understanding of the mathematics problem.

Error Analysis

Error analysis is another effective instructional planning technique that provides information on many aspects of a student's deeper understandings and misunderstandings in mathematics (Allsopp et al., 2008; Bender & Crane, 2011; Riccomini, 2005). Teachers at all grade levels are well prepared for this undertaking, as they have long used this procedure to understand students' insights into their mathematics work. That said, one of the strengths of the peer tutoring frameworks described previously involves having students help other students analyze their own errors. While peers should not be completely capable of in-depth error analysis on complex problems, they can easily use a scripted set of instructions such as those presented in the feature box titled CSTT Peer Tutoring Activity Directions on page 190 and help one another discuss their own errors.

> One strength of the peer tutoring frameworks involves having students help other students analyze their own errors.

Interviewing Students During Mathematics

Researchers have recommended various interviewing procedures for diagnosing problems in mathematics (Allsopp et al., 2008; Bender & Crane, 2011), and the MDA process involves in-depth interviewing both during and after a student solves a mathematics problem. As noted, having a student develop a physical representation of a problem and describe how they did so can provide deep insight for the teacher about the student's problem-solving processes. In fact, a major strength of the MDA process is the way in which each of these techniques—understanding students' interests, using CRA to represent problems, analyzing errors, and interviewing during problem solving—enriches the others. Using the MDA process two or three times each year or when students seem to be experiencing particular difficulties can allow teachers just the understanding they need to scaffold appropriate instructional strategies and help the students move forward (Allsopp et al., 2007; Allsopp et al., 2008).

A Case Study: RTI in Mathematics

Figure 8.4 presents a case study RTI for a tenth-grade student in mathematics involving problem solving for story problems. This intervention reflects a problem many teachers in the higher grades face: a student who is several grade levels behind in his problem-solving capabilities.

In one sense, this case study represents the actual results for most Tier 2 interventions; in the majority of cases, a well-planned Tier 2 intervention results in successful remediation of the academic problem, a result RTI research has shown repeatedly (Foegen, 2008; Fuchs et al., 2008; Maccini & Gagnon, 2006; Thompson, 2009). In

Student: Tremain Foster Initiating Teacher: Mrs. Deb Ferrell	Age: 16 School: Coppertown High School	Date: 10/17/2011 Grade: 10

1. Student Difficulty and Summary of Tier 1 Instruction:

I've noticed since the beginning of the year that Tremain was having difficulty in the most basic one-step story problems in my first-period general mathematics class. While he struggles on some operations (both multiplication and division), his most pressing problem is a weakness in problem-solving skills. I've assigned him to work as a peer buddy on sets of story problems, and I've provided some individual tutoring on two occasions. He still doesn't get it, and the state assessment results from last year indicated a weakness on problem solving. On that assessment, he scored 4.1 on mathematics applications, while scoring 6.3 on operations. It seems Tremain needs a more intensive intervention focused on solving story problems. I shared these concerns with Ms. Johnson, the department chair for mathematics, and suggested a Tier 2 intervention on story problems for Tremain.

Mrs. Deb Ferrell, 10/17/11

---

2. Tier 2 Intervention Plan:

As the chair for mathematics at Coppertown High, I consult with teachers on students who are struggling in mathematics, and I often complete any Tier 2 interventions that may be necessary. I routinely teach classes that are somewhat smaller than the other mathematics classes to accommodate the need for various Tier 2 interventions at Coppertown High School.

After Mrs. Ferrell shared her concerns with me about Tremain Foster, we determined that Tremain needed a Tier 2 intervention on story problems. Initially, I evaluated him (along with eight other students who needed assistance) using a short (six-problem) pretest on one- and two-step story problems. On that assessment, he missed two single-step story problems and all three two-step problems. I've recorded those scores as a pretest on story problems and will begin the intervention with instruction on single-step story problems using the STAR strategy. I will then move into multistep word problems.

Figure 8.4: RTI documentation form for Tremain in mathematics.   Continued➔

To teach the STAR strategy, I plan on reviewing it each day during the intervention and then demonstrating it prior to having the students practice on a story problem individually. I will hang a poster representing that strategy on my wall for the students to refer to.

Nine students need a Tier 2 intervention of this nature during the next grading period, and all nine will come to my room during their lunch or study hall. Working in pairs for twenty minutes each day, they will complete a series of one- or two-step story problems using the STAR strategy. They can complete this work while I lead my class in other work, and given only one or two pairs in my room at any single period, I will have time to provide some individual tutoring assistance as they need it. Tremain and the other students in this Tier 2 intervention will complete this work daily, and they will score each daily worksheet they and their peer buddy complete. On Friday of each week, I will provide the students with five single-step or two-step story problems selected from the school curriculum, which they will complete individually. I will collect and chart those data for each student. We will continue this intervention for nine weeks, until the end of the current grading period, and then re-evaluate Tremain's progress along with that of the others.

Faculty have presented this intervention plan to each student's parents by telephone and have sent home a note explaining it.

Ms. Sharon Johnson, 10/19/11

3. Observational Notes of Student in Tier 2 Intervention:

[Coppertown High School does not generally conduct observations of Tier 2 interventions when the reading or mathematics coach does the intervention.]

4. Tier 2 Intervention Summary and Recommendations:

The student support team reviewed Tremain's progress on the Tier 2 intervention on story problems [presented in fig. 8.5, page 210]. The team noted that Tremain was able to master the STAR strategy within only two weeks of beginning the intervention and that he quickly mastered one-step story problems. The data further indicate that he has now mastered two-step story problems. Mrs. Ferrell has also indicated that Tremain is now much more enthusiastic in her mathematics class and that she has seen an improvement in both his attitude and his grades. Because the peer buddy idea worked so well with Tremain, Mrs. Ferrell has decided to implement that variation of peer tutoring for her entire general mathematics class.

Given Tremain's success, the student support team believes he will no longer require this Tier 2 intervention and that he can successfully complete his general mathematics class without Tier 2 support. Thus we recommend termination of this successful Tier 2 intervention for Tremain Foster.

Mrs. Toni Buncomb, chair of student support team, 11/12/11

Figure 8.4: RTI documentation form for Tremain in mathematics.

such cases, no Tier 3 intervention is needed, and students should resume their normal coursework in the general education classes, as this example recommended.

Of course, to obtain successful results, Tier 2 interventions must incorporate several specific aspects. First, the intervention must address the student's specific problem—in this case, difficulty on one- and two-step story problems. Broad interventions that do not focus on the student's exact problem are not likely to have an immediate and positive impact.

Next, explicit instruction using a research-proven intervention tactic typically informs successful interventions in mathematics. In this case, learning and using the STAR strategy systematically allowed the student to become fluent not only in determining the structure of the story problem (that is, whether it was a one- or two-step problem) but also in completing those steps appropriately.

Finally, successful Tier 2 interventions will usually reflect repeated assessment that allows the teacher to determine how the intervention is working. Note in figure 8.5 (page 210) that Ms. Johnson was able to determine exactly when Tremain mastered one-step story problems, which allowed her to move on in a timely fashion to two-step story problems. This timely instructional delivery in response to actual student performance is a major strength of the RTI instructional approach.

Using Math Coaches for Tier 2 Interventions

Another aspect this case demonstrates involves the actual delivery of the Tier 2 intervention. Rather than using double periods, the mathematics instructional coach delivered the Tier 2 interventions in mathematics. In this example, Ms. Johnson had somewhat smaller classes during her normal instructional periods, which allowed her to deliver Tier 2 interventions as needed for many students who received Tier 1 instruction from other mathematics teachers. This is yet another scheduling option that should help schools plan for the delivery of highly effective Tier 2 and 3 interventions.

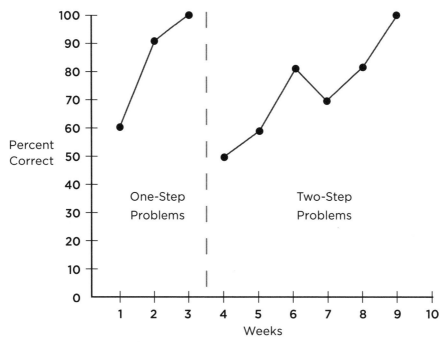

Figure 8.5: Tremain Foster's Tier 2 intervention data.

Conclusion

This chapter has presented information on RTI and differentiated instructional strategies for mathematics classes in middle and high schools. Given the difficulties that many upper-grade students experience in mathematics, one might well anticipate a national effort at RTI implementation in that area in the near future. Furthermore, while many middle and high school mathematics classes already reflect these differentiated instructional innovations, others do not, and teachers may have to expand their skill sets to incorporate these instructional innovations. In particular, experts encourage teachers to explore peer tutoring, since this offers not only an effective instructional option but also provides a mechanism for addressing students' fears of mathematics. Students do seem to be a bit more comfortable working on difficult problems with peer buddies, so this is an excellent choice.

Of course, instructional ideas in reading, writing, and mathematics are essential, but schools also need to develop a long-term plan to emphasize these basic tools more comprehensively throughout the middle and high school curricula. The epilogue recaps planning suggestions for educators that will foster increased emphasis on RTI procedures as well as differentiated instructional strategies as the Tier 1 instructional option of choice. As discussed previously, professional learning communities are the strongest basis for planning and facilitating these changes, and the recommendations presented next will help all educators as we move together to embrace these 21st century instructional practices.

Moving Into RTI and Differentiated Instruction

RTI implementation and differentiated instruction in middle and high school core content areas, coupled with the infusion of modern teaching technologies, will likely bring an end to traditional whole-group lessons. They will also likely mark the beginning of a more responsive, highly individualized instructional approach across the upper grade levels. Some middle and high school teachers are already "there" in terms of implementing RTI, differentiated instruction, and the recent technological innovations. Others, however, are not yet on board, and integrating these various changes in education provides interesting opportunities to redevelop one's teaching practices.

What's Next?

What steps should educators take to facilitate and guide these coming changes in appropriate directions? What activities can PLCs undertake to facilitate this transition to modern, 21st century instruction? How should media specialists, special education teachers, administrators, department heads, district-level administrators, team leaders, mentor teachers, and other educational leaders respond to these changes? In addition to using the school leadership team to drive this reform effort, following are several suggestions.

Develop Rigorous RTI Implementation Procedures

Knowing the RTI pyramid and actually implementing RTI across subject areas and all grade levels are quite different. As mentioned previously, most proponents of RTI recommend a three- or five-year plan for such rigorous implementation (Buffum et al., 2009). While research on RTI in the upper grade levels is lacking, model program descriptions and sample RTIs such as those presented here are available to guide middle and high school educators in their RTI planning.

Increase the Use of Technology

Technology applications are one of the most important factors with the greatest impact, and teams should plan and budget for enhanced technology in the core content areas. These modern teaching tools will provide instructional opportunities for students that cannot be provided otherwise and will truly prepare them for the 21st century world.

Train Teachers in These Technologies

It is not sufficient to purchase computers and software for all classes. Teachers and other educators must also learn to use those technologies in their various subject areas. It is safe to assume that unused technology is useless technology and that teacher training in technology is the key to effective technology applications (Partnership for 21st Century Skills, 2007).

Emphasize Differentiated Instruction

Middle and high schools have not implemented differentiated instructional practices as quickly as have elementary schools, and over the next five to ten years, an emphasis on differentiation in the higher grade levels will become increasingly apparent. As teachers and administrators alike seek new ways to reach and motivate students, differentiated instruction should be the norm rather than the exception.

Focus Firmly on Moving Forward

Educators can easily get lost in new technology applications or the newest trends in instruction. RTI, differentiated instruction, and technology-based teaching, however, are more than trends; these are long-term changes in instructional practice that should become the focus of educators for many years to come. We must stress these changes in instructional procedures for the right reasons—that these modifications work for all students in our classrooms and move many more students toward success in their schoolwork, and ultimately toward success in life.

Our primary goal in making any changes in education must be to enhance achievement and overall success for our students and not merely follow the educational fad or strategy of the moment. Research has documented that these innovations will facilitate learning, and in that sense, we undertake these changes in instruction to ultimately help our students succeed.

Conclusion

If instruction in our middle and high school classrooms has not changed drastically within the last three to five years, we are not offering best instructional practices. While the concept of differentiated instruction is now more than a decade old, both RTI and many of the technologies described in this book are much more recent, and we simply must offer these innovations to our struggling students. This is both our calling as teachers and our obligation to our students.

The interaction of these three instructional innovations—RTI, differentiated instruction, and technology—will continue to drastically improve instruction for our students, and in that sense, modern teachers are better prepared than ever before to assist all students in learning. This is what education for our students can be and should be, and ultimately, all educators will agree that we owe our students no less than the absolute best instruction possible.

References and Resources

Abernathy, S. (2008). *Responsiveness to instruction: An overview.* Accessed at www .ncpublicschools.org/docs/ec/development/learning/responsiveness/rtima terials/problem-solving/rtioverview-training-present.ppt on September 9, 2008.

Allen, J. P., Alexander, R. M., Mellard, D. F., & Prewett, S. L. (2011, February). *National review of current middle school RTI practices.* Paper presented at the National Association of School Psychologists, San Francisco, CA.

Allsopp, D. H. (1997). Using class wide peer tutoring to teach beginning algebra problem-solving skills in heterogeneous classrooms. *Remedial and Special Education, 18*(6), 367–379.

Allsopp, D. H., Kyger, M. M., & Lovin, L. H. (2007). *Teaching mathematics meaningfully: Solutions for struggling learners.* Baltimore: Paul H. Brookes.

Allsopp, D. H., Kyger, M. M., Lovin, L. H., Gerretson, H., Carson, K. L., & Ray, S. (2008). Mathematics dynamic assessment: Informal assessment that responds to the needs of struggling learners in mathematics. *Teaching Exceptional Children, 40*(3), 6–16.

Artiles, A. J., Kozleski, E. B., Trent, S. C., Osher, D., & Ortiz, A. (2010). Justifying and explaining disproportionality, 1968–2008: A critique of underlying views of culture. *Exceptional Children, 76*(3), 279–299.

Ash, K. (2010). Building on a decade of 1-to-1 lessons. *Education Week, 29*(26), 12–15.

Aubusson, P., Fogwill, S., Barr, R., & Perkovic, L. (1997). What happens when students do simulation-role-play in science? *Research in Science Education, 27*(4), 565–579.

Bender, W. N. (2008). *Differentiating instruction for students with learning disabilities: Best teaching practices for general and special educators* (2nd ed.). Thousand Oaks, CA: Corwin Press.

Bender, W. N. (2009a). *Beyond the RTI pyramid: Solutions for the first years of implementation.* Bloomington, IN: Solution Tree Press.

Bender, W. N. (2009b). *Differentiating math instruction* (2nd ed.). Thousand Oaks, CA: Corwin Press.

Bender, W. N., & Crane, D. (2011). *RTI in math: Practical guidelines for elementary teachers.* Bloomington, IN: Solution Tree Press.

Bender, W. N., & Larkin, M. J. (2009). *Reading strategies for elementary students with learning difficulties: Strategies for RTI* (2nd ed.). Thousand Oaks, CA: Corwin Press.

Bender, W. N., & Shores, C. (2007). *Response to intervention: A practical guide for every teacher.* Thousand Oaks, CA: Corwin Press.

Bender, W. N., & Waller, L. (2011). *RTI and differentiated reading in the K–8 classroom.* Bloomington, IN: Solution Tree Press.

Berkeley, S., Bender, W. N., Peaster, L. G., & Saunders, L. (2009). Implementation of response to intervention: A snapshot of progress. *Journal of Learning Disabilities, 42*(1), 85–95.

Biancarosa, C., & Snow, C. E. (2006). *Reading next—A vision for action and research in middle and high school literacy: A report to the Carnegie Corporation of New York* (2nd ed.). Washington, DC: Alliance for Excellent Education.

Boyer, L. (2008, June). *The West Virginia model for RTI: An update.* Paper presented at the annual Sopris West Educational Conference, Morgantown, WV.

Bradley, R., Danielson, L., & Doolittle, J. (2007). Responsiveness to intervention: 1997–2007. *Teaching Exceptional Children, 39*(5), 8–12.

Buffum, A., Mattos, M., & Weber, C. (2009). *Pyramid response to intervention: RTI, professional learning communities, and how to respond when kids don't learn.* Bloomington, IN: Solution Tree Press.

Bulgren, J., Deshler, D. D., & Lenz, B. K. (2007). Engaging adolescents with LD in higher order thinking about history concepts using integrated content enhancement routines. *Journal of Learning Disabilities, 40*(2), 121–133.

Busch, A. (2010, March 7). Jackson schools using federal stimulus funds to improve reading; Cape using money to help autistic students. *Southeast Missourian.* Accessed at www.semissourian.com/story/1616504.html on July 11, 2011.

Caine, R. N., & Caine, G. (2006). The way we learn. *Educational Leadership, 64*(1), 50–54.

Canter, A., Klotz, M. B., & Cowan, K. (2008). Response to intervention: The future for secondary schools. *Principal Leadership, 8*(6), 12–15. Accessed at www.nasponline.org/resources/principals/RTI%20Part%201-NASSP%20February%2008.pdf on March 23, 2010.

Castellani, J., & Jeffs, T. (2001). Emerging reading and writing strategies using technology. *Teaching Exceptional Children, 33*(5), 60–67.

Chalk, J. C., Hagan-Burke, S., & Burke, M. D. (2005). The effects of self-regulated strategy development on the writing process for high school students with learning disabilities. *Learning Disabilities Quarterly, 28*(1), 75–87.

Chamberlain, S. P. (2006). An interview with Don Deshler: Perspectives on teaching students with learning disabilities. *Intervention in School and Clinic, 41*(5), 302–306.

Christensen, C. M., Horn, M. B., & Johnson, C. W. (2008). *Disrupting class: How disruptive innovation will change the way the world learns.* New York: McGraw-Hill.

Clark, F. L., Deshler, D. D., Schumaker, J. B., Alley, G. R., & Warner, M. M. (1984). Visual imagery and self-questioning: Strategies to improve comprehension of written material. *Journal of Learning Disabilities, 17*(3), 145–149.

Cole, J. E., & Wasburn-Moses, L. H. (2010). Going beyond "The Math Wars": A special educator's guide to understanding and assisting with inquiry-based teaching in mathematics. *Teaching Exceptional Children, 42*(4), 14–20.

Conderman, G., & Strobel, D. (2006). Problem solving with guided repeated oral reading instruction. *Intervention in School and Clinic, 42*(1), 34–39.

Connor, D. J., & Lagares, C. (2007). Facing high stakes in high school: 25 successful strategies from an inclusive social studies classroom. *Teaching Exceptional Children, 40*(2), 18–27.

Cote, D. (2007). Problem-based learning software for students with disabilities. *Intervention in School and Clinic, 43*(1), 29–37.

Davis, M. R. (2010). Solving algebra on smartphones. *Education Week, 29*(26), 20–23.

Day, V. P., & Elksnin, L. K. (1994). Promoting strategic learning. *Intervention in School and Clinic, 29*(5), 262–270.

De La Paz, S., Morales, P., & Winston, P. M. (2007). Source interpretation: Teaching students with and without LD to read and write historically. *Journal of Learning Disabilities, 40*(2), 134–144.

Denton, C. A., Fletcher, J. M., Anthony, J. L., & Francis, D. J. (2006). An evaluation of intensive intervention for students with persistent reading difficulties. *Journal of Learning Disabilities, 39*(5), 447–466.

Denton, C. A., Wexler, J., Vaughn, S., & Bryan, D. (2007). Intervention provided to linguistically diverse middle school students with severe reading difficulties. *Learning Disabilities Research and Practice, 23*(2), 79–89.

Deshler, D. D., Schumaker, J. B., Lenz, B. K., Bulgren, J. A., Hock, M. F., Knight, J., et al. (2001). Ensuring content-area learning by secondary students with learning disabilities. *Learning Disabilities Research and Practice, 16*(2), 96–108.

Doidge, N. (2007). *The brain that changes itself: Stories of personal triumph from the frontiers of brain science.* New York: Penguin.

Donovan, M. S., & Cross, C. T. (Eds.). (2002). *Minority students in special and gifted education.* Washington, DC: National Academies Press.

Druyan, S. (1997). Effects of the kinesthetic conflict on promoting scientific reasoning. *Journal of Research in Science Teaching, 34*(10), 1083–1099.

Duffy, H. (n.d.). *Meeting the needs of significantly struggling learners in high school: A look at approaches to tiered intervention.* Accessed at www.rti4success.org/images /stories/high_school.pdf on January 25, 2010.

DuFour, R., DuFour, R., & Eaker, R. (2008). *Revisiting professional learning communities at work: New insights for improving schools.* Bloomington, IN: Solution Tree Press.

DuFour, R., DuFour, R., Eaker, R., & Many, T. (2006). *Learning by doing: A handbook for professional learning communities at work.* Bloomington, IN: Solution Tree Press.

Dwyer, T., Sallis, J. F., Blizzard, L., Lazarus, R., & Dean, K. (2001). Relation of academic performance to physical activity and fitness in children. *Pediatric Exercise Science, 13*(3), 225–237.

Elder-Hinshaw, R., Manset-Williamson, G., Nelson, J. M., & Dunn, M. W. (2006). Engaging older students with reading disabilities: Multimedia inquiry projects supported by reading assistive technology. *Teaching Exceptional Children, 39*(1), 6–11.

Ellis, E. S. (1994). Integrating writing strategy instruction with content area instruction: Part I—orienting students to organizational devices. *Intervention in School and Clinic, 29*(3), 169–179.

Espin, C. A., Cevasco, J., van den Broek, P., Baker, S., & Gersten, R. (2007). History as narrative: The nature and quality of historical understanding for students with LD. *Journal of Learning Disabilities, 40*(2), 174–182.

Espin, C. A., & Foegen, A. (1996). Validity of general outcome measures for predicting secondary students' performance on content-area tasks. *Exceptional Children, 62*(6), 497–514.

Espin, C. A., Shin, J., & Busch, T. W. (2005). Curriculum-based measurement in the content areas: Vocabulary-matching as an indicator of progress in social studies learning. *Journal of Learning Disabilities, 38*(4), 353–363.

Espin, C., Wallace, T., Lembke, E., Campbell, H., & Long, J. D. (2010). Creating a progress-monitoring system in reading for middle-school students: Tracking progress toward meeting high-stakes standards. *Learning Disabilities Research and Practice, 25*(2), 60–75.

Faggella-Luby, M. N., & Deshler, D. D. (2008). Reading comprehension in adolescents with LD: What we know; what we need to know. *Learning Disabilities Research and Practice, 23*(2), 70–78.

Ferriter, W. M. (2010). Preparing to teach digitally. *Educational Leadership, 67*(8), 88–89.

Fleischner, J. E., & Manheimer, M. A. (1997). Math interventions for students with learning disabilities: Myths and realities. *School Psychology Review, 26*(3), 397–413.

Foegen, A. (2008). Algebra progress monitoring and interventions for students with learning disabilities. *Learning Disability Quarterly, 31*(2), 65–78.

Fry, W. (1997). Spanish humor: A hypotheory, a report on initiation of research. *International Journal of Humor Research, 10*(2), 165–172.

Fuchs, D., & Deshler, D. D. (2007). What we need to know about responsiveness to intervention (and shouldn't be afraid to ask). *Learning Disabilities Research and Practice, 22*(2), 129–136.

Fuchs, D., Fuchs, L. S., & Stecker, P. M. (2010). The "blurring" of special education in a new continuum of general education placements and services. *Exceptional Children, 76*(3), 301–323.

Fuchs, D., Fuchs, L. S., Thompson, A., Svenson, E., Loulee, Y., Al Otaiba, S., et al. (2001). Peer-assisted learning strategies in reading: Extensions for kindergarten, first grade, and high school. *Remedial and Special Education, 22*(1), 15–21.

Fuchs, L. S., & Fuchs, D. (2007). A model for implementing responsiveness to intervention. *Teaching Exceptional Children, 39*(5), 14–20.

Fuchs, L. S., Fuchs, D., Powell, S. R., Seethaler, P. M., Cirino, P. T., & Fletcher, J. M. (2008). Intensive intervention for students with mathematics disabilities: Seven principles of effective practice. *Learning Disability Quarterly, 31*(2), 79–92.

Gajria, M., Jitendra, A. K., Sood, S., & Sacks, G. (2007). Improving comprehension of expository text in students with LD: A research synthesis. *Journal of Learning Disabilities, 40*(3), 210–225.

Gately, S. E. (2008). Facilitating reading comprehension for students on autism spectrum. *Teaching Exceptional Children, 40*(3), 40–45.

Geisick, K., & Graving-Reyes, P. (2008). RTI in a secondary school setting: Riverbank High School story. Accessed at www.schoolsmovingup.net/events/rtisecondary on July 11, 2011.

Gibbs, D. P. (2008). *RTI in middle and high schools: Strategies and structures for literacy success.* Horsham, PA: Labor Relations Press.

Gijbels, D., Dochy, F., Van den Bossche, P., & Segers, M. (2005). Effects of problem-based learning: A meta-analysis from the angle of assessment. *Review of Educational Research, 75*(1), 27–61.

Glassman, R. B. (1999). Hypothesized neural dynamics of working memory: Several chunks might be marked simultaneously by harmonic frequencies within an octave band of brain waves. *Brain Research Bulletin, 50*(2), 77–93.

Goldman, S. R. (1989). Strategy instruction in mathematics. *Learning Disability Quarterly, 12*(1), 43–55.

Greene, J. F. (1996). LANGUAGE! Effects of an individualized structured language curriculum for middle and high school students. *Annals of Dyslexia, 46*(1), 97–121.

Greene, J. F. (1999). *LANGUAGE! The comprehensive literacy curriculum* (2nd ed.). Longmont, CO: Sopris West.

Greenwood, C. R., Delquadri, J. C., & Carta, J. J. (1997). *Together we can! Classwide peer tutoring to improve basic academic skills.* Longmont, CO: Sopris West.

Gregory, G. H. (2008). *Differentiated instructional strategies in practice: Training, implementation, and supervision* (2nd ed.). Thousand Oaks, CA: Corwin Press.

Gregory, G. H., & Kuzmich, L. (2005). *Differentiated literacy strategies for student growth and achievement in grades 7–12.* Thousand Oaks, CA: Corwin Press.

Hannaford, C. (1995). *Smart moves: Why learning is not all in your head.* Arlington, VA: Great Oceans.

Harper, G. F., & Maheady, L. (2007). Peer-mediated teaching and students with learning disabilities. *Intervention in School and Clinic, 43*(2), 101–107.

Harper, G. G., Maheady, L., Mallett, B., & Sacca, M. (1992). *Classwide student tutoring teams: Instructor's manual.* Fredonia: State University of New York at Fredonia.

Harris, K. R., & Graham, S. (1996). *Making the writing process work: Strategies for composition and self-regulation.* Cambridge, MA: Brookline.

Hasbrouck, J. E., Ihnot, C., & Rogers, G. H. (1999). "Read Naturally": A strategy to increase oral reading fluency. *Reading Research and Instruction, 39*(1), 27–37.

High School Tiered Interventions Initiative. (2010). The High School Tiered Interventions Initiative: Progress monitoring [Webinar]. *National Center on Response to Intervention.* Accessed at www.rti4success.org/webinars/video/902 on June 14, 2011.

Hoover, J. J., Baca, L., Wexler-Love, E., & Saenz, L. (2008). *National implementation of response to intervention (RTI): Research summary.* Alexandria, VA: National Association of State Directors of Special Education. Accessed at www.nasdse.org/portals/0/national-implementation-or-RTI-Research-Summary.pdf on April 2, 2009.

Hoover, J. J., & Patton, J. R. (2008). The role of special educators in a multitiered instructional system. *Intervention in School and Clinic, 43*(4), 195–202.

Horton, S. V., Lovitt, T. C. & Bergerud, D. (1990). The effectiveness of graphic organizers for three classifications of secondary students in content area classes. *Journal of Learning Disabilities, 23*(1), 12–22, 29.

Hughes, C., & Dexter, D. D. (2008). *Field studies of RTI programs.* Accessed at www .rti-network.org/learn/research/fieldstudies on November 20, 2008.

Husman, J., Brem, S., & Duggan, M. A. (2005). Student goal orientation and formative assessment. *Academic Exchange Quarterly, 9*(3), 355–359.

Igo, L. B., Bruning, R., McCrudden, M., & Kauffman, D. F. (2003). InfoGather: A tool for gathering and organizing information from the web (pp. 282–298). In R. Bruning, C. A. Horn, & L. M. PytlikZillig (Eds.), *Web-based learning: What do we know? Where do we go?* Greenwich, CT: Information Age.

Igo, L. B., Riccomini, P. J., Bruning, R. H., & Pope, G. G. (2006). How should middle school students with LD approach online note taking? A mixed methods study. *Learning Disability Quarterly, 29*(2), 89–100.

Ihnot, C., Mastoff, J., Gavin, J., & Hendrickson, I. (2001). *Read Naturally.* St. Paul, MN: Read Naturally.

Jacobson, L. T., & Reid, R. (2010). Improving the persuasive essay writing of high school students with ADHD. *Exceptional Children, 76*(2), 157–174.

James, D. (2010, January 24). RTI initiative designed to ID and help struggling students. *Journal Gazette & Times Courier.* Accessed at www.jg-tc.com/arti cles/2010/1/24/news/doc4b5d167ed7de7919688382.txt on January 26, 2010.

Jitendra, A. (2002). Teaching students math problem-solving through graphic representations. *Teaching Exceptional Children, 34*(4), 34–38.

Johnson, E. S., & Smith, L. (2008). Implementation of response to intervention at middle school: Challenges and potential benefits. *Teaching Exceptional Children, 40*(3), 46–52.

Kame'enui, E. J. (2007). A new paradigm: Responsiveness to intervention. *Teaching Exceptional Children, 39*(5), 6–7.

Katz, L. A., Stone, C. A., Carlisle, J. F., Corey, D. L., & Zeng, J. (2008). Initial progress of children identified with disabilities in Michigan's Reading First schools. *Exceptional Children, 74*(2), 235–256.

King, K., & Gurian, M. (2006). Teaching to the minds of boys. *Educational Leadership, 64*(1), 56–61.

King-Sears, M. E., & Bowman-Kruhm, M. (2010). Attending to specialized reading instruction for adolescents with mild disabilities. *Teaching Exceptional Children, 42*(4), 30–40.

Knowlton, D. S. (2003). Preparing students for enhanced living: Virtues of problem-based learning across the higher education curriculum. In D. S. Knowlton & D. C. Sharp (Eds.), *Problem-based learning for the information age: New directions for teaching and learning* (pp. 5–12). San Francisco: Jossey-Bass.

Kolonay, D. J., & Kelly-Garris, K. (2009). The reading-ready brain. *Principal Leadership, 10*(4), 48–53.

Korinek, L., & Bulls, J. A. (1996). SCORE A: A student research paper writing strategy. *Teaching Exceptional Children, 28*(4), 60–63.

Kortering, L. J., deBettencourt, L. U., & Braziel, P. M. (2005). Improving performance in high school algebra: What students with learning disabilities are saying. *Learning Disability Quarterly, 28*(3), 191–203.

Kroeger, S. D., & Kouche, B. (2006). Using peer-assisted learning strategies to increase response to intervention in inclusive middle math settings. *Teaching Exceptional Children, 38*(5), 6–13.

Larmer, J., Ross, D., & Mergendollar, J. R. (2009). *PBL starter kit: To-the-point advice, tools, and tips for your first project in middle or high school.* San Francisco: Buck Institute for Education.

Lee, J., Grigg, W., & Dion, G. S. (2007). *The nation's report card: Mathematics 2007* (NCES 2007-494). Washington, DC: National Center for Education Statistics, Institute of Education Sciences, U.S. Department of Education.

Lee, S., Wehmeyer, M. L., Soukup, J. H., & Palmer, S. B. (2010). Impact of curriculum modifications on access to the general education curriculum for students with disabilities. *Exceptional Children, 76*(2), 213–233.

Lenz, B. K. (2006). Creating school-wide conditions for high-quality learning strategy classroom instruction. *Intervention in School and Clinic, 41*(5), 261–266.

Lenz, B. K., Adams, G. L., Bulgren, J. A., Pouliot, N., & Laraux, M. (2007). Effects of curriculum maps and guiding questions on the test performance of adolescents with learning disabilities. *Learning Disability Quarterly, 30*(4), 235–244.

Linan-Thompson, S., Vaughn, S., Prater, K., & Cirino, P. T. (2006). The response to intervention of English language learners at risk for reading problems. *Journal of Learning Disabilities, 39*(5), 390–398.

Lolich, E., Stover, G., Barker, N., Jolley, M., VanKleek, L., & Kendall, S. (2010). Response to intervention: Helping all students succeed [Video]. Accessed at www.rtinetwork.org/professional/virtualvisits on March 3, 2010.

Lovett, M. W., De Palma, M., Frijters, J., Steinbach, K., Temple, M., Benson, N., et al. (2008). Interventions for reading difficulties: A comparison of response to intervention by ELL and EFL struggling readers. *Journal of Learning Disabilities, 41*(4), 333–352.

Lovitt, T. C., & Horton, S. V. (1994). Strategies for adapting science textbooks for youth with learning disabilities. *Remedial and Special Education, 15*(2), 105–116.

MacArthur, C. A., & Philippakos, Z. (2010). Instruction in a strategy for compare-contrast writing. *Exceptional Children, 76*(4), 438–456.

Maccini, P., & Gagnon, J. C. (2006). Mathematics instructional practices and assessment accommodations by secondary special and general educators. *Exceptional Children, 72*(2), 217–234.

Maccini, P., & Hughes, C. A. (2000). Effects of a problem-solving strategy on the introductory algebra performance of secondary students with learning disabilities. *Learning Disabilities Research and Practice, 15*(1), 10–21.

Maccini, P., & Ruhl, K. L. (2000). Effects of a graduated instructional sequence on the algebraic subtraction of integers by secondary students with learning disabilities. *Education and Treatment of Children, 23*(4), 465–489.

Mahdavi, J. N., & Beebe-Frankenberger, M. E. (2009). Pioneering RTI systems that work: Social validity, collaboration, and context. *Teaching Exceptional Children, 42*(2), 64–72.

Mann, D., Shakeshaft, C., Becker, J., & Kottkamp, R. (1999). *West Virginia story: Achievement gains from a statewide comprehensive instructional technology program.* Santa Monica, CA: Milken Exchange on Education Technology.

Manzo, K. K. (2010a). Portable playlists for class lessons. *Education Week, 29*(26), 16–17.

Manzo, K. K. (2010b). Mobilizing the research. *Education Week, 29*(26), 34–36.

Marzano, R. J. (2007). *The art and science of teaching: A comprehensive framework for effective instruction.* Alexandria, VA: Association for Supervision and Curriculum Development.

Marzano, R. J. (2009). Teaching with interactive whiteboards. *Educational Leadership, 67*(3), 80–82.

Marzano, R. J. (2010). Representing knowledge nonlinguistically. *Educational Leadership, 67*(8), 84–86.

Marzano, R. J., & Haystead, M. (2009). *Final report on the evaluation of the Promethean technology.* Englewood, CO: Marzano Research Laboratory.

Mason, L. H., & Graham, S. (2008). Writing instruction for adolescents with learning disabilities: Programs of intervention research. *Learning Disabilities Research and Practice, 23*(2), 103–112.

Mastropieri, M. A., Leinart, A., & Scruggs, T. E. (1999). Strategies to increase reading fluency. *Intervention in School and Clinic, 34*(5), 278–283, 292.

McCoy, L. P. (1996). Computer-based mathematics learning. *Journal of Research on Computing in Education, 28*(4), 438–460.

McDuffie, K. A., Mastropieri, M. A., & Scruggs, T. E. (2009). Differential effects of peer tutoring in co-taught and non-co-taught classes: Results for content learning and student–teacher interaction. *Exceptional Children, 75*(4), 493–510.

Mellard, D. F., McKnight, M., & Woods, K. (2009). Response to intervention screening and progress-monitoring practices in 41 local schools. *Learning Disabilities Research and Practice, 24*(4), 186–195.

Merzenich, M. M. (2001). Cortical plasticity contributing to child development. In J. L. McClelland & R. S. Siegler (Eds.), *Mechanisms of cognitive development: Behavioral and neural perspectives* (pp. 67–96). Mahwah, NJ: Erlbaum.

Merzenich, M. M., Tallal, P., Peterson, B., Miller, S., & Jenkins, W. M. (1999). Some neurological principles relevant to the origins of—and the cortical plasticity-based remediation of—developmental language impairments. In J. Grafman & Y. Christen (Eds.), *Neuronal plasticity: Building a bridge from the laboratory to the clinic* (pp. 49–87). Berlin: Springer-Verlag.

Moran, S., Kornhaber, M., & Gardner, H. (2006). Orchestrating multiple intelligences. *Educational Leadership, 64*(1), 22–27.

Morgan, P. L., & Fuchs, D. (2007). Is there a bidirectional relationship between children's reading skills and reading motivation? *Exceptional Children, 73*(2), 165–183.

Morgan, P. L., & Sideridis, G. D. (2006). Contrasting the effectiveness of fluency interventions for students with or at risk for learning disabilities: A multilevel random coefficient modeling meta-analysis. *Learning Disabilities Research and Practice, 21*(4), 191–210.

National Association of State Directors of Special Education. (2006). *Myths about response to intervention (RTI) implementation.* Alexandria, VA: Author. Accessed at www.casecec.org/pdf/rti/Myths%20about%20RTI.pdf on November 21, 2008.

National Center on Response to Intervention. (n.d.a). *Ask the expert: Don Deshler.* Accessed at www.rti4success.org/index.php?option=com_content&task=view&id=1441 on February 25, 2010.

National Center on Response to Intervention. (n.d.b). *Ask the expert: John Hosp.* Accessed at www.rti4success.org/index.php?option=com_content&task =view&id=1545 on July 29, 2010.

National Council of Teachers of Mathematics. (2006). *Curriculum focal points for mathematics in prekindergarten through grade 8.* Reston, VA: Author.

National High School Center, National Center on Response to Intervention, & Center on Instruction. (2010). *Tiered interventions in high schools: Using preliminary "lessons learned" to guide ongoing discussions.* Washington, DC: American Institutes for Research. Accessed at www.betterhighschools.org/pubs/docu ments/HSTII_LessonsLearned.pdf on November 1, 2010.

National Mathematics Advisory Panel. (2008). *Foundations for success: The final report of the National Mathematics Advisory Panel.* Washington, DC: Author. Accessed at www.ed.gov/MathPanel on December 16, 2008.

Nunnery, J. A., & Ross, S. M. (2007). The effects of the School Renaissance program on student achievement in reading and mathematics. *Research in the Schools, 14*(1), 40–59.

Nunnery, J. A., Ross, S. M., & McDonald, A. (2006). A randomized experimental evaluation of the impact of Accelerated Reader/Reading Renaissance implementation on reading achievement in grades 3 to 6. *Journal of Education for Students Placed at Risk, 11*(1), 1–18.

O'Connor, R. W., White, A., & Swanson, H. L. (2007). Repeated reading versus continuous reading: Influences on reading fluency and comprehension. *Exceptional Children, 74*(1), 31–46.

Okolo, C. M., Englert, C. S., Bouck, E. C., & Heutsche, A. M. (2007). Web-based history learning environments: Helping all students learn and like history. *Intervention in School and Clinic, 43*(1), 3–11.

Orosco, M. J., & Klingner, J. (2010). One school's implementation of RTI with English language learners: "Referring into RTI." *Journal of Learning Disabilities, 43*(3), 269–288.

Partnership for 21st Century Skills. (2007). *21st century curriculum and instruction.* Accessed at www.21stcenturyskills.org/documents/21st_century_skills_cur riculum_and_instruction.pdf on November 18, 2009.

Partnership for 21st Century Skills. (2009). *21st century learning environments.* Accessed at www.21stcenturyskills.org/documents/1e_white_paper-1.pdf on November 18, 2009.

Podhajski, B., Mather, N., Nathan, J., & Sammons, J. (2009). Professional development in scientifically based reading instruction: Teacher knowledge and reading outcomes. *Journal of Learning Disabilities, 42*(5), 403–417.

Pro, J. C., & Thompson, M. J. (2010, March). *Response to intervention: Implementation at the secondary level.* Presented at the annual meeting of the National Association of School Psychologists, Chicago, IL. Accessed at www.nasponline .org on March 23, 2010.

Protheroe, N. (2010). Response to intervention in secondary schools. *Principal's Research Review, 5*(2), 1–7.

Rebora, A. (2010). Tools of the trade. *Education Week Teacher PD Sourcebook, 3*(2), 28–31.

Riccomini, P. J. (2005). Identification and remediation of systematic error patterns in subtraction. *Learning Disability Quarterly, 28*(3), 233–242.

Rinaldi, C., & Samson, J. (2008). English language learners and response to intervention: Referral considerations. *Teaching Exceptional Children, 40*(5), 6–14.

Robelen, E. W. (2010). Boys trail girls in reading across states. *Education Week, 29*(27), 10.

Roberts, G., Torgesen, J. K., Boardman, A., & Scammacca, N. (2008). Evidence based strategies for reading instruction of older students with learning disabilities. *Learning Disabilities Research and Practice, 23*(2), 63–69.

Rozalski, M. E. (2009, February). Response to intervention: A rural high school's attempt to improve reading achievement. *CEC Today.* Accessed at www .cec.sped.org?AM/Template.cfm?Section=Response_to_Intervention&CO NTENDID=11752&TEMPLATE=/CM/ContentDisplay.cfm on January 21, 2010.

Rushkoff, D., & Dretzin, R. (Writers). (2010, February 2). Digital nation: Life on the virtual frontier [Television series episode]. In R. Dretzin (Producer), *Frontline.* Boston: Public Broadcasting System.

Salend, S. J. (2009). Technology-based classroom assessments: Alternatives to testing. *Teaching Exceptional Children, 41*(6), 48–58.

Shaffer, D. W. (2007). Epistemic games as career preparatory experiences for students with disabilities. *Journal of Special Education Technology, 22*(3), 57–69.

Shapiro, M. (2010). Embracing Wikipedia. *Education Week, 29*(31). Accessed at www .edweek.org/ew/articles/2010/05/07/31shapiro.h29.html on April 21, 2011.

Silver, H., & Perini, M. (2010). Responding to the research: Harvey Silver and Matthew Perini address learning styles. *Education Update, 52*(5), 6–7.

Simmons, D. C., Coyne, M. D., Kwok, O., McDonagh, S., Harn, B. A., & Kame'enui, E. J. (2008). Indexing response to intervention: A longitudinal study of reading risk from kindergarten through third grade. *Journal of Learning Disabilities, 41*(2), 158–173.

Simos, P. G., Fletcher, J. M., Sarkari, S., Billingsley-Marshall, R., Denton, C. A., & Papanicolaou, A. C. (2007). Intensive instruction affects brain magnetic activity associated with oral word reading in children with persistent reading disabilities. *Journal of Learning Disabilities, 40*(1), 37–48.

Skylar, A. A., Higgins, K., & Boone, R. (2007). Strategies for adapting WebQuests for students with learning disabilities. *Intervention in School and Clinic, 43*(1), 20–28.

Slavin, R. E., Cheung, A., Groff, C., & Lake, C. (2008). Effective reading programs for middle and high schools: A best-evidence synthesis. *Reading Research Quarterly, 43*(3), 290–322.

Smutny, J. F., & von Fremd, S. E. (2010). *Differentiating for the young child: Teaching strategies across the content areas, prek–3* (2nd ed.). Thousand Oaks, CA: Corwin Press.

Sousa, D. A. (2005). *How the brain learns to read.* Thousand Oaks, CA: Corwin Press.

Sousa, D. A. (2008). *How the brain learns mathematics.* Thousand Oaks, CA: Corwin Press.

Sousa, D. A. (2009). *How the brain influences behavior: Management strategies for every classroom.* Thousand Oaks, CA: Corwin Press.

Sousa, D. A. (Ed.). (2010). *Mind, brain, and education: Neuroscience implications for the classroom.* Bloomington, IN: Solution Tree Press.

Sousa, D. A., & Tomlinson, C. A. (2011). *Differentiation and the brain: How neuroscience supports the learner-friendly classroom.* Bloomington, IN: Solution Tree Press.

Spectrum K–12 School Solutions. (2009). *Response to intervention (RTI) adoption survey 2009.* Washington, DC: Author. Accessed at www.spectrumk12.com /uploads/file/RTI%202009%20Adoption%20Survey%20Final%20Report .pdf on April 21, 2011.

Spectrum K–12 School Solutions/Council of Administrators of Special Education. (2008). *RTI adoption survey.* Washington, DC: Author.

Stefanoni, A. B. (2009, November 15). Pittsburg Middle School earns honors. Accessed at www.joplinglobe.com/local/x546219236/Andra-Bryan-Ste fanoni-Pittsburg-Middle-School-earns-honors on January 21, 2010.

Stein, B., Hardy, C. A., & Totten, H. (1984). The use of music and imagery to enhance and accelerate information retention. *Journal of the Society for Accelerative Learning and Teaching, 7*(4), 18–26.

Sternberg, R. J. (1985). *Beyond IQ: A triarchic theory of human intelligence.* New York: Cambridge University Press.

Sternberg, R. J. (2006). Recognizing neglected strengths. *Educational Leadership, 6*(1), 30–35.

Stevens, R. J., & Slavin, R. E. (1995). The cooperative elementary school: Effects on students' achievement, attitudes, and social relations. *American Educational Research Journal, 32*(2), 321–351.

Strobel, J., & van Barneveld, A. (2009). When is PBL more effective? A meta-synthesis of meta-analyses comparing PBL to conventional classrooms. *Interdisciplinary Journal of Problem-Based Learning, 3*(1), 44–58.

Tate, M. L. (2005). *Reading and language arts worksheets don't grow dendrites: 20 literacy strategies that engage the brain.* Thousand Oaks, CA: Corwin Press.

Temple, E., Deutsch, G. K., Poldrack, R. A., Miller, S. L., Tallal, P., Merzenich, M., et al. (2003). Neural deficits in children with dyslexia ameliorated by behavioral remediation: Evidence from functional MRI. *Proceedings of the National Academy of Sciences of the United States of America, 100*(5), 2860–2865.

Therrien, W. J., Hughes, C., Kapelski, C., & Mokhtari, K. (2009). Effectiveness of a test-taking strategy on achievement in essay tests for students with learning disabilities. *Journal of Learning Disabilities, 42*(1), 14–23.

Therrien, W. J., Wickstrom, K., & Jones, K. (2006). Effect of a combined repeated reading and question generation intervention on reading achievement. *Learning Disabilities Research and Practice, 21*(2), 89–97.

Thompson, C. J. (2009). Preparation, practice, and performance: The impact of standards-based instruction on secondary students' math and science achievement. *Research in Education, 81,* 53–62.

Tilly, W. D. (2003, December). *How many tiers are needed for successful prevention and early intervention? Heartland Area Education Agency's evolution from four to three tiers.* Paper presented at the National Research Center on Learning Disabilities Responsiveness-to-Intervention Symposium, Kansas City, MO.

Tomlinson, C. A. (1999). *The differentiated classroom: Responding to the needs of all learners.* Alexandria, VA: Association for Supervision and Curriculum Development.

Tomlinson, C. A. (2001). *How to differentiate instruction in mixed-ability classrooms* (2nd ed.). Alexandria, VA: Association for Supervision and Curriculum Development.

Tomlinson, C. A., Brimijoin, K., & Narvaez, L. (2008). *The differentiated school: Making revolutionary changes in teaching and learning.* Alexandria, VA: Association for Supervision and Curriculum Development.

Tomlinson, C. A., & McTighe, J. (2006). *Integrating differentiated instruction and understanding by design: Connecting content and kids.* Alexandria, VA: Association for Supervision and Curriculum Development.

Torgesen, J. K. (2007). *Using an RTI model to guide early reading instruction: Effects on identification rates for students with learning disabilities.* Tallahassee: Florida Center for Reading Research. Accessed at www.fcrr.org/science/pdf/torgesen /Response_intervention_Florida.pdf on December 12, 2008.

Troia, G. A., Graham, S., & Harris, K. R. (1999). Teaching students with learning disabilities to mindfully plan when writing. *Exceptional Children, 65*(2), 235–252.

Vandenberg, A., Boon, R., Fore, C., & Bender, W. N. (2008). The effects of repeated readings on the reading fluency and comprehension for high school students with specific learning disabilities. *Learning Disabilities: A Multidisciplinary Journal, 15*(1), 11–20.

van Garderen, D. (2007). Teaching students with LD to use diagrams to solve mathematical word problems. *Journal of Learning Disabilities, 40*(6), 540–553.

Vaughn, S., & Roberts, G. (2007). Secondary interventions in reading: Providing additional instruction for students at risk. *Teaching Exceptional Children, 39*(5), 40–46.

Vaughn, S., Wanzek, J., Murray, C. S., Scammacca, N., Linan-Thompson, S., & Woodruff, A. L. (2009). Response to early reading intervention: Examining higher and lower responders. *Exceptional Children, 75*(2), 165–183.

Wahl, M. (2006). *Read Naturally.* Tallahassee: Florida Center for Reading Research. Accessed at http://fcrr.org/FCRRReports/PDF/ReadNaturally.pdf on April 27, 2010.

Waller, L. (2011). Is your kid's classroom connection high speed? Six easy ways to engage students with technology in reading! *Teacher's Workshop Newsletter, 4*(1), 1–3.

Wang, F., & Hannafin, M. J. (2005). Design-based research and technology-enhanced learning environments. *Educational Technology Research and Development, 53*(4), 5–23.

Waters, J. C. (2008). *Blood oath.* Toccoa, GA: Currahee.

Webb, D., & Webb, T. (1990). *Accelerated learning with music.* Norcross, GA: Accelerated Learning Systems.

Weinberger, N. (1998). Creating creativity with music. *MuSICA Research Notes, 5*(2), 2.

Welsch, R. G. (2007). Using experimental analysis to determine interventions for reading fluency and recalls of students with learning disabilities. *Learning Disability Quarterly, 30*(2), 115–130.

Williams, D. L. (2010). The speaking brain. In D. A. Sousa (Ed.), *Mind, brain, and education: Neuroscience implications for the classroom* (pp. 85–109). Bloomington, IN: Solution Tree Press.

Williams, J. P., Nubla-Kung, A. B., Pollini, S., Stafford, K. B., Garcia, A., & Snyder, A. E. (2007). Teaching cause-effect text structure through social studies content to at-risk second graders. *Journal of Learning Disabilities, 40*(2), 111–120.

Willis, J. (2010). The current impact of neuroscience on teaching and learning. In D. A. Sousa (Ed.), *Mind, brain, and education: Neuroscience implications for the classroom* (pp. 45–66). Bloomington, IN: Solution Tree Press.

Witzel, B. S., Mercer, C. D., & Miller, M. D. (2003). Teaching algebra to students with learning difficulties: An investigation of an explicit instruction model. *Learning Disabilities Research and Practice, 18*(2), 121–131.

Witzel, B. S., Riccomini, P. J., & Schneider, E. (2008). Improving CRA with secondary students with learning disabilities in math. *Intervention in School and Clinic, 43*(5), 270–276.

Wolgemuth, J. R., Cobb, R. B., & Alwell, M. (2008). The effects of mnemonic interventions on academic outcomes for youth with disabilities: A systematic review. *Learning Disabilities Research and Practice, 23*(1), 1–10.

Wood, C. L., Mackiewicz, S. M., Norman, R. K., & Cooke, N. L. (2007). Tutoring with technology. *Intervention in School and Clinic, 43*(2), 108–115.

Woodward, J., & Stroh, M. (2004). *Transitional Mathematics: Making sense of rational numbers.* Longmont, CO: Sopris West.

Yeh, S. S. (2007). The cost-effectiveness of five policies for improving student achievement. *American Journal of Evaluation, 28*(4), 416–436.

Index

proven, 26

D

DARE, 171, 172

Davis, M. R., 119

De La Paz, S., 172

departmentalized schools, RTI in,
  43–45

Deshler, D., 43, 142, 143, 170

diagrams, use of, 197–199

differentiated instruction
  See also Tier 1, differentiation in
  brain-compatible, 71–76
  gender differences, 77–79
  learning styles/preferences, 67–71
  need for emphasis on, 212
  origins of, 65–66
  role of RTI with, 100–101
  SHEMR tool, 80–86
  Tomlinson's recommendations for,
    66–67

disproportionality, 16–17

double dippers, 25–26

Dretzin, R., 104

E

Education Podcast Network, 118

emotional ties to content, 82–83

empowerment, teacher, 17

error analysis, 206

Espin, C. A., 150

F

Facebook, 169

Fast ForWord, 26, 145–146

Florida Center for Reading Research,
  19

fMRI (functional magnetic resonance

imaging), 71

G

Gaggle, 120

gender differences, 77–79

Gibbs, D. P., 52, 55

goals, RTI and yearly progress, 16

Graham, S., 171

Grammar Girl, 118

Greenwood, C. R., 188–189

Gurian, M., 77, 78, 79

H

Hardy, C. A., 73

Harris, K. R., 171

High School Tiered Interventions
  Initiative, 18

humor, 82

I

IES What Works Clearinghouse, 19

Igo, L. B., 175, 176

International Society for Technology in
  Education, 111

Internet4Classrooms, 113

iPads, 107–108

J

Jacobson, L. T., 171

James, D., 50

Jeffs, T., 178

Jenkins, B., 145

K

Kansas Institute for Positive Behavior
  Support, 19

King, K., 77, 78, 79

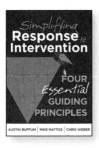

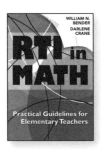